WORLD TRADE ISSUES

WORLD TRADE ISSUES

LAMBERT S. MARTIN

Nova Science Publishers, Inc.
New York

Senior Editors: Susan Boriotti and Donna Dennis
Coordinating Editor: Tatiana Shohov
Office Manager: Annette Hellinger
Graphics: Wanda Serrano
Editorial Production: Jennifer Vogt, Matthew Kozlowski and Maya Columbus
Circulation: Ave Maria Gonzalez, Indah Becker and Vladimir Klestov
Communications and Acquisitions: Serge P. Shohov
Marketing: Cathy DeGregory

Library of Congress Cataloging-in-Publication Data
Available Upon Request

ISBN: 1-59033-307-1.

400 Oser Ave, Suite 1600
Hauppauge, New York 11788-3619
Tele. 631-231-7269 Fax 631-231-8175
e-mail: Novascience@earthlink.net
Web Site: http://www.novapublishers.com

Printed in the United States of America

CONTENTS

PREFACE

The interaction among national economies is critical to today's globalized society; no country can survive without trade. Major international organizations like the World Trade Organization attempt to oversee and regulate these important relations. The United States, as the world's leading economic power is intimately involved with other countries and its own policies impact each nation. This book presents analyses of major international trade issues, emphasizing their effects and relevance to the U.S. This overview is valuable to understanding the status of the global economy and America's role in it.

Chapter 1

NORMAL TRADE RELATIONS (MOST FAVORED NATION) POLICY OF THE UNITED STATES

Vladimir N. Pregelj

SUMMARY

Legislation was enacted in 1998 to replace in U.S. statutes the misleading term "most-favored-nation" (MFN) with "normal trade relations" (NTR) or another appropriate term, but the former is still in general international use. The United States accords general MFN (nondiscriminatory) treatment as a matter of statutory policy to all trading partners except those whose MFN tariff status has been suspended by specific legislation. Virtually all such suspensions have been carried out under the mandate of the Trade Agreements Extension Act of 1951.

MFN tariff status can be restored to and retained temporarily by most of these countries under Title IV of the Trade Act of 1974 if they conclude with the United States a trade agreement containing a reciprocal MFN clause, and if they are (and remain) in compliance with the requirements of the Act's Jackson-Vanik (J-V) provision.

The trade agreement must be approved by a joint resolution, and the required presidential semiannual reports confirming full compliance with the J-V free-emigration provision, or annual recommendations for extensions of the authority to waive it, are annually subject to possible disapproval by joint resolution. Trade agreements are triennially self-renewable, but their renewal is also subject to presidential confirmation.

MFN status of a country can also be changed by specific legislation. In 19 instances, MFN status was restored under the waiver provisions of Title IV; in 17 of these cases, restoration trader the waiver was changed to one subject to determination of full compliance and, in eight cases, such restoration was later made permanent by enactment. Permanent MEN status was restored directly to four former non-MFN countries, while six countries are still denied it altogether.

In recent years, permanent NTR status was extended to Mongolia in July 1999, to Albania and Kyrgyzstan in June 2000, and to Georgia in December 2000, and measures to restore it to Kazakhstan and Cuba have been introduced in 2001, but not yet further considered.

In mid-January and in early July 2001, the President reported to Congress continued compliance with the Jackson-Vanik requirements by 9 former Soviet republics. A Jackson-Vanik waiver for Vietnam, in effect since 1998, has been extended in early June

2001 and a resolution to disapprove the extension has been defeated. A trade agreement with Vietnam, signed in July 2000, containing reciprocal grant of NTR, has been approved by law (P.L. 107-52), but not yet implemented.

MOST RECENT DEVELOPMENTS

In January 2001, the President reported to Congress continued full compliance with the requirements of the Jackson-Vanik (J- V) amendment by nine former Soviet republics and, in July 2001, made a similar report regarding the same nine countries. On June 1, 2001, the President extended for a year the J- V waiver for Vietnam, and on June 8, 2001, transmitted to Congress for approval the trade agreement with Vietnam, signed on July 13, 2000, and containing, among other provisions, reciprocal extension of the NTR status (still subject to J-V amendment). Legislative action to approve the agreement was initiated by the introduction of S.J.Res. 16 (June 11, 2001) and H.J.Res. 51 (June 12, 2001); S.J.Res. 16 was reported favorably on July 27, 2001, and H.J.Res. 51 on September 5, 2001. H.J.Res. 51 was passed the following day by the House and on October 3, 2001, by the Senate, and signed into law (P.L. 107-52) by the President on October 16, 2001, but not yet implemented.

A resolution (H.J.Res. 55) to disapprove Vietnam's waiver extension, introduced on June 21, 2001, and reported adversely on July 23, 2001, was defeated on July 26, 2001. A J-V waiver (and extension of NTR treatment) for Belarus, which had not been extended by the June 3; 2001, deadline, was issued anew on July 2, 2001.

Permanent NTR status was extended by specific law to Albania and Kyrgyzstan effective June 29, 2000, and to Georgia, effective December 29, 2000. Measures to restore it to Kazakhstan and Cuba have been introduced but not yet considered.

BACKGROUND AND ANALYSIS

What is Normal-Trade-Relations (Most-Favored-Nation) Treatment?

Although legislation has been enacted to replace the term "most-favored-nation" treatment in existing and future legislation with the term "normal trade relations" or another appropriate expression, the former term is still used in this issue brief for reasons of historical continuity and because of its continued universal use in international trade relations as well as in several U.S. bilateral trade treaties and agreements at present in force.

In international trade, the expression "most-favored-nation," usually abbreviated "MFN," status (or treatment) has a specific meaning quite at variance with what it appears to mean. While suggesting special and exclusive privileges granted to one country, it means in reality equal treatment of all countries. More specifically, it denotes the extension by a country of any concessions, privileges, or immunities granted, or yet to be granted, in a trade agreement to one country that is, or would be, the "most favored" in this respect, to all countries to which it accords MFN treatment. As a consequence, all countries to which a country extends MFN treatment are, or would be, treated equally by the extending country. Most-favored-nation treatment in fact means equal treatment, and the terms "most-favored-nation" and "non-discriminatory" are often used interchangeably.

In practice, the principal benefit a country gains from being accorded MFN status by another country is that the latter's imports from the former are dutied at concessional (often referred to as "MFN", and listed in the tariff schedules as "General") rather than full rates. Thus, the extension of MFN treatment to a country can often mean a significantly lower cost and, hence, greater competitiveness of its products in the extending country's markets.

U.S. Most-Favored-Nation Policy

There are three basic, often overlapping, ways in which the United States accords general MFN treatment to its trading partners. One is by means of a bilateral compact (e.g., a "friendship, commerce, and navigation" or similar treaty, or an executive trade agreement) in which MFN status is accorded reciprocally. Another, much broader in its reach, is through being a member of the World Trade Organization (WTO), which, as a rule, carries with it the obligation of according MFN treatment to all other members.

In addition, the United States specifically accords to all foreign countries any concession on tariffs or other import restrictions agreed to in reciprocal negotiations with any trading partner by its own law, first enacted in 1934 and now contained in Section 126 of the Trade Act of 1974 (19 U.S.C. 2136). U.S. legislation provides no specific procedure for extending MFN status to a country (except in the case of restoration of the status mentioned below) nor is there an official list of countries with MFN status. All countries other than those to which MFN treatment is specifically denied by taw have MFN status.

The policy of general application of MFN treatment was modified when the President, as required by Section 5, Trade Agreements Extension Act of 1951 (65 Stat. 75), suspended, in 1951 and 1952, the application of MFN tariff rates to the Soviet Union and to all countries or areas under the control of international communism (in practice, the suspension applied to all countries of the then Sino-Soviet bloc but not to Yugoslavia). This action resulted in the increase of customs duties assessed on the U.S. imports from the countries involved from the concessional levels resulting from trade agreements with third countries to considerably higher levels as enacted by the highly protectionist Tariff Act of 1930.

The countries and areas initially denied MFN tariff treatment under Section 5 were: Albania, Bulgaria, China (any part under Communist domination or control), Czechoslovakia, Estonia, Germany (Soviet Zone and Soviet Sector of Berlin), Hungary, Indochina (any part of Cambodia, Laos, or Vietnam under Communist domination or control), Korea (any part under Communist domination or control), Kurile Islands, Latvia, Lithuania, Outer Mongolia, Poland and areas under Polish domination or control, Rumania, Southern Sakhalin Island, Soviet Union, Tanna Tuva, and Tibet.

Subsequently, Poland's MFN tariff status was restored by the President in December 1960, while Cuba's was suspended in May 1962. Also in 1962, a list of "Communist countries" (all "Section 5" countries except Poland), to which MFN tariff status was being currently denied, was included in the newly revised Tariff Schedules of the United States, enacted by the Tariff Classification Act of 1962.

Section 231 of the Trade Expansion Act of 1962 (P.L. 87-794; 76 Stat. 876) applied the Section 5 suspension to "any country or area dominated by Communism" mad thereby placed in jeopardy MFN status of Yugoslavia as well as Poland. The implementation of this directive was delayed and the law was later amended by allowing any country with MFN status at the time of its enactment (December 16, 1963) to retain it if the President determines it to be in the national interest. Such determination was made on March 26, 1964, for both countries.

The Trade Expansion Act of 1962 also made impossible the restoration of MFN status to a country subject to Section 5 suspension except by legislation. Such a law was enacted as part of the Trade Act of 1974, which in its Section 401 requires the continuation in force of the then existing suspensions of MFN tariff status, but also, in the remainder of its Title IV, authorizes the President to restore MFN status to a "non-market economy" (NME) country and maintain it in effect. The restoration may take place and is continued in force if: (l) the President determines and reports to Congress initially and then semiannually that such country is not in violation of the requirements of the freedom-of-emigration ("Jackson-Vanik") amendment, or if he waives full compliance with such requirements under specified conditions, and his waiver authority and the existing waivers are renewed every mid-year; and (2) the country has concluded with the United States a trade agreement providing for reciprocal MFN treatment and containing other provisions as required by law, and the agreement is approved by a joint resolution enacted under a specific fast-track procedure.

The President's initial and any year-end report of full compliance with (no violation of) the free-emigration requirements or his annual mid-year recommendation of renewal of the waiver authority can be disapproved by a fast-track enactment of a joint resolution. A trade agreement with an NME country remains in effect for 3-year periods and is extended automatically under its own terms unless denounced; each such extension also requires a presidential determination of satisfactory reciprocation of the benefits extended by the United States under its MFN policy to the NME country. Triennial extensions of an agreement do not require congressional approving action.

Poland's MFN tariff status was suspended again in October 1982, after the Polish martial-law government increased its repressive measures, but was restored in February 1987, after most such measures had been repealed. In January 1986, Afghanistan's MFN status was suspended by specific law; it can be restored, under specified conditions, by executive action without congressional involvement. In 1989 the designation "Communist countries" was omitted from the title of the list of countries denied MFN tariff treatment in the newly enacted Harmonized Tariff Schedule of the United States and the designation of the countries themselves was streamlined to reflect the actual World War II border changes, except for Estonia, Latvia, and Lithuania, which remained listed individually, since their incorporation into the USSR had not been recognized by the United States. The suspension of East Germany's MFN tariff status automatically ended with the unification of the two Germanies on October 3, 1990. By the end of 1990, MFN status had been restored on an annual basis under the waiver provisions of Title IV to Romania (1975), Hungary (1978), China (including Tibet) (1980), and Czechoslovakia (1990). Romania, however, in 1988, renounced the continuation of its MFN tariff status subject to the conditions of Title IV.

Much activity related to MFN tariff status of U.S, trading partners took place during the 102nd through 105th Congresses (1991-1998).

The status was restored temporarily under the waiver provision of Title IV to Bulgaria and Mongolia in November 1991, and permanently by law in December 1991 to previously non-MFN countries Estonia, Latvia, and Lithuania, after they declared their independence from the Soviet Union, and, in April 1992, to Czechoslovakia (later split into the Czech Republic and Slovakia) and Hungary (both of which already had MFN status under Title IV). After the dissolution of the Soviet Union in late December 1991, the suspension of MFN tariff status continued in force individually with respect to its other (than the three Baltic) 12 former constituent republics. Most of these had their MFN status restored within the next two years under the waiver provision of Title IV and by acceding to the U.S.-Soviet Union trade agreement of June 1, 1990, modified to apply to each individual republic. Thus, MFN status was restored to Armenia in April 1992, Russia and Ukraine in June 1992, Moldova in July 1992, Kyrgyzstan in August 1992, Belarus and Kazakhstan in February 1993, Georgia in August 1993, Turkmenistan in October 1993, Tajikistan in November 1993, and Uzbekistan in January 1994. Azerbaijan was the only former Soviet republic whose restoration of MFN status under Title IV was still awaiting at the end of 1994 (since April 1993) the approval of that country's parliament.

During the same period, MFN tariff status also was regained under Title IV waiver provision by Albania (November 1992) and Romania (November 1993, following the September 1992 refusal of the House to restore it). MFN status of Bulgaria and the Russian Federation, restored earlier under the waiver provision, was continued in force by presidential determinations of full compliance with the freedom-of-emigration requirements (made, respectively, in June 1993 and September 1994).

Although President Bush issued in October 1992 a notice of intention to restore MFN status to Afghanistan, no action to that effect has as yet been taken.

Also, in October 1992, legislation was enacted to withdraw MFN tariff status from Serbia and Montenegro (constituent republics of Yugoslavia in its reduced size). The status may be restored by the President to either republic 30 days after he certifies to the Congress that it had ceased its warlike activities in the former Yugoslavia.

In April 1995, MFN tariff status was extended to Azerbaijan under the Jackson-Vanik waiver provision, and permanent and unconditional MFN tariff status was restored in late 1996 by specific law to three countries: Bulgaria, and Romania (both of which at the time already had MFN status under the full-compliance provision of the Jackson-Vanik amendment), respectively in October and November, and Cambodia (then a non-MFN country) in October.

Measures introduced to restore MFN tariff status, either temporarily or permanently, to a number of other countries were not given further consideration, nor were measures denying or restricting MFN status of certain countries in a variety of circumstances. The Senate did approve, however, a bill to substitute in all U.S. statutes the often misunderstood term "most favored nation treatment" with "normal trade relations;" a similar House bill, using the term "standard trade relations," remained pending. (Also suggested during the consideration of this change were other replacement terms, among them the actually more accurate terms "standard tariff relations" and "standard tariff treatment.")

In 1996, the President renewed his determinations of full compliance with the Jackson-Vanik amendment requirements for Bulgaria, Romania (both since granted permanent MFN status), and Russia, and made the initial determination for Mongolia. The President also confirmed 3-year extensions of trade agreements with 12 NME countries, with some of them after considerable delay.

During the 105th Congress, several bills affecting the MFN status of U.S. trading partners were introduced, but none enacted. Most legislative action involved bills permanently restoring MFN tariff status to Mongolia (passed by the House and favorably reported in the Senate) and Laos (favorably reported in the Senate). Introduced but not further considered was a bill granting permanent nondiscriminatory status to Kyrgyzstan and one that would grant, under certain conditions, permanent MFN status to any country still without it. On the other hand, bills also were introduced which would withdraw MEN tariff treatment from certain countries.

The President, at the appropriate times, extended all the existing Jackson-Vanik waivers, determined full compliance with the free emigration requirements by all but two (Belarus, and China) countries then still subject to the waiver, and subsequently reconfirmed such compliance. The President also issued, in April 1998, the initial Jackson-Vanik waiver for Vietnam. Joint resolutions to disapprove this waiver were introduced in both houses and reported unfavorably, whereupon the House resolution was defeated, allowing Vietnam's waiver to remain in force.

During the entire period since mid-1989, the most controversial issue of the U.S. MFN policy has been the MFN status of China. Yet, despite strong opposition in Congress to the President's annual renewals of China's Jackson-Vanik waiver and MFN status, joint resolutions introduced every year in the aftermath of the June 1989 Tiananmen Square events to disapprove such renewals have not been adopted. Two bills to subject China's MFN status to additional restrictions, passed during the 2nd session of the 102nd Congress, were vetoed by the President and in both cases, the veto was upheld by the Senate. Similar legislation as well as joint resolutions disapproving China's waiver in subsequent Congresses have not reached enactment.

Without actually affecting the practical application of MFN tariff treatment, legislation was enacted in 1998 (Section 5003 of the Internal Revenue Service Restructuring and Reform Act of 1998) to replace the term " most-favored-nation" in seven specific statutes with "normal trade relations" or another similar appropriate term. The term "most-favored-nation" continues to be used in international practice and in U.S. trade agreements with other countries.

In view of the, then prospective, accession of the Kyrgyz Republic (Kyrgyzstan) to the World Trade Organization (which eventually took effect on December 20, 1998) and the obligation of a WTO member to accord permanent and unconditional most-favored-nation treatment to all WTO members, the United States on October 12, 1998, invoked Article XIII of the WTO Agreement. The article allows the non-application of the entire WTO Agreement (and not merely of one part of it) between any current WTO member and the acceding member, upon written notice to the WTO by either, before the latter's accession. Without invoking Article XIII, the United States would be in violation of its WTO obligation toward the Kyrgyz Republic because of the latter's MFN status being subject to the Jackson-Vanik amendment. (Identical action had been taken in similar circumstances on July 11, 1996, with respect to Mongolia, then a candidate for WTO membership. After Mongolia's accession to the WTO (January 29, 1997) and the extension of permanent MFN status to Mongolia by the United States, U.S. recourse to Article XIII was rescinded by the United States with respect to Mongolia on July 7, 1999).

Developments during the 106th and 107th Congresses

In the 106th Congress, legislation to extend permanent MFN status to Mongolia, Albania, Kyrgyzstan, and Georgia was enacted and implemented; and the required report of full compliance with the requirements of the Jackson-Vanik provision by ten former Soviet Union republics was made by the President in mid-2000, as was the renewal of Jackson-Vanik waivers for Belarus and Vietnam; joint resolutions to disapprove the latter extension, introduced in both houses, failed in the House. In January and June 2001, the full compliance reports were made with regard to nine FSU republics, Kyrgyzstan meanwhile having been granted permanent NTR status.

A comprehensive trade agreement with Vietnam was signed in July 2000, and approved by Congress, but still requires approval by Vietnam legislature. Also introduced--without further action--was legislation to grant permanent nondiscriminatory status to Cuba, and several measures to reform unilateral economic sanctions legislation (including MFN policy).

Extensions of permanent nondiscriminatory tariff status were enacted and implemented as follows:

(1) Mongolia-- enacted June 25, 1999, by Section 2424 of the Miscellaneous Trade and Technical Corrections Act of 1999 (P.L. 106-36) and implemented by Presidential Proclamation 7207, effective July 1, 1999.
(2) Albania, and Kyrgyzstan -- enacted May 18, 2000, respectively, by Sections 301 and 302 of the Trade and Development Act of 2000 (P.L. 106-200) and implemented by Presidential Proclamation 7326, effective June 29, 2000.
(3) Georgia -- enacted November 9, 2000, as Title III of the Miscellaneous Trade and Technical Corrections Act of 2000 (P.L. 106-476) and implemented by Presidential Proclamation 7389, effective December 29, 2000.

Legislation to extend permanent NTR status to Cuba (S. 401; H.R. 796) and Kazakhstan (S. 168; H.R. 1318) was introduced, respectively, February 27 and 28, and January 24 and March 29, 2001, but not yet considered. Joint resolutions to approve the trade agreement with Vietnam (S.J.Res. 16; H.J.Res. 51) were introduced, respectively, on June 11 and 12, 2001, and a hearing on the U.S.-Vietnam trade agreement was held by the Senate Finance Committee on June 26, 2001.

The required Presidential semiannual determinations of continued full compliance with the requirements of the Jackson-Vanik amendment were made, occasionally with some delay, in early and mid-1999 and in early and mid-2000. Since, in the meantime, several countries once subject to the amendment have been granted permanent NTR treatment, the most recent determination (July 2, 2001) involved only nine countries, all former republics of the Soviet Union.

On June 3, 1999, the President recommended one-year extensions of Jackson-Vanik waivers for Belarus, China, and Vietnam, triggering the introduction of joint resolutions disapproving the extension for Vietnam (and China). The Vietnam resolution failed to pass the House August 3, 1999. Similarly, Presidential mid-2000 (June 2) recommendations (Presidential Determinations Nos. 2000-21, -22, and -23) to extend the waivers for Vietnam, Belarus (and China) were followed by the introduction of H.J.Res. 99 and S.J.Res. 47 to disapprove the extension of Vietnam's waiver. A hearing by the Ways and Means Trade Subcommittee on U.S.-Vietnam trade relations, including the renewal of Vietnam's waiver, took place June 15, 2000. H.J.Res. 99 was reported adversely (H.Rept. 106-794) and defeated (91 - 332) July 26, 2000. Vietnam's (but – apparently an oversight – not Belarus') Jackson-Vanik waiver was extended for another year on June 1, 2001 (Presidential Determination No. 2001-17; 66 FR 30633); a resolution (H.J.Res. 55) to disapprove it was introduced on June 21, 2001, reported adversely on July 23,2001 (H.Rept. 107-154) and defeated (91 - 324) on July 26, 2001.

A comprehensive bilateral trade agreement, containing among many other provisions a reciprocal grant of nondiscriminatory status, which is still subject to the annual extensions of the J-V waiver, was signed with Vietnam on July 13, 2000, and transmitted by the President to Congress on June 8, 2001, for legislative approval, which was enacted (P.L. 107-52) on October 16, 2001.

The earlier invocation of the non-application Article XIII of the WTO Agreement with respect to Kyrgyzstan was rescinded on July 20, 2000; and, on January 8,2001, the September 30, 1999, recourse by the United States to Article XIII with respect to Georgia (whose accession to the WTO took effect June 14, 2000) was disinvoked upon the implementation of PNTR for that country. In view of the impending accession of Moldova to the WTO (eventually approved by the WTO General Council on May 8, 2001, and taking effect on July 26, 2001), the United States, on May 2, 2001, invoked the application of Article XIII with respect to Moldova (since Moldova is still subject to the conditional MFN treatment under Title IV of the 1974 Trade Act).

Present Status

In view of the statutory general applicability of MFN status to U.S. trading partners under Section 126 of the Trade Act of 1974, there is no official specific list of countries with MFN status; all countries other than those to which MEN tariff status has been specifically denied by law or extended conditionally under Title IV of the Trade Act of 1974, have permanent and unconditional MFN status.

Countries to which, at present, MFN tariff status is denied are Afghanistan, Cuba, Laos, North Korea, Vietnam, and Yugoslavia (Serbia and Montenegro).

Countries to which MFN tariff status is at present being extended after having been conditionally restored temporarily under the provisions of Title IV of the Trade Act of 1974 are:

(1) under the presidential waiver of Jackson-Vanik amendment requirements, which must be extended annually and the extension of which is subject to disapproval by joint resolution of Congress: Belarus, and China (with Tibet). (A waiver is also in effect for Vietnam, and the restoration of its MFN tariff status, contained in the bilateral agreement, but still subject to the J-V amendment, has been approved by law (P.L. 107-52). The entry into force of the agreement, still remains contingent its ratification by Vietnam's National Assembly, and bilateral exchange of notices of acceptance); and

(2) under the presidential determination of continued compliance with the Jackson-Vanik amendment requirements, which, after the initial one, must be renewed semiannually and is subject to disapproval by joint resolution of Congress at the time of year-end renewal: Armenia, Azerbaijan, Kazakhstan, Moldova, Russia, Tajikistan, Turkmenistan, Ukraine, and Uzbekistan.

Restoration of permanent NTR status to Mongolia has been enacted (P.L. 106-36) and implemented by Presidential Proclamation 7207, effective July 1, 1999, and permanent nondiscriminatory treatment was restored to Albania and Kyrgyzstan by Sections 301 and 302 of P.L. 106-200, signed May 18, 2000, and implemented by Presidential Proclamation 7326, effective June 29, 2000. Legislation to grant PNTR to Georgia (Title III, P.L. 106-476) was signed on November 9, 2000, and implemented by Presidential Proclamation 7389, effective December 29, 2000.

The Jackson-Vanik waiver for Vietnam was extended on June 1, 2001, for one year by the President (Pres. Det. No. 2001-17; 66 F.R. 30633); H.J.Res. 55 to disapprove the extension was introduced on June 21, 2001, reported adversely on July 23, 2001 (H.Rept. 107-154) and defeated on July 26, 2001 (91 - 324). Belarus' Jackson-Vanik waiver, which-apparently through an oversight-was not extended by the June 3 deadline, was issued anew on July 2, 2001 (Executive Order 13220; 66 F.R. 35527).

Legislation (S.J.Res. 16 and H.J.Res. 51) was introduced, respectively, on June 11 and 12, 2001, to approve the comprehensive trade agreement with Vietnam, signed on July 13, 2000, and transmitted on June 8, 2001, by the President to Congress for approval. A hearing on the U.S.-Vietnam trade relations was held by the House Ways and Means Trade Subcommittee on June 15, 2000, and on the trade agreement by the Senate Committee on Finance on June 26, 2001; S.J.Res. 16 was reported favorably on July 27, 2001 (S.Rept. 107-49), and H.J.Res. 51 was reported favorably on September 5, 2001 (H.Rept. 107-198), and passed in the House by voice vote on the following day and in the Senate (88 - 12) on October 3, 2001. It was signed into law (P.L. 107-52) on October 16, 2001, but not yet implemented, still requiring approval by the Vietnam National Assembly

MFN status can be restored to Afghanistan and Yugoslavia -- countries not subject to the Jackson-Vanik amendment -- by executive action under conditions specified in the legislation suspending the status.

Presidential determinations of satisfactory reciprocity, which the law requires for extending the triennial terms of bilateral trade agreements with NME countries, have in recent years been published with delays or, in one instance, not at all. At present, there are no extant published determinations extending the agreements with the NME countries to which this provision applies past the expiration dates of their previous determinations (10 fairly recent, 1 of several years ago). This omission does not in practice affect the NTR status of these countries, since they are all still treated as having NTR status, apparently on the basis of the standard provision for automatic triennial renewal in the trade agreements themselves.

Legislation, enacted in 1998, requires that the term "most-favored-nation" in existing mad future legislation be replaced with "normal trade relations" or another appropriate term. The MFN term, however, is still being used in practice internationally and in U.S. trade agreements; in some of the latter, both terms are used in parallel.

LEGISLATION

P.L. 107-52, H.J.Res. 51 (Armey)

Approves extension of nondiscriminatory treatment to Vietnam. H.J.Res. 51 and S.J.Res. 16 introduced, respectively, on June 12 and 11, 2001; referred to House Committee on Ways and Means, and to Senate Committee on Finance, respectively. A hearing on the U.S.-Vietnam trade agreement was held by the Senate Finance Committee on June 26, 2001, and S.J.Res. 16 reported favorably on July 27, 2001 (S.Rept. 107-49). H.J.Res. 51 was reported favorably on September 5, 2001 (H.Rept. 107-198) and passed in the House by voice vote on the following day and in the Senate (88-12) on October 3, 2001. It was signed into law (P.L. 107-52) on October 16, 2001.

H.J.Res. 55 (Rohrabaeher)

Disapproves the annual extension of Vietnam's Jackson-Vanik waiver. Introduced on June 5, 2001; referred to the Ways and Means Committee; reported adversely on July 23, 2001 (H.Rept. 107-154) and defeated on July 27, 2001 (91 - 324).

H.R. 796 (Rangel)/S. 401 (Baucus)

(United States-Cuba Act of 2001) Terminates the application of Title IV of the Trade Act of 1974 to Cuba and extends permanent nondiscriminatory treatment to imports from Cuba. Introduced, respectively, February 28 and 27, 2001, and referred to House Committee of Ways and Means, and Senate Committee on Finance, respectively.

H.R. 1318 (Pitts)/S. 168 (Brownback)

Terminates the application of Title IV of the Trade Act of 1974 to Kazakhstan and extends permanent nondiscriminatory treatment to imports from Kazakhstan. Introduced, respectively, March 29 and January 24, 2001, and referred to House Committee of Ways and Means, and Senate Committee on Finance, respectively.

CHRONOLOGY

10/16/01 – H.J.Res. 51 signed into law (P.L. 107-52).

10/03/01 – H.J.Res. 51 passed in the Senate (88-12).

09/06/01 – H.J.Res. 51 to approve the extension of nondiscriminatory treatment to Vietnam (see 09/05/01) passed in the House by voice Vote.

09/05/01 – H.J.Res. 51 to approve the extension of nondiscriminatory treatment to Vietnam see 07/26/01) reported favorably by House Ways and Means Committee (H.Rept. 107-198).

07/27/01 – S.J.Res. 16 to approve the extension of nondiscriminatory treatment to Vietnam see 06/11/01) reported favorably by Senate Finance Committee (S.Rept. 107-49).

07/26/01 – H.J.Res. 55 to disapprove extension of the Jackson-Vanik waiver for Vietnam defeated in the House (91 - 324).

07/23/01 –	J.Res. 55 to disapprove extension of the Jackson-Vanik waiver for Vietnam reported adversely by House Ways and Means Committee (see entry for 06/21/01).
07/02/01 –	Since Belarus' Jackson-Vanik waiver had not been extended by the June 3 deadline; the President issued a new waiver for Belarus (E.O. 13220; 66 F.R. 35527; H.Doc. 107-97).
–	The President determined and reported to Congress that 9 former Soviet Republics subject to the Jackson-Vanik amendment (all except Belarus) continue to be in full compliance with the Jackson-Vanik requirements (H.Doc. 107-98).
06/26/01 –	Senate Committee on Finance held a hearing on the U.S.-Vietnam trade agreement.
06/21/01 –	H.J.Res. 55 introduced to disapprove the extension of the Jackson-Vanik waiver for Vietnam (see entry for June 1, 2001).
06/12/01 –	H.J.Res. 51 introduced to approve extension of nondiscriminatory treatment to Vietnam. (identical with S.J.Res. 16).
06/11/01 –	S.J.Res. 16 introduced to approve extension of nondiscriminatory treatment to Vietnam (identical with H.J.Res. 51).
06/08/01 –	The President transmitted to Congress the trade agreement with Vietnam and its proclamation (Pres. Proc. 7449) (H.Doc. 107-85).
06/01/02 –	The President extended the Jackson-Vanik waiver for Vietnam for one year (Pres. Det. No. 2001-17; 66 F.R. 30633).
05/02/01 –	The United States invoked the WTO non-application Article XIII with respect to Moldova.
03/29/01 –	H.R. 1318 (identical with S. 168) introduced to extend permanent nondiscriminatory treatment to Kazakhstan.
02/28/01 –	H.R. 796 (identical with S. 401) introduced to extend permanent nondiscriminatory treatment to Cuba.
02/27/01 –	S. 401 (United States-Cuba Act of 2001) introduced to extend permanent nondiscriminatory treatment to Cuba.
01/24/01 –	S. 168 introduced to extend permanent nondiscriminatory treatment to Kazakhstan.
01/17/01 –	The President determined and reported to Congress that 9 former Soviet Republics subject to the Jackson-Vanik amendment (all except Belarus) continue to be in full compliance with the Jackson-Vanik requirements (H.Doc. 107-17).
12/29/00 –	Permanent nondiscriminatory treatment extended to Georgia by Pres. Proclamation 7389 (66 F.R. 703).
11/09/00 –	H.R. 4868 (Miscellaneous Trade and Technical Corrections Act of 2000; P.L. 106-476), including permanent NTR status for Georgia, signed by the President.
10/26/00 –	H.R. 4868 (as amended by the House) passed by the Senate.
10/25/00 –	H.R. 4868 passed by the House with an amendment.
10/13/00 –	Senate version of H.R. 4868, with language of H.R. 4782 added, passed.

07/26/00 –	H.J.Res. 99, to disapprove the extension of the Jackson-Vanik waiver for Vietnam, reported adversely (H.Rept. 106-704) and defeated (91 - 331) in the House, permitting the waiver to remain in force for another year.
07/20/00 –	S. 2896 introduced to extend permanent nondiscriminatory treatment to Cuba.
–	The United States rescinded the invocation (on June 29, 1999, under WTO Article XIII) of the application of the WTO Agreement with respect to Kyrgyzstan (see entry for 06/29/00).
07/13/00 –	A comprehensive trade agreement between the United States and Vietnam, including reciprocal extension of NTR, was signed. Agreement must still be approved by a joint resolution of Congress and by Vietnam's National Assembly.
–	H.R. 4856 introduced to extend permanent nondiscriminatory treatment to Cuba.
06/30/00 –	The President determined and reported to Congress that 10 former Soviet Republics (all except Belarus) continue to be in full compliance with the Jackson-Vanik requirements.
06/29/00 –	Permanent nondiscriminatory treatment extended to Albania and Kyrgyzstan by Pres. Proclamation 7326 (63 FR 41547).
–	H.R. 4782 introduced to extend permanent nondiscriminatory treatment to Georgia.
06/15/00 –	House Ways and Means Trade Subcommittee held a hearing on U.S.-Vietnam relations, including Vietnam's Jackson-Vanik waiver.
06/06/00 –	H.J.Res. 99 and S.J.Res. 47 introduced to disapprove the President's extension of the Jackson-Vanik waiver for Vietnam.
06/02/00 –	The President issued Presidential Determinations 2000-21 and 2000-22, extending for one year Jackson-Vanik waivers, respectively, for Vietnam and Belarus.
05/18/00 –	The President signed H.R. 434 (P.L. 106-200), containing provisions (Secs. 301 and 302) authorizing the President to extend nondiscriminatory treatment to Albania and Kyrgyzstan.
05/11/00 –	The Senate agreed (77-19) to the conference report on H.R. 434.
05/04/00 –	Conference report on H.R. 434 (Trade and Development Act of 2000) (H.Rept. t06- 606) filed, including the authority for extending unconditional nondiscriminatory treatment to Albania and Kyrgyzstan in Sees. 301 and 302, respectively.
–	Conference version of H.R. 434 passed by the House (309 - 110).
02/09/00 –	The President determined and reported to Congress (H.Doc. 106-195) that Albania continues to be in full compliance with the Jackson-Vanik requirements.
01/07/00 –	The President determined and reported to Congress that 11 former Soviet Republics (all except Belarus) continue to be in full compliance with the Jackson-Vanik requirements (Weekly Compilation of Presidential Documents, v. 36, No. 2, Jan. 17, 2000, p. 29.

CONGRESSIONAL HEARINGS, REPORTS, AND DOCUMENTS

U.S. Congress. Conference Committees. Trade and Development Act of 2000; conference report (to accompany H.R. 434). Washington, U.S. Govt. Print. Off., May 4, 2000. 146 p. At head of tire: 106th Congress, 2d Session. H.Rept. 106-606.

U.S. Congress. House. Committee on Ways and Means. Approval of the extension of nondiscriminatory treatment with respect to the products of the Socialist Republic of Vietnam; report together with additional views (to accompany H.J.Res. 51). Washington, U.S. Govt. Print Off., Sept. 5, 2001. 11 p. At the head of title: 107th Congress, 1st session. H.Rept. 107-198.

— Disapproval of normal trade relations treatment to the products of Vietnam; adverse report (to accompany H.J.Res. 55). Washington, U.S. Govt. Print. Off., July 23, 2001. 8 p. At head of title: 107th Congress, 1st Session. H.Rept. 107-154).

— Disapproval of normal trade relations treatment to the products of Vietnam; adverse report (to accompany H.J.Res. 55). Washington, U.S. Govt. Print. Off., August 2, 1999. 8 p. At head of title: 106th Congress, 1st Session. H.Rept. 106-282.

— Disapproving the extension of waiver authority contained in Section 402(c) of the Trade Act of 1974 with respect to Vietnam; adverse report (to accompany H.J.Res. 99). Washington, U.S. Govt. Print. Off., July 26, 2000.8 p. At head of title: 106th Congress, 2d Session. H.Rept. 106-794.

— Subcommittee on Trade. United States-Vietnam trade relations; hearing ... June 15, 2000. (Serial 106-106). Washington, U.S. Govt. Print. Off., 2000. 78 p.

— Subcommittee on Trade. Written comments on the extension of normal trade relations to the Kyrgyz Republic. Washington, U.S. Govt. Print. Off., February 10, 1999. 6 p. At head of tire: 105th Congress, 2nd session. Committee print WMCP: 105-12.

— Subcommittee on Trade. Written comments on the extension of unconditional normal trade relations to the Kyrgyz Republic. Washington, U.S. Govt. Print. Off., November 4, 1999. 11 p. At head of title: 106th Congress, 1st session. Committee print WMCP: 106-5.

— Written comments on the extension of normal trade relations to the Lao People's Democratic Republic. Washington, U.S. Govt. Print. Off., November 4, 1999. 44 p. At head of title: 106th Congress, 1st session. Committee print WMCP:106-6.

— U.S. Congress. Senate. Committee on Finance. Approving the extension of nondiscriminatory treatment (normal trade relations) to the products of the Socialist Republic of Vietnam; report (to accompany S.J.Res. 16). Washington, U.S. Govt. Print. Off., July 27, 2001. 13 p. At head of title: 107th Congress. 1st session. H.Rept.107-49.

— Miscellaneous Trade and Technical Corrections Act of 1999; report (to accompany S. 262). Washington, U.S. Govt. Print. Off., February 3, 1999. 81 p. [p. 73]. At head of title: 106th Congress, 1st session. S.Rept. 106-2.

— U.S. President, 1993-2001 (Clinton). An update on the emigration laws and policies of Albania; communication from the President of the United States... Washington, U.S. Govt. Print Off., 1999. 3 p. (106th Congress, 1st session. H.Doc. 106-16). Communication dated February 2, 1999.

— Emigration laws and policies of Albania; message from the President of the United States... Washington, U.S. Govt. Print. Off., 1999. 3 p. (106th Congress, 1st session. H.Doc. 106-98). Message dated July 19, 1999.

— Emigration laws and policies of Mongolia; communication from the President of the United States... Washington, U.S. Govt. Print Off., 1999. 3 p. (106th Congress, 1st session. H.Doc. 106-19). Communication dated February 11, 1999.

— Report concerning emigration laws and policies of Albania; message from the President of the United States... Washington, U.S. Govt. Print. Off., 2001 5 p., (106th Congress, 2d Session. H.Doc. 106-195). Message dated Feb. 9, 2000.

— A report to Congress concerning the extension of waiver authority for Belarus; communication from the President of the United States... Washington, U.S. Govt. Print. Off., 1999. 4 p. (106th Congress, 1st session. H.Doc. 106-76). Communication dated June 3, 1999.

— A report to the Congress concerning the extension of waiver authority for Vietnam; communication from the President of the United States... Washington, U.S. Govt. Print. Off., 1999. 6 p. (106th Congress, 1st session. H.Doc. 106-78). Communication dated June 3, 1999.

U.S. President, 2001- (Bush). An agreement between the United States and the Socialist Republic of Vietnam on trade relations: message from the Preside/at of the United States... Washington, U.S. Govt. Print. Off., 2001. 128 p. (107th Congress, 1st Session. H.Doc. 107-85). Message dated June 8, 2001.

— Emigration laws and policies; communication from the President of the United States...Washington, U.S. Govt. Print. Off., 2001.7 p. (107th Congress, 1st Session. H.Doc. 107-98). Communication dated July 2, 2001.

— A report concerning a waiver of Jackson-Vanik amendment for the Republic of Belarus; communication from the President of the United States ... Washington, U.S. Govt. Print. Off., 2001. 4 p. (107th Congress, 1st Session. H.Doc. 107-97). Communication dated July 2, 2001.

Chapter 2

THE WORLD TRADE ORGANIZATION: THE DOHA MINISTERIAL

Lenore Sek

ISSUE

Trade ministers from member countries of the World Trade Organization are scheduled to meet November 9-13, 2001, in Doha, Qatar, where they will consider whether to begin a new round of trade negotiations. A draft ministerial declaration was released on October 27. It reflects the range of priorities among WTO members and will be the basis for trade ministers' decisions on an agenda for a new round. India and other developing countries have been cool to a new round, in some cases because they believe they received few benefits from the last round. It remains to be seen whether a new round will be launched.

BACKGROUND

Trade ministers from member countries of the World Trade Organization (WTO) must meet at least every two years, according to the agreement that established the WTO. These meetings, called Ministerial Conferences, are the highest level of decision-making in the WTO. Since the WTO was established in 1995, there have been three Ministerial Conferences, and the fourth is scheduled for November 9-13 in Doha, Qatar.

The scheduled ministerial comes at a time when economic activity worldwide is slowing and business and consumer confidence is declining. These developments no doubt have been exacerbated by the September 11 terrorist attacks on the United States and continuing terrorist threats to the United States and other countries.

Although a new round of global trade liberalization agreements, according to a University of Michigan study, could be expected to add a $700 billion stimulus to the world economy and boost U.S. family income by $2,500 annually, these results would take years to materialize given the normal pace of such negotiations. Nevertheless, given today's tense environment, the launching of a new round (or conversely the failure to launch a new round) may have increased symbolic importance especially if decisions made in Doha affect nervous markets, or producer and consumer psychology, at home and abroad.

Given this environment, the key question for the Doha meeting may be whether countries will agree to begin a new "round" of trade negotiations on a broad range of topics. Negotiations are currently underway on agriculture and services trade, as required under agreements that resulted from the last comprehensive round of multilateral trade negotiations (the Uruguay Round, 1986-1994). Those negotiations formally began on February 25, 2000, (services) and March 23, 2000, (agriculture; see in this briefing book *Agriculture Trade Negotiations in the World Trade Organization*). There are no deadlines for completion. Some countries, including the United States, wanted to expand the agriculture and services talks to include other areas. Their argument was that broader negotiations not only will address other areas, but also will allow greater trade liberalization through trade-offs. They wanted WTO members to agree to start a new round of trade negotiations at the Doha Ministerial Conference.

Trade ministers had considered a new round of trade negotiations at the 1999 Ministerial Conference in Seattle, but they ended their meeting without agreeing on an agenda. Following the Seattle Ministerial, it was agreed that WTO officials would consult with member countries and discuss ways to bridge remaining differences. Much progress reportedly has been made toward reaching agreement on issues to be discussed at the Doha Ministerial and on items for a possible agenda.

A first draft of a ministerial declaration, which sets out a "future work programme," was released on September 26, 2001, by the Chairman of the WTO General Council, Stuart Harbinson. That draft was circulated for comment and was revised on October 27, 2001. This second version of the Harbinson text will be presented to trade ministers at Doha for their decisions. The U.S. Trade Representative commented on the October 27 draft: "The revised draft declaration makes additional progress towards a successful launch of negotiations at Doha, although we still have much work to do."

The October 27 draft declaration includes a future work program that would be an agenda for new negotiations. The future work program includes the following topics: agriculture; services; market access for non-agricultural (industrial) products; trade-related aspects of intellectual property rights; the relationship between trade and investment; the interaction between trade and competition policy; transparency in government procurement; trade facilitation; WTO rules; dispute settlement understanding; trade and environment; electronic commerce; small economies; trade, debt and finance; trade and transfer of technology; technical cooperation and capacity building; least developed countries; and special and differential treatment. On the issue of labor standards, which was highly controversial at the Seattle Ministerial, the Harbinson draft says little: it reaffirms the Singapore Ministerial Declaration, which recognized the International Labor Organization (ILO) as the "competent body to set and deal with these [labor] standards" and notes "...work under way in the [ILO] on the social dimension of globalization."

Launching a new round will depend on agreements and accommodations made by the United States, the European Union, Japan, and the developing countries. The Harbinson draft poses opportunities as well as challenges for each of these key players.

The United States has much to gain from the emphasis of the draft on market access proposals that would tend to open up trade opportunities for agriculture and services, the two sectors where the United States enjoys competitive advantages. At the same time, market access proposals that could accelerate developing country exports of textile and apparel products to the United States, as well as proposals to "weaken" antidumping and countervailing duty laws could prove politically sensitive.

The European Union has also much to gain from the liberalization of trade in services, but much greater sensitivity on agricultural liberalization. With much of the rest of the world wanting WTO members to commit to eliminating agricultural export subsidies, the EU seeks to devise a compromise that will allow its liberalization to proceed at a pace consistent with its internal political dynamics. The EU's other key sensitivities are on the environment (see Environment in the WTO in this briefing book) and food safety. The EU also is pushing for a broad agenda that includes competition and investment.

Japan has much to gain from trade liberalization generally, but has focused primarily on political sensitivities relating to agriculture and steel. Accordingly, it has not supported a trade liberalizing agricultural agenda, nor has it shown much flexibility in supporting the U.S. effort to keep antidumping and countervailing duty laws off the negotiating table. According to U.S. Trade Representative Robert Zoellick not only has Japan not led in the run-up to Doha, it has not even been a "respectable follower."

Developing countries have been reluctant to agree to new trade negotiations. They say they have not yet received the benefits that were promised from the Uruguay Round. They are now a large proportion of total WTO membership (about three-fourths), and any new negotiations would depend on their participation. The draft declaration includes several topics of interest to developing countries in the future work program, but developing countries want up-front concessions from developed countries. They want developed countries to address concessions that they feel they should have received under the Uruguay Round agreements but haven't, and technical or other assistance to help them meet obligations they agreed to under existing trade agreements. Such issues are being called "implementation issues." General Council Chairman Harbinson released a separate text addressing these issues. The Harbinson text proposes action on implementation issues at the Doha ministerial meeting in connection with the start of new negotiations and over a longer time as part of the negotiations.

Domestically, there is both opposition to and support for new WTO negotiations. The AFL-CIO reports that labor groups throughout the world are planning a day of action on the opening day of the Doha meeting to express their view that globalization is hurting workers. On the other hand, the Business Roundtable says that the United States has the most to gain from removing foreign barriers through trade agreements and the most to lose if barriers continue.

LEGISLATION

Although the executive branch conducts trade negotiations in the WTO, Congress has an important role in how the United States participates in multilateral trade negotiations through its constitutional responsibility for the conduct of foreign commerce. In the past, Congress has prescribed trade objectives for U.S. negotiators and has required the executive branch to consult with it as a condition for expedited procedures for legislation to implement trade agreements. Trade promotion authority (TPA) legislation with these provisions is currently under consideration in the 107th Congress. Some observers had argued that congressional approval of negotiating authority before the Doha meeting was critical if the United States was to play a leadership role in getting the negotiations started. Others argued that past multilateral rounds started without the executive branch having trade negotiating authority without any major problem. The Doha Ministerial will begin without congressional approval of TPA. However, a vote on TPA legislation might occur before the end of the session. Finally, after negotiations are finished and if an agreement is reached, Congress ultimately decides whether or not to approve the trade agreement and implementing legislation.

Chapter 3

TRADE AND THE AMERICAS

Raymond J. Ahearn

SUMMARY

The Summit of the Americas, held in Miami in December 1994, led to ongoing congressional interest in three inter-related trade policy issues. The first involves an invitation extended to Chile to join the North America Free Trade Agreement (NAFTA). The second focuses on preferential tariff treatment for Caribbean and Central American countries. The third concerns movement towards a Free Trade Area of the Americas (FTAA), the concept of making the entire hemisphere a free-trade zone. A fourth issue has subsequently arisen concerning a request by the Andean countries to extend the Andean Trade Preferences Act (ATPA) beyond its scheduled December 4, 2001, expiration date. Following the Miami Summit, the U.S., Canada, and Mexico invited Chile to enter into negotiations to accede to NAFTA. Envisioned as a first step towards creation of an FTAA, preliminary negotiations started in July 1995. Chile, how- ever, shortly thereafter suspended the negotiations pending renewal of U.S. "fast-track" negotiating authority. In August 1999, Chile proposed to restart discussions on a bilateral free trade agreement (not NAFTA accession), and negotiations eventually commenced December 6-7, 2000 in Washington. The Bush Administration has continued the negotiations with the hope of reaching an agreement by early this year. A second issue concerns the treatment of the Caribbean and Central American countries that may have been hurt in trade and investment terms as a result of the implementation of NAFTA. After many years of consideration, Congress in May 2000 enacted the Caribbean Basin Trade Partnership Act (Title 11 of P.L. 106-200) that provides benefits for CBI beneficiary countries that are similar to the tariff benefits afforded Mexico. The new law, in particular, offers expanded access and preferential tariff treatment to certain textile and apparel products assembled from U.S. fabric, under specified conditions. To date, the program has been implemented with respect to 14 countries, but several interim customs rules implementing the law remain controversial. The third issue involves movement towards hemispheric free trade.

Nearly four years after the 1994 Summit of the Americas, hemispheric leaders formally launched the FTAA negotiations in 1998. The course of the negotiations has been affected by political and economic problems in the hemisphere and the continued absence of U.S. fast trade authority. At the third Summit of the Americas held in Quebec City on April 20-22, 2001, hemispheric leaders did agree to complete the negotiations by January

1, 2005 and to implement the agreement no later than the end of 2005. A preliminary draft and bracketed text of the nine chapters that have been negotiated to date are now available to the public on the FTAA website. Negotiators will strive to eliminate brackets in the text to the extent possible before the seventh Ministerial in Quito, Ecuador, to be held by October 2002. A fourth issue that has arisen involves a request from Bolivia, Colombia, Ecuador, and Peru to extend the ATPA beyond its December 4, 2001 expiration date, to reduce the list of products excluded from tariff benefits, and to add Venezuela as a beneficiary country. The 1991 ATPA granted Andean countries tariff preferences for 10 years in an effort to help the countries fight narcotics trafficking. The House in 2001 approved an expansion and extension of the program (H.R. 3009). Less expansive legislation has been reported out of the Senate Finance Committee, but the full Senate has not taken up the bill yet.

MOST RECENT DEVELOPMENTS

In a speech on January 16, 2002, President Bush announced that his administration wishes to negotiate a free trade agreement with the five countries of Central America - Costa Rica, Honduras, Guatemala, El Salvador, and Nicaragua.

Brazilian President Cardoso charged on December 10, 2001, that the House passed trade promotion bill will doom any prospects for approval of the Free Trade Area of the Americas. He objected strenuously to a provision of the bill that removes import-sensitive agricultural products from the President's tariff proclamation authority.

The House on December 6, 2001, approved a bill (H.R. 3005) to provide the President with trade promotion authority, formerly known as fast track. In an effort to win support for the bill, House Republican leaders pledged to bring no future trade bills to the House floor until legislative action is taken to assure that apparel assembled in Caribbean and Central American countries for export to the United States is made from fabric that is dyed, printed, or finished in the United States.

On November 16, 2001, the House passed (H.R. 3009), a bill to extend and expand the Andean Trade Preference Act (ATPA).

Chilean Ambassador to the United States, Andres Bianchi, stated on September 27, 2001, that completing negotiations on a U.S.-Chile free trade agreement was certainly a "tall order." U.S. Trade Representative Robert Zoellick on July 3, 2001, welcomed the release of a draft Free Trade Area of the Americas bracketed text of the nine chapters that have been negotiated to date.

BACKGROUND AND ANALYSIS

Summit of the Americas: Trade Results

At the Summit of the Americas held December 9-11, 1994, in Miami, 34 hemispheric democracies agreed to create a "Free Trade Area of the Americas (FTAA)." Under the Declaration of Principles, the countries committed to "begin immediately" construction of the free trade area and to complete negotiations no later than the year 2005.

The Declaration stated that concrete progress toward the FTAA will occur before the close of the century. Based on the view that substantial progress towards economic integration in the hemisphere has already been made, the declaration called for building on "existing sub-regional and bilateral arrangements in order to broaden and deepen hemispheric economic integration and to bring the agreements together." At the same time, the declaration recognized the need to "remain cognizant" of the "wide differences in the levels of development and size of economies" in the Hemisphere in moving toward tighter economic integration.

If created, the FTAA would have 34 members (Cuba is not included) with over 800 million people. This population would be more than twice the 375 million of the now 15-nation European Union.

In the 7 years following the 1994 Miami Summit, Western Hemisphere trade ministers have met six times under the FTAA process. The first meeting was held in Denver in June 1995; the second in Cartagena, Colombia in March 1996; the third in Belo Horizonte, Brazil in May 1997; the fourth in San Jose, Costa Rica in March 1998; the fifth in Toronto, Canada in November 1999, and the sixth in Argentina from April 6-7, 2001.

At the San Jose meeting, the 34 Ministers responsible for trade in the Hemisphere unanimously recommended that the Leaders formally launch the negotiation of the FTAA at the Second Summit of the Americas in Santiago. As provided by the San Jose Declaration, ministers agreed that negotiating groups were to achieve considerable progress by the year 2000, with a conclusion set for December 31, 2004. The San Jose Declaration also provided recommendations on the initial structure, objectives, venues, and principles of the negotiations.

Canada was designated as the Chair of the overall negotiating process for the initial 18 months (May 1, 1998-Oct. 31, 1999) and the United States and Brazil were named co-chairs during the final two years of the negotiations (November 1, 2002-December 31, 2004). As head of both the Ministerial and Trade Negotiations Committee (TNC), the Chair will provide overall direction and management of the negotiations.

The Ministers elected to establish nine initial negotiating groups, which cover all the tariff and non-tariff barrier issue areas identified by the Leaders at the Miami Summit of the Americas. These groups are market access, agriculture, services, government procurement, investment, intellectual property, subsidies, competition policy, and dispute settlement. In addition, the Ministers created two committees and a consultative group. A Committee on Electronic Commerce, comprised of both government and private sector experts, was established to make recommendations on how to increase and broaden the benefits to be derived from the electronic marketplace. A Committee on Civil Society was established to receive input at the hemispheric level from labor and environmental groups, and academic, consumer, and other non-governmental groups. And a Consultative Group on Smaller Economies was established to bring to the attention of the TNC the interests and concerns of the smaller economies.

The United States (Miami) provided the venue for the negotiating groups and the administrative secretariat supporting those meeting during the first three years. The last four years of the negotiations are being held in Panama and Mexico.

The San Jose Declaration contains General Principles for the Negotiations, as well as General and Specific Objectives. In addition to transparency during the negotiations, the Ministers agreed that the FTAA should improve upon WTO rules and disciplines wherever possible and appropriate. This provision was an attempt to ensure that any final agreement will break down the most serious trade barriers in the region and provide a single set of roles for hemispheric trade. It was agreed that bilateral and sub-regional agreements such as NAFTA and Mercosur can coexist with the FTAA only to the extent that the fights and obligations under those agreements are not covered or go beyond those of the FTAA. It was also agreed that the negotiations will be a "single undertaking," in the sense that signatories to the final FTAA Agreement will have to accept all parts of it (i.e. cannot pick and choose among the obligations.)

At the Second Summit of the Americas, held in Chile in April 1998, President Clinton and 21 other presidents and 12 prime ministers of the Western Hemisphere agreed to begin the trade negotiations, and to make "concrete progress" toward the free trade goal by 2000. Since then, some progress has been made in developing a variety of customs-related business facilitation measures to expedite the conduct of trade even before the negotiations are completed. In terms of the negotiations, considerable progress has been made in some of the groups; much less in others.

The sixth ministerial meeting, held April 6-7, 2001, in Buenos Aires, established a more precise time frame for conclusion and entry into force of the FTAA agreement. These deadlines, which include that the FTAA countries must agree on how to conduct the market-opening portion of the talks by April 1, 2002; start negotiations no later than May 15, 2002; and produce an agreement that should enter into force no later than December 2005, were approved by 33 Heads of State at the Quebec City Summit. Only Venezuela declined to endorse the timeline, arguing that the leaders' declaration as worded did not reflect the process under its national laws for ratifying the agreement. The leaders also added a new pledge that only democracies would be able to participate in the trade bloc and agreed to make public the preliminary negotiated texts. (The preliminary draft text coveting nine chapters negotiated is now available on the FTAA website in the four official languages of the FTAA: English, Spanish, French, and Portuguese).

The seventh Ministerial will be held in Quito, Ecuador by October 2002. Ministers have instructed negotiators from all FTAA governments to undertake work to revise the draft chapters of the FTAA text, eliminating brackets in the texts to the maximum extent possible before the Quito Ministerial.

Vision of Free Trade in the Americas

The vision of free trade in the Americas was put forth initially by President George Bush in June 1990. Proposed as the cornerstone of the Enterprise for the Americas Initiative (EAI), President Bush envisaged the creation of a " free trade system that links all of the Americas: North, Central, and South ... a free trade zone stretching from the port of Anchorage to the Tierra del Fuego" (the southern tip of Chile). The free trade vision was enthusiastically received in Latin America.

Bush Administration officials at the time emphasized that the goal of hemispheric free trade was long-term, and could take a decade or more to come to fruition. Moreover, the hemispheric free trade vision entailed a variable pattern of economic integration, perhaps involving a number of free trade agreements with individual countries or with the region's economic groupings. Given that the timing, terms, and actual dimensions of the proposal were uncertain, its main significance was an offer of a special relationship with the countries of the Western Hemisphere.

Upon assuming office, President Clinton supported the hemispheric free trade concept. Like his predecessor, Clinton viewed movement towards hemispheric economic integration as supportive of U.S. economic and political interests.

Initially, Clinton Administration efforts to clarify the process by which it would work toward creation of a hemispheric free trade area awaited the outcome of the congressional vote on NAFTA, a trade agreement that was touted as a first step in moving towards the vision of hemispheric free trade. Since NAFTA was approved in late 1993, the Administration restated its intention of negotiating a free trade agreement with Chile first, but declined from naming other specific countries as candidates for future free trade agreements.

The 1994 Clinton Summit of the Americas in Miami helped create a political consensus in the Administration to take further steps in moving towards hemispheric integration. In remarks delivered at the Summit, President Clinton hailed the proposal to build a free trade area from Alaska to Argentina as producing more jobs in the United States and improving the quality of life for residents of the Western Hemisphere.

Since Miami, the vision of hemispheric free trade has been promoted both by the formal negotiations held as a part of the FTAA process, and by the expansion of sub-regional groups and the proliferation of bilateral free trade agreements. Under the former approach, the trade ministers of the hemisphere laid the groundwork for the formal launching of the negotiations, which was agreed to at the Second Summit of the Americas in Santiago. Under the latter approach, Mercosur (the Southern Cone Common Market) has expanded and countries such as Chile and Mexico have negotiated bilateral free trade agreements. Lacking fast-track negotiating authority, the Clinton Administration was not active under this process.

President George W. Bush, who is a strong supporter of promoting close economic ties with Latin America, has enthusiastically backed the FTAA process. At the Quebec City meeting, he committed to obtaining fast-track authority by the end of 2001, thereby giving the FTAA process, which was in danger of stalling, another push forward.

U.S. Interests and Concerns

Supporters view hemispheric integration as bolstering U.S. economic and political interests in a variety of ways. Movement towards freer markets is viewed as supportive of U.S. prosperity, while the strengthening of democratic regimes is viewed as supportive of U.S. values and security. Closer economic ties are also seen improving cooperation on a range of bilateral issues, including environmental concerns and anti-drug efforts.

In most general terms, a reciprocal reduction of trade barriers by two or more countries usually contributes to improved efficiency and higher living standards for both. As average tariffs in Latin America are roughly three times higher than U.S. tariffs (12% compared to 3%), supporters argue that the lowering of tariffs and other trade barriers should facilitate significant increases in U.S. exports.

Supporters point out that the Western Hemisphere (which includes Canada and Mexico) has become the largest regional destination for U.S. exports of goods over the past three years. The region usually accounts for about 40% of total U.S. merchandise exports. Excluding Canada and Mexico, U.S. exports to the region have grown 38 percent faster than to countries outside the hemisphere, reaching $59 billion in 2000.

Supporters also believe that a higher degree of economic integration should contribute to the consolidation of economic and political reforms that have taken place throughout the hemisphere. They maintain that the reforms have not only contributed to an improved economic performance in Latin America overall, but they have also made Latin America a more attractive setting for U.S. foreign investment. Similarly, they maintain that the stronger Latin America becomes economically, the more likely democratic institutions will continue to proliferate and deepen.

Opponents of an FTAA are concerned that hemispheric free trade would lead to the export of jobs that otherwise would be in the United States. Some critics believe that an FTAA will induce an outflow of American capital to take advantage of much lower wages and weak safety and environmental standards. Many opponents of the FTAA have argued that free trade with poorer countries will put pressure on the United States to lessen its workforce protections and environmental requirements.

Other critics are concerned that an FTAA will inevitably involve the United States in the instabilities, class tensions, and economic turmoil of many southern hemisphere societies. Some cite Mexico's financial crisis in 1995 as an example of potential costs. According to this view, costs include a deterioration in the U.S. trade balance, an increase in immigration pressures, and the need to extend a large amount of credit.

From a very different perspective, some opponents also argue that hemispheric free trade could undermine the achievement of a stronger and more open multilateral trading system. According to this perspective, regional free trade agreements that may weaken the multilateral trading system do not serve the interests of the United States because it has major commercial interests in all regions of the world – Asia, Europe, and North America, and Latin America. Furthermore, this argument is that a multilateral agreement offers far greater economic benefits than regional agreements.

Latin American Interests and Concerns

Over the last few years, Latin American nations have made considerable progress in implementing far-reaching trade reforms and opening their economies to outside competition. The prospects of hemispheric economic integration have spurred new sub- regional integration schemes and breathed life into sub-regional groups that had lost their stamina. Most importantly, the political commitment at the Miami Summit to create an FTAA by the year 2005 was a product largely of pressures from many of the countries in the region.

If the 1980s were Latin America's lost decade, the 1990s, particularly the first five years, may be the catch-up years. Since 1991, the economies of the region have averaged roughly 3.5% growth, up from 1.1% in the 1980s. Inflation has been reduced dramatically, averaging around 10% in recent years compared to 550% in 1990. And fiscal deficits are now approximately 2% of gross domestic product, compared to 9% in 1983.

One of the central aspects of the economic transformation of the region has been impressive market-oriented reforms and unilateral trade liberalization. This trend has been, until Argentina's financial crisis of 2001-2002, complemented by a surge of sub-regional integration efforts and growing hemispheric interdependence.

Since 1990, four sub-regional groups have made considerable progress breaking down intra-regional trade barriers. MERCOSUR, the Common Market of South, consists of Argentina, Brazil, Paraguay, and Uruguay and is the second largest preferential trading group in the Western Hemisphere. Argentina's recent financial crisis and devaluation, however, is severely challenging the viability of Mercosur today. The Andean Community, consisting of Bolivia, Colombia, Ecuador, and Venezuela (Peru dropped out in 1997), currently is the third largest preferential trading group in the Western Hemisphere. Acting unilaterally as well as under the auspices of the Community (formerly the Andean Pact), individual members have liberalized their own trade and investment regimes in recent years. The Caribbean Community and Common Market (CARICOM), consisting of 13 English-speaking Caribbean nations, has agreed to implement a common external tariff over a period of six years, although members will be allowed to maintain their own non-tariff barriers. The Central American Common Market, (CACM), originally established in 1961, gained new stimulus after a 1990 Summit of Central American Presidents. Within CACM, the Central American Group of four – El Salvador, Guatemala, Honduras, and Nicaragua – has taken measures to liberalize and harmonize their trade regimes.

The likelihood of eventual hemispheric free trade could provide a further boost to the economies of the region. Hemisphere-wide free trade could boost the region's economic growth through increased trade and inflows of foreign investment.

Most Latin American leaders generally support the establishment of a hemispheric free trade area, believing that an FTAA will help bring about greater prosperity, competition, and entrepreneurial activity. A number of critics, however, caution that the United States will benefit the most from the arrangement.

Similarly, many Latin Americans understand that negotiating a free trade agreement with the United States opens themselves to increased trade competition and potential U.S. involvement in such issues as environmental standards, workers' rights, and intellectual property rights protection. Some worry that as tariffs fall the United States would increasingly resort to other procedural ways (such as the imposition of anti-dumping or countervailing duties) to protect its producers and workers. Consequently, some nations might not be willing to move as quickly as others toward the goal of free trade. And others, such as Brazil, may attach greater importance and priority to the consolidation and strengthening of sub-regional trade groups before moving towards a hemispheric free trade area.

Beyond that, opposition to hemispheric free trade could grow if the region's unemployment and staggering poverty does not begin to decline. Despite the overall improvement in economic growth in the 1990s, the number of people living in poverty (defined as less than $1 a day) has remained at an alarming 40% of the population. As a result, too many Latin Americans have seen little evidence that the shift towards freer trade and more open markets has improved their living standards.

POLICY ISSUES AND CONGRESSIONAL ACTIONS

Chile: Negotiating A Free Trade Agreement

Canada's Prime Minister Jean Chretien was widely quoted at the conclusion of the first Summit of the Americas on the invitation to Chile from the United States, Canada, and Mexico to join NAFTA: "For one year we have been the three amigos. Starting today, we will be the four amigos."

Accession negotiations were formally initiated on June 7, 1995 in Toronto, but they remained preliminary due to the fact that the Clinton Administration lacked fast- track negotiating authority. Chile elected not to negotiate on any "sensitive" issues unless fast track authority is renewed to cover the negotiations (Chile subsequently negotiated an FTA with Canada and already had one with Mexico). Such authority allows the Administration to negotiate a trade agreement with assurances that the legislation implementing the agreement will be treated under special, expedited floor procedures. Differences between most House Democrats, on the one hand, and most Republican, on the other hand, on the inclusion of labor and environmental objectives in future free trade agreements was a major obstacle to the renewal of fast- track in 1995, 1996, 1997, and again in 1998. The most recent attempt to pass a fast track bill occurred on September 25, t998, when the House defeated H.R. 2621 by a vote of 180 to 243. In 1999 and 2000, no comprehensive fast-track bills were reintroduced. This year to date, major bills have been introduced in both the House (H.R. 2149) and Senate (S. 1104).

From 1995-1999, the significance of the inability of the Clinton Administration to carry through on its pledge to negotiate Chilean accession to NAFTA or to negotiate a bilateral free trade agreement was mostly political, not economic. In economic terms, NAFTA accession or a free trade agreement would unlikely have any demonstrable effect on the overall U.S. economy because trade between the two countries, although growing, is a minuscule percent of overall U.S. trade flows (approximately ½ of 1 percent). Chile ranks as the 32nd most important market for U.S. exports worldwide, accounting for $3.5 billion in 2000. U.S. imports from Chile also totaled $3.2 billion in 2000, representing the 40th largest supplier. As a country of only 13 million people, with an economy the size of Dallas, and located some 4,000 miles from the United States, Chile is unlikely to become a major trading partner of the United States.

In political terms, the Clinton Administration's inability to carry through on its promise to achieve a free trade agreement with Chile perhaps weakened its negotiating leverage in the context of the FTAA. The promise of Chilean accession to NAFTA, for some interest groups, was that NAFTA obligations and rules could be adopted to serve as the foundation for hemispheric integration. After Chile acceded, it was believed that other countries would be eager to join NAFTA when they were ready as well. Lacking fast track, the Administration, however, arguably was forced to make a number of compromises concerning the objectives and structure of the FTAA negotiations as enunciated in the San Jose Declaration.

Despite the obvious setbacks and delays, the idea of free trade negotiations with Chile took an unexpected turn on August 10, 1999. On this day, Chile's Foreign Minister Juan Gabriel Valdes announced that Chile was prepared to start preliminary discussions on a bilateral FTA with the United States without fast track negotiating authority in place. The United States termed the proposal "constructive" and "positive" at the October 5-6, 1999, meeting of the U.S.-Chile Joint Commission on Trade in Investment in Santiago, Chile. And on November 29, 2000, President Clinton proposed that formal negotiations begin. Chile accepted and the negotiations formally commenced December 6-7, 2000, in Washington, D.C.

The Bush Administration, which continued the negotiations during March 26-30, 2001, in Chile, has indicated that it does not expect an agreement to be reached until early this year. Differences on how to handle labor and environmental issues are likely to be significant. Through January 2002, ten rounds of negotiations have taken place in the context of seventeen negotiating groups covering such areas as market access, agriculture, services, and investment. In the area of services, U.S. industry hopes that Chile will agree to broad commitments in a number of sectors so that other countries in later FTAA negotiations would have adhere to the same obligations. Chile has indicated that it wants the bilateral agreement to be more extensive than either the NAFTA accord or the proposed FTAA. Both sides have already exchanged initial proposals for tariff reductions. Chile has proposed a tariff phase-out that take effect immediately on some products, and after 5 and 10n years on others. The U.S. has proposed a slightly different timeframe of immediately, 4, and 8 years.

While the Chilean economy is relatively open, it still has a number of agricultural barriers. Chile uses a price band system that keeps the price of food imports level by applying a charge on top of its regular tariff. Chile's sanitary and phytosanitary measures do not recognize U.S. meat grading system nor allow unprocessed livestock plants not inspected by Chile's agriculture department to enter the country. And some U.S. industries, such as sugar and fruits and vegetables, want limits placed on Chile's access to the U.S. market.

For its part, Chile is pushing for better access for its professionals to work in the United States. In addition, Chile is expected to try to negotiate a waiver from U.S. antidumping laws and to end certain U.S. farm payments that are said to distort trade. Reportedly, negotiators from both sides are confident that they can resolve these issues pending passage of a trade promotion authority bill by Congress.

Implementing the Caribbean Basin Trade Partnership Act

Ever since NAFTA was proposed in the early 1990s, Caribbean Basin leaders have expressed concern that Mexico's more preferential trading status would erode its own preferential access to the U.S. market as provided by the 1984 Caribbean Basin Economic Recovery Act (CBERA). At the Summit of the Americas, President Clinton and key legislators supported legislation to address the concerns of the CBERA countries. Legislation to prevent an erosion of the CBERA countries' preferential access to the U.S. market has been introduced in every Congress since 1993, but it was not until 2000 that legislation was enacted.

The CBERA, which is commonly referred to as the Caribbean Basin Initiative or CBI, was enacted in 1983 in an effort to bolster the economic development and political stability of this strategically important region. A key objective was to help these countries diversify their exports away from traditional agricultural and raw material based exports such as petroleum, sugar cane, coffee, cocoa, bananas, and aluminum ores.

The centerpiece of this U.S. government program is a unilateral, non-reciprocal, grant of duty-free or reduced duty access for certain Caribbean exports to the U.S. market. Most textiles and apparel, certain footwear, canned tuna, petroleum and petroleum derivatives, and certain watches are not eligible for any preferential treatment. The CBERA was amended by Caribbean Basin Economic Recovery Act of 1990, so-called CBI II. This act made the trade benefits permanent and included measures to promote tourism and establish a scholarship assistance program for the region.

Currently, 24 Caribbean, and Central and South American countries enjoy these trade preferences. (Four countries -- Anguilla, Cayman Islands, Suriname, and Turks and Caicos Islands – are eligible to become a CBERA beneficiary country, but have not requested to be designated). Benefits under CBI are conditioned on various mandatory and discretionary conditions, including intellectual property rights protection, investment protection, improved market access for U.S. exports, and workers rights. In its 18-year history, CBERA has been popular with Caribbean exporters, and in recent years about one-fifth of overall U.S. imports from CBERA countries have entered the U.S. under CBERA preferential provisions.

"NAFTA parity" or CBI enhancement bills introduced in Congress since 1993 have been premised, in part, on the notion that Mexico's more favorable tariff treatment under NAFTA would lead to a diversion of exports and investment, particularly in the textile and apparel sectors, from the CBERA region. To remedy potential trade and investment diversion, most bills proposed extending NAFTA equivalent provisions to CBERA countries for products that did not enjoy equivalent preferential treatment under CBERA.

In the 106th Congress, both the House and Senate passed bills that provided a form of parity. The House bill (H.R. 984) provided more expansive benefits than the Senate bill (S. 1389). The differences related most basically to the minimum U.S.-origin content under which textile apparel assembled in a CBI country would qualify for the preference. After protracted informal negotiations between the two houses, the final language was agreed to, passed by both houses and signed into law on May 18, 2000 (Caribbean Basin Trade Partnership Act -Title II, P.L. 106-200; Trade and Development Act of 2000).

The Caribbean Basin Trade Partnership Act (CBTPA) focuses primarily on the preferential treatment of textile and apparel products. Articles accorded duty-free and quota-free treatment include apparel assembled in a beneficiary country from fabric wholly formed and cut in the United States from U.S. made yarn, or from a fabric made in the United States from U.S. made yam, cut in a beneficiary country and sewn together there with U.S. made yarn. Other items granted preferential treatment include hand-loomed, handmade, and folklore articles.

The preferential treatment becomes effective for each beneficiary country when the U.S. Trade Representative determines that the country has satisfied the statutory eligibility customs requirements for such treatment. Such determinations have to date been made for 14 countries. How to allocate the expanded benefits has been among the most controversial implementation issues. In addition, U.S. Customs Service rulings on how to interpret a number of provisions have led to continuing controversy.

One of the most controversial provisions involves whether Caribbean textile and apparel can qualify for duty-free treatment if the dyeing and finishing process is done outside the United States. U.S. yarn spinners and cotton growers have argued that allowing these processes to take place in CBI countries would allow more trade because it would speed the process from greige goods to finished garments. This position is supported by U.S. apparel importers but opposed by U.S. textile manufacturers who want the U.S. Customs Service to issue a ruling that fabric must be dyed and finished in the United States to qualify as U.S. fabric. A Customs interim ruling on "knit -to-shape" items such as socks and sweaters whose components are knit in the United States and shipped overseas for assembly has also been controversial. Customs ruled that these knit-to-shape articles were excluded from unlimited, duty-free treatment.

The dye and finishing provision took on added significance in the House debate on H.R. 3005, a bill to provide the President trade promotion authority. House leaders pledged in writing to bring no future trade bills to the House floor until legislative action is taken to assure that apparel assembled in Caribbean and Central American countries for export to the United States is made from fabric that is dyed, printed, or finished in the United States. They also promised that the same requirement would be included in any Andean Trade Preference Act renewal measure containing textile preferences before it would be considered on the floor. Before the end of the 2001 legislative session, the House had not yet moved legislation to implement this promise.

Movement Towards Hemispheric Free Trade

Since the 1994 Summit of the Americas, the goal of hemispheric free trade has been advanced by two different processes. The first process involves the expansion of sub-regional groupings such as MERCOSUR and the proliferation of bilateral free trade agreements. Most all countries of the Western Hemisphere – except the United States – have been active ha this process.

The second process involves the formal negotiations among 34 democratic countries of the hemisphere to create an FTAA. As described above, the March 1998 San Jose Declaration formulated a framework for the negotiations and the Leaders formally launched the FTAA negotiations during the second Summit meeting in Santiago in April 1998. And at the third Summit of the Americas held April 20-22, 2001, in Quebec City, leaders agreed to complete the negotiations by January 2005, with the agreement entering into force no later than

December 2005. Only Venezuela declined to endorse the timeline, arguing that the leaders' declaration as worded did not reflect the process under its national laws for ratifying an agreement.

Assessments differ on whether this combined movement toward hemispheric free trade is "on-track" or "off-track." The former perspective maintains that a solid foundation and structure for FTAA negotiations has been agreed to and that on-going efforts to expand sub-regional groupings are accelerating hemispheric integration. The tatter perspective holds that the United States, lacking fast-track authority, has been unable to provide the kind of leadership that is necessary to ensure that the FTAA negotiations proceed according to schedule or in a manner that is supportive of U.S. interests.

Those who see positive developments over the past several years point to the accomplishments of the San Jose Trade Ministerial and the Second Summit of the Americas in getting the FTAA negotiations off to an official start. While some critics doubt much progress can be made in the negotiations until the U.S. President obtains fast track negotiating authority, others point to agreement on a range of business facilitation measures to date. These include temporary admission of certain goods related to business travelers, express shipments, simplified procedures for low value shipments, compatible data interchange systems, harmonized commodity description and coding system, hemispheric guide on customs procedures, codes of conduct for customs officials, and risk analysis/targeting methodology. The development of a draft "bracketed" text is also considered a major accomplishment, providing an opportunity for political negotiations to begin anytime. Moreover, the "Action Plan" agreed to at the Quebec City Summit also specified deadlines for interim steps in the negotiations to be completed. And the leaders also agreed to help build public support by publishing the draft bracketed text in its current form.

The "on-track" perspective also points to a continuing trend of greater market opening at both the bilateral and sub-regional level as contributing to an expansion of trade flows. In recent years, intra-hemispheric trade has been growing more rapidly than exports to the rest of the world. This trade growth, in turn, has bolstered the economic performance of the countries of the region and enabled Latin American leaders to negotiate with the United States more confidently, as well as to embrace the long-term goal of hemispheric free trade.

Those who judge that the process is "off-track" make several points. The first is that more than seven years have passed since the commitment was made to create an FTAA and that only modest progress has been made since then. Negotiators have established a framework for negotiations and have produced a heavily bracketed text, but the differences among the key countries on basic issues remain large. Most of the hard negotiating work remains to be done. The United States, lacking fast-track authority, has not been able to provide strong leadership to making greater progress.

Most importantly, Brazil and the United States, the two key countries in the negotiation, remain far apart on key issues. Much of Brazilian industry is not supportive of the FTAA. Long protected by high tariffs and quotas, many Brazilian companies are wary that they would be overwhelmed by U.S. competition if the FTAA were to come to fruition. The United States, for its part, is determined to maintain protection in sectors most coveted by Brazil, including textiles, steel, and agriculture. And Brazil has made it clear that it will not begin negotiations on sensitive issues until the U.S. President has fast-track implementing authority.

Public support for hemispheric free trade appears to be low both in the United States and in Latin America. Labor and environmental interest groups in the United States oppose free trade agreements that lack strong protections for basic labor and environmental standards. And many Latin American businesses and citizens fear the effects of greater exposure to the competitive pressures of large U.S. companies.

Extending the Andean Trade Preferences Act

The Andean Trade Preferences Act (ATPA) authorizes the President to grant certain unilateral preferential tariff benefits to Bolivia, Colombia, Ecuador, and Peru. The ATPA, which went into effect on December 4, 1991, expired on December 4, 2001. Often referred to as the trade component of then President Bush's "war on drugs," the ATPA attempted to encourage the economic development of Andean countries and economic alternatives to drug production and trafficking.

The Andean countries have asked the United States to extend the program beyond its expiration date for more than three years, and to reduce the list of products excluded from tariff benefits, and to add Venezuela as a beneficiary country. Colombian President Andres Pastrana in his February 27, 2001, visit to Washington urged the U.S. to expand coverage to agriculture, leather goods, apparel, and footwear.

The Clinton Administration did argue that the APTA has been successful in encouraging a move away from narcotics trade to legitimate business in the region and in increasing U.S. exports. Since APTA was passed in 1991, the four Andean countries have increased their exports to the United States by about 80%. Products benefiting from ATPA tariff preferences include cut flowers from Colombia, Ecuador, and Bolivia; precious metals and jewelry from Colombia, Bolivia, and Peru; and fish and fish products from Ecuador. By some estimates, the ATPA has created some 140,000 new jobs for these four countries since its inception.

ATPA countries hope that any extension will provide preferences for their textile and apparel products. They want unlimited duty-free access for apparel articles made from regional fabric and regional yarn, as well as duty-free treatment for other products currently excluded- such as tuna, dairy products, leather, meat, and sugar- could create an additional 200,000 jobs over the next four years.

On November 16, 2001, the House passed a bill (H.R. 3009) that extends the program through December 31, 2006, and provides similar, but more expansive benefits to those in the Senate version (S. 525). H.R. 3009 provides apparel items assembled in beneficiary countries from U.S.-made fabrics using U.S.-made yam with unlimited duty-free access, as would processed tuna. Apparel items assembled from regional fabrics using U.S.-made yam would get quantity-limited duty-free access. Other product groups excluded from duty-Bee treatment, such as footwear and petroleum, would be eligible for duty-free treatment provided the President determines that they are not "import sensitive."

On November 29, 2001, the Senate Finance Committee reported S. 525 with an amendment in the nature of a substitute for language in H.R. 3090, the Economic Security and Recovery Act This would amend and extend the program through September 30, 2005. The bill allows new unlimited duty-Bee access to non-knit-to-shape apparel assembled in a beneficiary country from entirely U.S.-made fabrics and yams. The bill awaits Senate action on the floor.

Chronology

10/05/01 – The House Ways and Means Committee reported out by a voice vote a bill (H.R. 3009) to extend the Andean Trade Preference Act.

08/21/01 – U.S. Trade Representative Robert Zoellick announced that he will meet with the trade ministers of Argentina, Brazil, Paraguay, and Uruguay to pursue a common interest in free trade as an engine of economic growth.

07/02/01 – A draft FTAA bracketed text of the nine chapters negotiated to date was released to the public.

06/15/01 – The United States and Chile concluded the fifth round of talks on an FTA with both sides saying that substantial progress has been made in consolidating their respective proposals.

05/01/01 – The Bush Administration announced that it supports an expansion of the Andean Trade Preferences Act to provide the broadest possible benefits for Colombia, Bolivia, Peru, and Ecuador.

04/22/01 – The Third Summit of Americas, held in Quebec City, concluded with an agreement to complete the negotiations by January 2005 and to implement the agreement by year-end 2005.

03/26/01 – U.S. Trade Representative Robert Zoellick said that he does not believe that it is likely that FTAA negotiations could be accelerated and completed by 2003.

02/01/01 – U.S. Trade Representative Robert Zoellick stated that the U.S. would look for alternatives to the FTAA for promoting trade in the hemisphere if it proves impossible to revive the lagging initiative.

01/08/01 – Chile and the United States begin formal negotiations to establish a free trade agreement.

07/10/00 – The United States and Chile have agreed on a work program aimed at identifying issues that would have to be addressed in a free trade negotiation. No decision on beginning a bilateral negotiation is expected to be made until after the U.S. presidential election.

05/18/00 – President Clinton signed into law (P.L. 106-200) legislation aimed at expanding U.S. trade with African and Caribbean Basin Initiative countries. The conference bill (H.R. 434) was approved by the House on May 4, 2000 by a vote of 309-110 and by the Senate on May 11, 2000, by a vote of 77-19.

05/04/00 – By a vote of 309-110, the House approved the conference report on H.R. 434, the Trade and Development Act of 2000. Title II expands trade preferences for Caribbean Basin exports of apparel products.

02/18/00 – Brazilian Foreign Minister Luiz Felipe Lampreia announced that Brazil is not going to commit to an FTAA until it sees what the final package is and whether the U.S. Congress will approve it.

10/7-8/00 – A U.S.-Chile Joint Commission on Trade and Investment met in Santiago to explore possible negotiations on a free trade agreement.

08/10/99 – Chile's Foreign Minister Juan Gabriel Valdes announced that Chile was ready to start preliminary work on a bilateral free trade agreement without U.S. fast-track negotiating authority in place.

07/28/99 – At a meeting of the Trade Negotiations Committee (TNC) of the FTAA, representatives of 27 countries reached agreement on nine business facilitation measures. The measures will be reviewed at the November 1999 ministerial summit in Canada.

06/22/99 – The Senate Finance Committee reported out a CBI bill, S. 1389 (Roth), by voice vote.

06/10/99 – The House Ways and Means Committee reported out a CBI bill, H.R. 984 (Crane), by voice vote.

05/18/99 – The Ways and Means Trade Subcommittee approved H.R. 984, the U.S.-Caribbean Trade Partnership Act, by voice vote without amendments.

03/04/99 – Congressman Philip Crane (R-Il) introduced the "United States-Caribbean Trade Partnership Act. Title I of the bill offers additional incentive for economic development in the region through enhancement of the CBI trade program.

09/25/98 – The House defeated H.R. 2621, a Republican leadership sponsored fast-track bill, by a vote of 180 to 243.

06/11/98 – Commerce Secretary William Daley expressed doubts that the 2005 deadline for completion of the FTAA can be met given an enormous negotiating agenda and the large number of diverse economies involved in the process.

04/19/98 – 34 Leaders meeting at the second Summit of the Americas in Santiago, Chile agree to formally launch FTAA negotiations.

03/19/98 – Trade ministers meeting in San Jose, Costa Rica agree on the principles, objectives, and venues that will guide the FTAA negotiations.

11/04/97 – The House defeated by a vote of 234-182 the United States-Caribbean Trade Partnership Act (H.R. 2644).

07/25/95 – Negotiations for Chilean accession to NAFTA officially began in Mexico City.

12/9-11/94 – Summit of the Americas held in Miami. Political commitment was made to negotiate a "Free Trade Area of the Americas" by the year 2005. In a separate action, the United States, Canada, and Mexico invited Chile to enter into negotiations to join NAFTA.

01/01/94 – The North American Free Trade Agreement entered into force.

LEGISLATION

H.R. 2149 (Crane)

A bill to provide to renew trade agreement authority according to fast-track legislative procedures. Introduced June 22, 2001; referred to Committees on Rules; and Ways and Means.

H.R. 3009 (Thomas)

A bill to expand and extend the Andean Trade Preference Act. Reported out of the Ways and Means Committee on October 5, 2001, by voice vote.

S. 138 (Gramm)

A bill to authorize negotiation for the accession of Chile to the North American Free Trade Agreement, and for other purposes. Referred to Committee on Finance.

S. 525 (Graham)

A bill to expand trade benefit to certain Andean countries, and for other purposes. Referred to Committee on Finance.

S. 586 (Dodd)

A bill to authorize negotiation for the accession of Chile to the North American Free Trade Agreement, to provide for fast-track consideration, and for other purposes. Referred to Committee on Finance.

S. 599 (Roberts)

A bill to amend the Omnibus Trade and Competitiveness Act of 1988 to establish permanent trade negotiating and trade agreement implementing authority. Referred to Committee on Finance.

S. 1104 (Graham and Murkowski)

A bill to renew trade agreement authority trader fast-track legislative procedures. Introduced June 26, 2001; referred to Committee on Finance.

Chapter 4

TRADE: LATIN AMERICA

J. F. Hornbeck

ISSUE

On April 20-22, 2001, leaders of 34 Western Hemisphere countries met in Quebec City for the third Summit of the Americas, There, the spotlight shone on the recently completed initial (bracketed) draft version of the Free Trade Area of the Americas (FTAA). The FTAA took a big step forward in Quebec City with the Heads of State supporting completion of the agreement by January 2005. The United States has a strong interest in Western Hemisphere integration, especially trade relations with Latin America. These relationships have expanded and deepened over the past decade, especially the unique long-term economic partnership with Mexico. Given the apparent rising expectations for pushing ahead on an FTAA and Mexico's prominence as the United States' second largest trade partner, U.S.-Latin American trade will continue to be an important part of the broader congressional agenda.

BACKGROUND

Trends in U.S.-Latin American Trade

Latin America is the fastest growing U.S. regional trading partner, Between 1990 and 2000, total U.S. merchandise trade (exports plus imports) with Latin America grew by 219% compared to 118% for Asia, 89% for Western Europe, 62% for Africa, and 125% for the world. Latin America has grown from 13.3% of total U.S. trade in 1990 to 18.8% in 2000, but this growth has not been uniform throughout the region.

Table 1. U.S. Merchandise Trade with Selected Latin American Countries, 1990-2000 ($ billions)

Country	1990	1992	1994	1996	1999	2000	% Change 1999-2000	% Change 1990-2000
U.S. Exports								
Brazil	5.1	5.8	8.1	12.7	13.2	15.4	16.7%	202.0%
Venezuela	3.1	5.4	4.0	4.8	5.4	5.6	3.7%	80.6%
Argentina	1.2	3.2	4.5	4.5	5.0	4.7	-6.0%	291.7%
Dom. Rep.	1.7	2.1	2.8	3.2	4.1	4.4	7.3%	158.8%
Colombia	2.0	33.3	4.1	4.7	3.6	3.7	2.8%	85.0%
Chile	1.7	2.5	2.8	4.1	3.1	3.5	12.9%	105.9%
Honduras	0.6	0.8	1.0	1.6	2.4	2.6	8.3%	333.3%
Costa Rica	1.0	1.4	1.9	1.8	2.4	2.5	4.2%	150.0%
Peru	0.8	1.0	1.4	1.8	1.7	1.7	0.0%	112.5%
Guatemala	0.8	1.2	1.4	1.6	1.8	1.9	5.6%	137.5%
Panama	0.7	1.1	1.3	1.4	1.7	1.6	-5.9%	77.8%
Ecuador	0.7	1.0	1.2	1.3	0.9	1.0	11.1%	42.9%
El Salvador	0.6	0.7	0.9	1.1	1.5	1.8	20.0%	200.0%
Jamaica	1.0	1.0	1.1	1.5	1.3	1.4	7.7%	40.0%
Other	4.5	4.6	5.5	6.4	5.0	7.5	50.0%	66.7%
Total LAC*	25.7	35.1	42.0	52.5	53.1	59.3	11.7%	130.7%
Mexico	28.3	40.6	50.8	56.8	86.9	111.7	28.5%	294.7%
Total LA	54.0	75.7	92.8	109.3	140.0	171.0	22.1%	216.7%
World	393.6	448.2	512.6	625.1	695.8	780.4	12.2%	98.3%
U.S. Imports								
Brazil	7.9	7.6	8.7	8.8	11.3	13.9	23.0%	75.9%
Venezuela	9.5	8.2	8.4	12.9	11.3	18.7	65.5%	96.8%
Argentina	1.5	1.3	1.7	2.3	2.6	3.1	19.2%	106.7%
Dom. Rep.	1.8	2.4	3.1	3.6	4.3	4.4	2.3%	144.4%
Colombia	3.2	2.8	3.2	4.3	6.3	7.0	11.1%	118.8%
Chile	1.3	1.4	1.8	2.3	3.0	3.2	6.7%	146.2%
Honduras	0.5	0.8	1.1	1.8	2.7	3.1	14.8%	520.0%
Costa Rica	1.0	1.4	1.7	2.0	4.0	3.6	-10.0%	260.0%
Peru	0.8	0.7	0.8	1.3	1.9	2.0	5.3%	150.0%
Guatemala	0.8	1.1	1.3	1.7	2.3	2.6	13.0%	225.0%
Panama	0.2	0.3	0.3	0.4	0.3	0.3	0.0%	50.0%
Ecuador	1.4	1.4	1.7	1.9	1.8	2.2	22.2%	57.1%
El Salvador	0.2	0.4	0.6	1.1	1.6	1.9	18.8%	850.0%
Jamaica	0.6	0.6	0.9	0.8	0.7	0.7	0.0%	16.7%
Other	3.1	3.2	3.2	3.6	3.2	6.6	106.3%	112.9%
Total LAC*	33.8	33.6	38.5	48.8	57.3	73.3	27.9%	116.9%
Mexico	30.2	35.2	49.5	74.3	109.7	135.9	23.9%	350.0%
Total LA	64.0	68.8	88.0	123.1	167.0	209.2	25.3%	226.9%
World	495.3	532.7	663.3	795.3	1,024.9	1,216.9	18.8%	147.5%

Source: CRS table created from U.S. Department of Commerce data presented in World Trade Atlas.

*LAC = Latin America and the Caribbean, except Mexico.

In 2000, U.S. exports to the world expanded by 12%, recovering from a 2% decline in 1999. Among the larger trade partners, U.S. exports increased by 22% to Korea; 24% to China, 14% to Japan 9% to Western Europe, and 8% to Canada. U.S. exports to Latin America rose by 21% ether a decline of 0. 4% in 1999 (see **table 1**). This increase reflects recovery from the 1999 recession in much of South America and a large increase (29%) in export growth to Mexico, the second largest foreign market for U.S. goods. U.S. export growth to the top six Latin American markets after Mexico was uneven. In order of export market size, exports grew by 17% to Brazil, 4% to Venezuela, -6% to Argentina, 7% to the Dominican Republic, 3% to Colombia, and 13% to Chile.

U.S. imports from the world increased by 19% in 2000, reflecting continuing strong demand in the U.S. economy. Imports grew by 13% from Western Europe, 16% from Canada, 23% from China, 29% from Korea, and 12% from Japan. Imports from Latin America grew in kind, by 24% on average. All countries benefited some as imports increased by 24% from Mexico, 23% from Brazil, 66% from Venezuela (reflecting the sharp rise in oil prices), 19% from Argentina, 2% from the Dominican Republic, 11% from Colombia, and 7% from Chile. Although the United States runs a trade surplus with most Latin American countries, there is a large deficit with Mexico and significant increases in deficits with Venezuela and Colombia, reflecting relatively high oil prices during 2000. Mexico made up 12.4% of U.S. world trade in 2000 and its dominance as a regional trade partner is evident in *Table 1*. It is not only the largest Latin American trading partner, accounting for two-thirds of the region's trade with the United States, but also is among the fastest growing. The rest of Latin America together made up only 6.4% of U.S. trade in 2000, but the trade growth has been brisk for much of the decade.

U.S.-Latin America Trade Issues

U.S.-Latin American trade issues are focused both very broadly, through the Free Trade Area of the Americas (FTAA) negotiations, and more narrowly through discussions on the U.S.-Chile bilateral free trade agreement and legislation to reauthorize the Andean Trade Preference Act (ATPA). The FTAA is a comprehensive agreement that includes 34 nations of the Western Hemisphere and is scheduled for completion by January 2005. The U.S.-Chile FTA, although also comprehensive, is moving ahead more quickly given the limited number parties involved, and some observers hope to see it concluded in early 2002. The ATPA is a unilateral trade preference agreement intended as part of a larger counter-narcotics effort that encourages the export of legally produced goods. All three have important implications for U.S. groups affected by trade relations.

From a purely commercial perspective, improving market access in Latin America is an important U.S. trade-negotiating goal. There are three generally recognized components to this objective. The first involves lowering barriers that allow improved market access for U.S. goods to occur, an issue that varies in significance with each country. The second is achieving a uniform trade regime throughout the Western Hemisphere [market access under the same rules as other Western Hemisphere countries], an increasingly complex goal given the ongoing trend toward bilateral and sub-regional agreements. The third entails guaranteeing that improvements are permanent, providing confidence to U.S. businesses that trade and investment can be undertaken in a predictable environment.

Tariffs as barriers to trade are still an important part of the U.S. trade policy agenda, despite the trend toward lower average tariffs throughout the region. There are three reasons for this. First, historically there has been selective backsliding in tariff reductions during times of economic hardship. Second, unilateral tariff reductions do not necessarily favor U.S. goods, as might be thought at first glance. Although Latin American countries have lowered their average tariff rates, they still exceed U.S. rates and in some cases, there are very high tariffs on automobiles and other capital goods that dominate U.S. exports. Third, U.S. businesses face higher tariffs than competing firms in cases where sub-regional pacts have been signed that do not include the United States. Latin American countries, however, are quick to note that although the U.S. has lower average tariffs, it does have very high peak rates on a few selected products compared to some countries.

Non-tariff barriers are another fertile area for negotiation. Although the United States has trade-related issues over Latin American legal and regulatory environments (e.g. intellectual property rights, government procurement), it is use of U.S. non-tariff barriers (e.g. trade remedy laws, farm price supports) that Latin Americans would like to see restricted in an FTAA. Although legal under World Trade Organization (WTO) guidelines unless successfully challenged, from the Latin American perspective, U.S. antidumping and countervailing duty action is a major impediment to trade because it is brought frequently and against their primary export products.

There is also considerable difference between some Latin American countries and the United States over broader social issues that have implications for trade policy, such as the perennial concerns over labor and environmental rules and standards. These particular issues point to the breadth of topics that now fall under trade negotiations, complicating negotiations and raising the question of whether the FTAA can meet expectations of becoming a hemispheric unifying force.

OUTLOOK

A critical step for completing an FTAA is the decision over passage of trade promotion authority (TPA), which is currently being debated in the 107th Congress. Without TPA, a formal Western Hemisphere trade agreement is unlikely to include the United States. At some point, however, if Congress believes that the FTAA is the preferred way to negotiate regional trade issues, it may consider whether TPA is critical to U.S. participation, because as the bargaining becomes more detailed, other hemispheric countries will be looking for authoritative U.S. representation with respect to specific promises and trade-offs made. The U.S.-Chile FTA is moving ahead quickly, with many observers hoping for passage with or with Out TPA, as was the case with the U.S.-Jordan FTA.

LEGISLATION: 107TH CONGRESS

The House Ways and Means Committee has marked up *H.R. 3008,* reauthorizing the Trade Adjustment Assistance Act through 2006 and *H.R. 3009*, reauthorizing and expanding the Andean Trade Preferences Act.

Chapter 5

ANDEAN REGIONAL INITIATIVE (ARI): FY 2002 ASSISTANCE FOR COLOMBIA AND NEIGHBORS

K. Larry Storrs and Nina M. Serafino

PRESIDENT BUSH'S ANDEAN REGIONAL INITIATIVE

In April 2001 budget submissions, President Bush requested $882.29 million in FY2002 economic and counter-narcotics assistance for Colombia and regional neighbors in an initiative called the "Andean Regional Initiative," with $731 million of the counter-narcotics assistance called the "Andean Counter-Drug Initiative." According to the Administration, there are two distinctive features of this program, compared to last year's Plan Colombia assistance,[1] both of which aim to promote peace and to stem the flow of cocaine and heroin from the Andean region. The differences are that the assistance for economic and social programs is roughly equal to the assistance for counter-narcotics programs, and that more than half of the assistance is directed at regional countries that are experiencing the spillover effects of illicit drug and insurgency activities.[2]

In presenting the Andean Regional Initiative to Andean regional leaders at Summit of the Americas III in Quebec City, Canada, in mid-April 2001, President Bush said: "The United States is responsible to fight its own demand for drugs. And we will expand our efforts to work with producer and transit countries to fortify their democratic institutions, promote

---

[1] "Plan Colombia" refers to the $1.3 billion in FY2000 emergency supplemental appropriations approved by the 106th Congress in the FY2001 Military Construction Appropriations bill (H.R. 4425, P.L. 106-246) for counter-narcotics and related efforts in Colombia and neighboring countries. There was no limitation on the fiscal year in which the funding could be obligated or spent; see Appendix C for a chart on the obligation of this and other funding to Colombia in FY2000 and FY2001. For more detail, see CRS Report RL30541, *Colombia: Plan Colombia Legislation and Assistance (FY2000-FY2001).*

[2] President Bush also requested $31.250 million from the International Affairs account for international narcotics control funding for Other Western Hemisphere countries, with $12 million for Mexico, $12.5 million for the Latin American Regional program, $4 million for Guatemala, $1.550 million for Jamaica, and $1.2 million for the Bahamas. He also committed to fully fund the Western Hemisphere Drug Elimination Act as incorporated into the Omnibus Consolidated and Emergency Supplemental Appropriations Act of 1998 (P.L. 105-277) by providing $278 million to upgrade drug interdiction efforts of the U.S. Coast Guard and Customs Service in Transportation and Administration of Justice accounts. See the Administration's February 200t Blueprint for New Beginnings, and April budget submission documents.

sustainable development, and fight the supply of drugs at the source....The United States appreciates the difficult challenges [Andean countries] face in fighting drugs - and stands ready to be their partner."[3]

Requested ARI funding of $882.29 million is to be distributed as follows, taking into account only international affairs funding:

Colombia: $399 million

- Socio-economic aid: $146.5 million for programs such as alternative development, judicial reform, human rights, anti-corruption measures, and support for the peace process.
- Counter-narcotics aid: $252.5 million for aviation and infrastructure support for air assets provided under Plan Colombia, training and equipping security forces, and interdiction and eradication efforts.

Peru: $206.15 million

- Socio-economic aid: $128.15 million for alternative development, promotion of democracy, health and education programs.
- Counter-narcotics aid: $78 million for upgrading helicopters and riverine interdiction efforts, eradication, and demand reduction and policy development.

Bolivia: $143.48 million

- Socio-economic aid: $88.48 million for programs such as alternative development, judicial reform, poverty alleviation, health and environment.
- Counter-narcotics aid: $55 million for ground-based and air interdiction support, eradication efforts, counter-narcotics training, and narcotics awareness and prevention programs.

Ecuador: $76.48 million

- Socio-economic aid: $56.48 million for border area development, poverty reduction, judicial reform, and environmental programs.
- Counter-narcotics aid: $20 million for northern border security, law enforcement and border checkpoints, and sea and airport control efforts.

Brazil: $26.18 million

- Socio-economic aid: $11.18 million for health and environmental programs.
- Counter-narcotics aid: $15 million for training and equipping border counter-narcotics forces, and for drug awareness and demand reduction programs.

Panama: $20.5 million

- Socio-economic aid: $8.5 million for judicial reform, watershed management, and economic growth opportunities.
- Counter-narcotics aid: $12 million for upgrading interdiction and law enforcement forces, and for modernizing criminal justice institutions.

---

[3] See U.S. Department of State International Information Programs Washington File, Fact Sheet: U.S. Andean Regional Initiative, April 21, 2001, and Appendix A in this report.

Venezuela: $10.5 million

- Socio-economic aid: $0.5 million for legal and judicial reform.
- Counter-narcotics aid: $10 million for law enforcement and interdiction reforms, efforts to counter money laundering, and demand reduction.

Another aspect of the Andean Regional Initiative is U.S. support for the extension and broadening of the Andean Trade Preferences Act (ATPA), expiring at the end of this year, that gives duty free or reduced-rate treatment to the products of Bolivia, Peru, Ecuador and Colombia. This was the centerpiece appeal of Colombian President Pastrana at his mid-April 2001 meeting with the President Bush, and the U.S. President replied that he favored extension of the Act and would work with Congress to broaden the coverage. President Bush repeated that pledge when he met with Andean leaders at the Summit of the Americas meeting in Canada. Colombia especially wants textiles and apparel to be covered, while Ecuador wants tuna to be covered. The countries are looking for parity with Central American and Caribbean preferences, provided in last year's U.S.-Caribbean Trade Partnership Act, which would prevent a diversion of trade and investment from the Andean region to Mexico, Central America, or the Caribbean.[4]

In a mid-May 2001 briefing on the Andean Regional Initiative, Administration spokesmen noted that democracy is under pressure in all regional countries, that economic development is in doubt, and that Andean countries pose a direct national security threat because they produce virtually all of the world's cocaine and increasing amounts of heroin. The policy makers suggested three overarching goals in the Andean Ridge that could be called the three D's - democracy, development, and drugs. The first goal is to promote and support democracy and democratic institutions by support for judicial reform, anti-corruption measures, human rights improvement, and the peace process in Colombia. The second goal is to foster sustainable economic development and trade liberalization through alternative economic development, protection of the environment, and renewal of the Andean Trade Preference Act (ATPA). The third goal is to significantly reduce the supply of illegal drugs to the United States at the source, while simultaneously reducing U.S. demand, through eradication, interdiction and other efforts.[5]

The Administration's Andean Regional Initiative if enacted as requested will significantly increase funding to some Latin American drug production countries. It would place Columbia, Peru, and Bolivia among the top eight U.S. foreign aid recipients in FY2002, with Columbia in third place, Peru in fifth place, and Bolivia in eighth place.[6]

Critics of the Andean Regional Initiative argue that it is a continuation of what they regard as the misguided approach of last year's Plan Colombia, with an overemphasis on military and counter-drug assistance, and with inadequate support for human rights and the peace process in Colombia. They argue that support for the military will weaken and

---

[4] For information on ATPA see CRS Report RL30790, *The Andean Trade Preference Act: Background and Issues for Reauthorization*, by J.F. Hornbeck For information on the U.S.- Caribbean Trade Partnership Act and other regional free trade agreements, see CRS Issue Brief IB95017, *Trade and the Americas*, by Raymond J. Ahearn.

[5] See U.S. Department of State International Information Programs Washington File, Fact Sheet: U.S. Policy Toward the Andean Region, and Transcript: State Department Briefing on Andean Regional Initiative, May 17, 2001, also available at the following website

[6] See CRS Report RL31011, *Appropriations for FY2002: Foreign Operations, Export Financing, and Related Programs*, p. 9, by Larry Nowels. For more information on past international narcotics control efforts by the United States, see CRS Issue Brief 13388093, *Drug Control: International Policy and Options*, by Raphael Perl.

undermine the peace process as the only viable solution, particularly if the military's ties to the paramilitary groups and human rights abuse are not ended. They also argue that forced eradication of crops through aerial spraying will cause environmental damage and internal displacement in the entire region, and is likely to fail ultimately as new sources of supply emerge elsewhere. Supporters argue that the Andean Regional Initiative continues needed assistance to Colombia when Plan Colombia assistance is just beginning to take effect, while providing more support for endangered regional neighbors and more assistance for social and economic programs.[7]

SITUATION IN COLOMBIA AND NEIGHBORING COUNTRIES

The Andean Regional Initiative is designed to provide assistance to seven important countries in the broadly defined Andean regions,[8] or what the Administration has called the Andean Ridge: Colombia (the major producer of cocaine and the central challenge); Peru and Bolivia (where past successes in reducing cocaine production could be threatened by expected progress in Colombia); Ecuador (the most exposed neighbor because of its proximity to Colombian areas controlled by drug producers and guerrillas); and Brazil, Venezuela and Panama (where the threat is primarily confined to common border areas with Colombia).

This area has some of the most heavily populated countries in Latin America, including the first (Brazil), third (Colombia), fifth (Peru), sixth (Venezuela), and eighth (Ecuador) most populous. It includes three major drug producing countries (Colombia, Bolivia, and Peru) where virtually all the world's cocaine, and more than two thirds of the heroin consumed in the U.S. East Coast are produced. It also includes two major oil-producing countries (Venezuela and Ecuador) which supply significant quantities of oil to the United States and are members of the Organization of Petroleum Exporting Countries (OPEC). While the designated countries have diverse trading relationships, the United States is the major trading partner by far for all of them. For the five traditional Andean countries (Colombia, Venezuela Ecuador, Peru, and Bolivia) the Andes mountain range that runs through South America poses geographical obstacles to intra-state and inter-state integration, but the countries are linked together in the Andean Community economic integration pact. While Colombia and Venezuela have largely European-Indian mixed race (mestizo) populations, Bolivia, Peru, and Ecuador have significant indigenous populations.

---

[7] For critical comments, see statements on the Center for International Policy's Colombia Project website [http://www.ciponline.org/colombia/] Under CIP Analyses, under U.S. Military and Police Aid (especially Other Groups' Analyses) and under U.S. Government Information (especially Legislators). For supportive comments, see statements on the same website under U.S. Military and Police Aid (especially Other Groups' Analyses), and U.S. Government Information (especially statements from Officials and Legislators).

[8] Panama and Brazil are not normally considered to be part of the Andean region; Bolivia is an Andean country but it does not share a border with Colombia For usage of the term "Andean Ridge" see citations under Plan Colombia on the website of the State Department's International Information Programs [http://usinfo.state.gov/regional/ar/colombia/].

Colombia

With a population of 42.8 million, Colombia is the third most populous country in Latin America after Brazil and Mexico, with a largely mixed race (mestizo) population, and a spacious territory separated by three parallel mountain ranges. It is known for a long tradition of democracy, but also for continuing violence, including guerrilla insurgency dating back to the 1960s, and persistent drug trafficking activity. Negotiated settlements were achieved with some of the guerrilla groups in the 1980s, but fell apart by 1990 when former guerrillas participating in political activities were assassinated. Recent administrations have had to deal with a complicated mix of leftist guerrillas, rightist paramilitary forces, and drug traffickers associated with both forces.

President Andres Pastrana was elected and inaugurated in 1998 for a four year term largely on the basis of pledges to bring peace to the country by negotiating with the guerrillas, strengthening the Colombian military and counter-narcotics forces, and seeking international support for these efforts and other reforms to address the country's unusually serious economic difficulties.[9]

In 1999, President Pastrana, with U.S. assistance, developed a $7.5 billion plan called Plan Colombia, with $4 billion to come from Colombia and $3.5 billion to come from international donors, although funding from Colombia and the international community has been lagging. In response to Colombian requests, the Clinton Administration developed and the U.S. Congress approved a $1.3 billion package of assistance in 2000, also called Plan Colombia assistance. Some $860.2 million or 67% of this assistance was to support programs in Colombia, with $416.9 million for helicopter, training, and other assistance to three Colombian Army counter-narcotics battalions. This plan was targeted mainly at Colombia and expenses for big ticket items were weighted toward support for military and counter-narcotics activities, although there was funding for alternative development, governance, and human rights programs, and conditions to encourage an improvement in the military's human rights performance.[10]

President Pastrana is approaching the end of his term, which expires in August 2002, and the selection process to determine his successor is under way. While peace talks had been reinvigorated by President Pastrana's direct talks with Revolutionary Armed Forces of Colombia (FARC) guerrilla leader Manuel Marulanda in February 2001, prospects are still very uncertain. Although many elements of Plan Colombia counter-drug assistance were just beginning to be put in place, the State Department reported in March 2001 that Colombian production of cocaine had increased 11% in the year 2000. Despite the FARCs murder in late September 2001 of the popular former Minister of Culture, President Pastrana decided in early October 2001 to extend the demilitarized zone through January 20, 2002, after the FARC agreed to stop random highway kidnappings and to discuss a ceasefire. Shortly thereafter, however, the Army accused the FARC of kidnapping six people on a highway in Narino province, and killing four others in an attack on a small town there.

---

[9] For information on the multi-faceted conditions in Colombia, see CRS Report RL30330, *Colombia: Conditions and U.S. Policy Options*, by Nina M. Serafino.

[10] For information on U.S. "Plan Colombia" assistance in FY2000-FY2001, including all Congressional action and congressionally imposed conditions, see CRS Report RL3054I, *Colombia Plan Colombia Legislation and Assistance (FY2000-FY2002)*, by Nina M. Serafino. This report also contains charts detailing U.S. assistance to Colombia Since 1989.

While international support for Plan Colombia had been lagging, with European countries previously pledging only about $200 million for social development (not military) projects, the shift in focus of the U.S. Andean Regional Initiative gained wider diplomatic support. In part because of the change in emphasis, the international community pledged an additional $580 million at the third meeting of the International Support Group for the Peace Process in Colombia on April 30, 2001, although some double counting may be involved. The European Union pledged $297 million, the United States pledged $146 million, the Andean Development Corporation pledged $100 million, and other countries pledged $37 million.

Under the Andean Regional Initiative, Colombia would receive $399 million, with $146.5 million in socio-economic aid for programs like alternative development, judicial reform, human rights, anti-corruption measures, and support for the peace process; and $252.5 million in counter-narcotics aid for aviation and infrastructure support for air assets provided under Plan Colombia, training and equipping security forces, and interdiction and eradication efforts.

Peru

With a population of 25.7 million (45% Indian, 37% mestizo, 15% European), Peru is the filth most populous country in Latin America. It has been in flux since the constitutionally questionable third term re-election in June 2000 of President Alberto Fujimori. Although President Fujimori had considerable support during his presidency (1990-2000) for restoring the economy, defeating the guerrilla insurgency, and reducing drug trafficking activity, he was criticized for corruption, human rights violations, and authoritarian tendencies. The political uncertainty in Peru was compounded when President Fujimori suddenly resigned and fled into exile in December 2000, following allegations of corruption associated particularly with security chief Vladimiro Montesinos.

Peru was governed by Acting President Valentin Paniagua during a transition period until president-elect Alejandro Toledo was inaugurated as President on July 28, 2001, following the well regarded two-round presidential elections in April and June 2001. Toledo, a longtime anti-Fujimori opposition leader, was elected on June 3, 2001, with 53% of the valid vote, against former left-leaning Peruvian President Alan Garcia with 47% of the vote.[11] President Toledo has promised to end corruption and to stabilize the economy, and most observers worry that the expectations of the populace, especially poor, indigenous groups, are almost impossible to achieve. Representatives of Peru and the United States launched an investigation into the circumstances and procedures leading to an accident on April 20, 2001, when a Peruvian military plane shot down a small plane, killing an American missionary woman and her infant daughter, after a CIA surveillance plane indicated that the small craft might be involved in drug trafficking activities. As a result of this accident, U.S. surveillance of drug-related flights in Peru and Colombia were suspended pending clarification of procedures. The State Department released the report of the U.S.-Peruvian investigative team on August 2, 2001, concluding that "communications systems overload" and "cumbersome procedures" played a role in the accident.

---

[11] For more details, see CRS Report RL30918, *Peru: Recovery from Crisis*, by Maureen Taft-Morales.

Peru is viewed as a success story in counter-narcotics efforts because six years of joint U.S.-Peru air and riverine interdiction operations, aggressive eradication efforts, and promising alternative development programs have reduced coca production by 70%. However, Peruvian spokesmen have worried about spillover effects of illicit drug activities from Colombia into Peru, and a possible increase in coca production. They have denounced Colombian plantings of coca and poppies in Peru, and international trafficking of arms through Peru to FARC guerrillas in Colombia. Because of these threats, Peru has moved a fleet of MI-17 helicopters from its border with traditional rival Ecuador, where tensions have diminished, to the border with Colombia.

As part of Plan Colombia funding, Peru received $25 million for KMAX helicopters for the Peruvian National Police, and benefited from regional interdiction funding.

Under the Andean Regional Initiative, Peru would receive $206.15 million in assistance, with $128.15 in socio-economic aid for alternative development, promotion of democracy, health and education programs; and $78 million in counter-narcotics aid for upgrading helicopters and riverine interdiction efforts, eradication, and demand reduction and policy development.

Bolivia

With a population of 7.9 million (roughly 60% indigenous and 40% mestizo and European), Bolivia is the eleventh most populous country in Latin America. It has been governed by President Hugo Banzer, elected and inaugurated in 1997, who was serving the second time as President, this time as a democratically elected President, following his earlier period of military rule in the 1970s. In late June 2001, President Banzer was diagnosed with lung and liver cancer and flew to the United States for treatment. Banzer resigned on August 6, and Vice President Jorge Quiroga became President on August 7, 2001, vowing to continue the economic reforms and to rid the country of coca production in line with his predecessor's promises.

With a large indigenous population, Bolivia experienced a significant social revolution under one party in the 1950s with sweeping land reform, universal suffrage, rural education, and nationalization of the country's important tin mines. The period of military control ran from the mid-1960s to the mid-1980s and was followed by a series of ineffective and largely corrupt governments with linkages to drug traffickers. Beginning in the mid-1990s, reformist governments in Bolivia carried out major privatization programs and put the country on a sound economic footing. President Banzer continued the economic reforms and set the goal of eliminating illegal coca cultivation and narco-trafficking during his five-year term. While Bolivia is actively involved with the Andean Community, it is an associate member of the Southern Common Market (Mercosur) formed by Brazil, Argentina, Paraguay and Uruguay. In support of Bolivia's counter-narcotics efforts, the United States has provided significant interdiction and alternative development assistance and it has forgiven all of Bolivia's debt for development assistance projects, and most of the debt for food assistance.

Bolivia, like Peru, is viewed by many as a counter-narcotics success story, with joint air and riverine interdiction operations, successful eradication efforts, and effective alternative development programs reducing coca cultivation to the lowest level in five years, with a net reduction of approximately 70%. Bolivia does not have a common border with Colombia, but the principal concern in Bolivia is that the successes of the last few years could be turned back and coca cultivation and drug trafficking could return to Bolivia to meet world-wide demand if counter-narcotics efforts are successful m Colombia. Some critics have also charged that, while eradication has been successful in dramatically reducing coca cultivation, it has hurt the overall economy.

As part of Plan Colombia funding, Bolivia received $25 million for regional interdiction assistance and $85 million in alternative development assistance.

Under the Andean Regional Initiative, Bolivia would receive $143.48 million. This includes $88.48 million in socio-economic aid for programs such as alternative development, judicial reform, poverty alleviation, health and environment; and $55 million in counter-narcotics aid for ground-based and air interdiction support, eradication efforts, counter-narcotics training, and narcotics awareness and prevention programs.

Ecuador

With a population of 12.6 million, Ecuador is the eighth most populous country in Latin America. While more than half of the population is mixed race mestizo, about a quarter of the population is indigenous. Ecuador is the most exposed neighbor in the region because it is situated adjacent to southern Colombian areas that are guerrilla strongholds and heavy drug producing areas. Ecuador is led by President Gustavo Noboa, the former Vice President who took office in January 2000, after an uprising by elements of the military and indigenous groups. He is the fifth president in five years, with several of the previous presidents leaving as a result of corruption charges. The country has experienced hyperinflation for several years in the past, and is still struggling with economic austerity following dollarization of the currency in early 2000.

According to press reports, Colombian guerrillas pass into Ecuadorian territory for rest, recuperation, and medical treatment, and there are reports that Colombians are buying ranches and farms in the Ecuadorian border region, possibly for drug cultivation. Ecuadorian officials say they have uncovered and destroyed several small cocaine processing labs in the area. The Ecuadorian border region is experiencing a constant flow of Colombian refugees into the poor areas, and fighters with Colombian paramilitary organizations have been arrested for running extortion rings in Ecuadorian border regions. The FARC has been accused of kidnapping people in Ecuador, although the FARC denies the allegations.[12]

As part of last year's Plan Colombia funding Ecuador received $20 million in U.S. assistance, of which $12 million is to support drug interdiction efforts, and $8 million is for alternative development assistance. Another $61.3 million has been allocated for the construction of a Forward Operating Location in Manta, Ecuador for counter-narcotics aerial surveillance. There have been numerous press reports that Ecuadorian officials have been requesting significantly increased U.S. assistance for some time.

Under the Andean Regional Initiative, Ecuador would receive a total of $76.48 million in assistance, with $56.48 million in socio-economic aid for border area development, poverty reduction, judicial reform, and environmental programs; and $20 million in counter-narcotics

---

[12] For more information, see CRS Report RS20494, *Ecuador: International Narcotics Control Issues*, by Raphael Perl.

aid for northern border security, law enforcement and border checkpoints, and sea and airport control efforts.

Brazil

With a population of 170 million (of European, African, and mixed stock), Brazil is the largest and most populous country in Latin America, with most of the population concentrated in the more developed southeastern areas of the country and along the Atlantic coast. The country is led by President Fernando Henrique Cardoso who is approaching the end of his second and final term. He is credited with leading the country into a period of growth after ending years of inflation with his Real Plan and after weathering the international financial crisis with IMF assistance in late 1998 and 1999. New presidential elections are approaching in 2002, with doubts about whether the governing coalition can hold together and carry out needed reforms. Brazilians have long been concerned about the sparsely populated territory in the huge Amazon region, and they have been fearful historically of foreign designs and intervention in this territory.

In an effort to exercise control over this vast territory Brazil has constructed a $1.4 billion radar project called the Amazon Vigilance System, or SIVAM from its acronym in Portuguese, and it has offered to share data from this system with neighbors and the United States. It has established a military base at Tabatinga, with 25,000 soldiers and policemen, with air force and navy support, to deal with spillover effects from Colombia. Press accounts suggest evidence of Colombian drug traffickers encouraging indigenous communities in Brazil to plant coca, and the threat of FARC incursions along the border. In one example in late 1998, the FARC captured a city on the Colombian border, forcing Colombian troops to withdraw into Brazilian territory, before recapturing the city. In another example, a plane from Suriname with arms for FARC guerrillas was discovered when it was forced to make an emergency landing in Brazil.

Brazil is not an illicit drug producing country, but it is a growing transit area for cocaine moving from the Andean Ridge to Colombia. Although Brazil was not designated as a recipient of Plan Colombia assistance, under the Andean Regional Initiative it would receive $26.18 million. This includes $11.18 million in socioeconomic aid for health and environmental programs; and $15 million in counter- narcotics aid for training mad equipping border counter-narcotics forces, and for drug awareness and demand reduction programs.

Venezuela

With a population of 23.5 million (of largely mestizo stock), Venezuela is the sixth most populous country in Latin America. The country is presently led by President Hugo Chavez, a former disgruntled military leader and a populist, who was initially elected in late 1998 on a campaign to rewrite the constitution, rid the country of corruption, and more adequately meet the needs of the people. During 1999, at Chavez's request, Venezuelan voters approved the creation of a National Constituent Assembly, elected members of the new assembly, and approved the newly written constitution, which lengthened and expanded presidential powers.

On July 30, 2000, ha a so-called mega-election, President Chavez easily won election to a new six-year term of office.[13] Because of his previous attacks on the legislature and other institutions, many observers fear that he has authoritarian tendencies somewhat like those of disgraced former President Fujimori in Peru. Chavez has established close ties with Fidel Castro and other leftist leaders, and he often employs anti-U.S. rhetoric. He has denounced Plan Colombia as a U.S.-dominated military strategy, and he has denied the United States over flight rights over Venezuela territory. Reports persist that he has established friendly relations with Colombian guerrillas.

At the April 2001 Summit of the Americas in Quebec City, President Chavez reserved the position of Venezuela in the Declaration of leaders committing to move forward to achieve a Free Trade Area of the Americas (FTAA) by January 2005, and he also expressed alternative views on U.S. policy and Plan Colombia.

Venezuela is not an illicit drug producing country but it is a transit route for cocaine and heroin from neighboring Colombia to the United States and Europe. Despite various policy disagreements with the United States, the Chavez government has cooperated with the United States in counter-narcotics efforts. While Venezuela was not designated specifically as a recipient of Plan Colombia assistance, under the Andean Regional Initiative, it would receive $10.5 million. This amount includes $0.5 million in socio-economic aid for legal and judicial reform; and $10 million in counter-narcotics aid for law enforcement and interdiction reforms, efforts to counter money laundering, and demand reduction.

Panama

With a population of 2.8 million (of largely mestizo and West Indian stock), Panama is the twentieth most populous country in Latin America. Its history has been heavily influenced by its strategic location and the transit of commerce through the Panama Canal in the center of the country where the major cities are located. It is led by Mireya Moscoso, elected and inaugurated in 1999, who has been dealing with economic difficulties in Panama, and Panamanian responsibilities for the Panama Canal since the U.S. withdrawal on the last day of 1999. Despite considerable effort in the period leading up to the U.S. withdrawal, Panama was unwilling to allow the United States to retain a formal military presence in Panama for counter-narcotics surveillance purposes.[14] This forced the United States to develop the Forward Operating Locations in El Salvador, Aruba/Curacao and Ecuador as substitute locations for such activities. Panama has been the scene of cross-border incursions by Colombian guerrillas and by Colombian paramilitary groups, and there is some evidence that paramilitary groups are being founded in Panama, with support from Colombian groups, because of the perception that the Panamanian government has left some areas unprotected.

Panama is not an illicit drug producing country, but it is a major transshipment point for illicit drugs, especially cocaine, smuggled from South America. In recent years, Panama has cooperated with the United States in bilateral counter-narcotics efforts, seizing significant amounts of illicit drugs and passing anti-money laundering legislation. While Panama was not

---

[13] For more details, see CRS Report RS20978, *Venezuela under Chavez: Political Conditions and U.S. Relations*, by Mark P. Sullivan; and Scott Wilson, "Chavez's Unfinished Revolution; Venezuelan's Accomplishments Fall Short of His Rhetoric," *Washington Post*, May 21, 2001, p. A1.

[14] For more detail, see CRS Report RL30981, *Panama-U.S. Relations*, by Mark P. Sullivan and M. Angeles Villarreal.

designated as a recipient of Plan Colombia assistance, under the Andean Regional Initiative, it would receive $20.5 million. This includes $8.5 million in socio-economic aid for judicial reform, watershed management; and economic growth opportunities; and $12 million in counter-narcotics aid for upgrading interdiction and law enforcement forces, and for modernizing criminal justice institutions.

MAJOR LEGISLATIVE ACTIVITY ON ANDEAN REGIONAL INITIATIVE AND RELATED ISSUES

Foreign Operations Appropriations, FY2002

House Action

On July 10, 2001, the House Appropriations Committee approved H.R. 2506, with a reduction of $55 million in the counter-narcotics "Andean Counter-Drug Initiative" (ACI) portion of the ARI after defeating several amendments to reduce the funding even more. On July 24, 2001, the House approved H.R. 2506, reducing counter-drug assistance by an additional $1 million, and approving amendments relating to caps on personnel in Colombia and a required report on the April 20 accidental shoot down of a missionary plane in Peru. As passed by the House, the bill provides $826 million for the ARI, of which $675 million is for the ACI, a reduction of $56 million from the President's request.

Subcommittee Action

On June 27, 2001, the House Appropriations Committee's Foreign Operations Subcommittee marked up and passed a $15.2 billion FY2002 foreign operations funding bill, which contained funding for the Bush Administration's Andean Regional Initiation (ARI). The subcommittee action funded the entire bill at the level requested by the President, but considerably reduced funding for the Andean Counter-Drug Initiative portion of the ARI.

The subcommittee action would provide $55 million less than the President's $731 million request for the State Department's International Narcotics Control "Andean Counter-Drug Initiative" portion, funding that account at $676 million. The subcommittee did not specify which among the initiative's programs were to be affected by the funding reduction. This would reduce funding for the total ARI from $882 million to $827 million.

Two amendments regarding Colombia were offered and withdrawn during the subcommittee mark-up. The Pelosi amendment would have limited funding for Colombia's military to no more than $52 million, and transferred the other approximately $100 million of funding requested for the Colombian military to a Child Survival account for infectious diseases. The Rothman amendment would have placed a temporary moratorium on U.S. supported fumigation efforts in Colombia until the State Department presented Congressional appropriations committees with conclusive evidence that the United States and Colombian governments had commenced implementation o friable alternative development plans in 75% of all communities that have signed alternative development pacts.

Committee Action

On July 10, the House Appropriations Committee passed H.R. 2506, retaining the subcommittee-approved $827 million funding level for the ARI, with the $676 million funding level for the Andean Counter-Drug Initiative. The Committee provided no explanation in the report (H.Rept. 107-142) for its action, but recommended there that the $55 million reduction "should be evenly distributed among all programs, projects, and activities referred to in the Administration's request for the Andean Counter-Drug Initiative." The bill itself recommends a limit of $14.24 million for administrative expenses. As reported by the committee, the bill also would exempt any programs supported through the ACI funds from the cap of 300 on civilian contractors established by the Plan Colombia legislation (Section 3204(b)(1)(B), P.L. 106-246). (It does not, however, exempt the cap of 500 on the number of U.S. military personnel in Colombia established by the same legislation.) The bill would also exempt ACI funds from the prohibition under Section 482 (b) of the Foreign Assistance Act of 1961, as amended, on the use of funds for the procurement of weapons and ammunition, with exceptions for counter-narcotics activities. The exceptions, requiring an advance notification to Congress, apply to the defensive arming of aircraft used for counter-narcotics activities, and the provision of firearms and related ammunition for defensive purposes to Department of State employees or contract personnel engaged in such activities. The Section 482(b) exemption was also contained in the Plan Colombia legislation.

The full committee rejected two Colombia-related amendments: (1) the Pelosi amendment, which had been withdrawn in subcommittee, to transfer approximately $100 million from the Colombian military to the Child Survival account, failed 22 to 39; and (2) the Obey amendment, to withdraw all Andean counter-drug funding and shift it to domestic drug treatment and prevention programs, failed 18 to 43.

In H.Rept. 107-142, however, the Committee adopted language requiring the Secretary of State to report to the appropriations committees by January 1, 2002, and quarterly thereafter, on the human health and environmental effects of the materials used in aerial eradication of coca and opium poppy in Colombia, and of the spraying of those illegal narcotic crops in Colombia. "Such reports shall include a description of the areas sprayed, materials and methods used, compliance with the spray guidelines, and the human and environmental impacts of such spraying."

The Committee also requested two semi-annual reports from the Secretary of State, both beginning March 1, 2002. One would provide information on all aircraft, vehicles, boats, and lethal equipment transferred to military and police forces under the ACI. This report is also to include the number of U.S. military personnel deployed or assigned to duty in the Andean region or other countries using fund provided under the ACI during the previous 180 days, and the length, purpose, costs, and risks of their deployment or assignment. Another would provide information on "the specific efforts being made by AID, the State Department and the Colombian government to expedite the delivery of non-cash assistance to communities in Colombia that have signed pacts to voluntarily eradicate their coca crops." This report is to include the percentages of available alternative development funds disbursed to Colombian communities that have signed such pacts.

The Appropriations Committee report also contains extensive language on Colombia and other Andean countries. On Colombia, the Committee stated that it believes that a negotiated settlement "offers the only viable resolution to the complex conflict" in Colombia, and that efforts to reduce the cultivation of illegal crops "will continue to face enormous challenges" until a peace accord is reached. The Committee strongly urged the Secretary of State "to work with all parties in the talks to encourage rapid progress toward a firm and lasting peace." Noting that "stronger trade between Colombia and the United States is crucial to managing the vulnerabilities of the Colombian economy," the Committee urged the President "to seek renewal and expansion of the Andean Trade Preference Act (ATPA)." It expressed concern that alternative development projects were not being implemented in a timely fashion in Southern Colombia.

For the Andean region in general, the Committee report called on the Department of State to ensure that all U.S. laws regarding human rights, including Section 556 of the bill, "are strictly applied in Colombia and each of the Andean nations." Regarding Bolivia, the Committee took "special note" of the country's progress in counter-narcotics efforts, and stated that its "enormous success" was due "in large part, to the support of the U.S. Government." It urged the Administration to continue to strongly support Bolivia "when deciding on its allocation of aid."

Floor Action

On July 24, the House adopted H.R. 2506, by a vote of 381-46. It reduced the ACI account by $1 million from the level approved by the Appropriations Committee, to $675 million, despite efforts to reduce it by much larger amounts, and altered committee provisions regarding the cap on civilian contractors. (See the first bullet under approved amendments, below.)

In floor action on July 24, three amendments pertaining to the ARI were approved, two were defeated, and two were withdrawn. Nine others, which had been printed in the record and therefore were eligible for debate under the initial rule were barred from debate under an order of procedure adopted in the course of floor consideration.

The three amendments **approved** were:

- An amendment offered by Rep. Conyers to allow the President to waive the 300 person cap on civilian contractors set by the Plan Colombia legislation, provided that the President certifies that the aggregate ceiling of 800 personnel (for military personnel and civilian contractors combined) set by that legislation would not be exceeded, and if Congress is informed of the extent to which the 300 civilian contractor limitation is exceeded. Agreed to by voice vote.
- Amendment 44 offered by Rep. Hoekstra to withhold $65 million of ACI funds until the Secretary of State submits to Congress a full report on the April 20, 2001, aircraft shoot-down by the Peruvian Air Force in which U.S. missionary Veronica "Roni" Bowers and her daughter were killed. Agreed to by voice vote.
- A substitute Kolbe amendment (to amendment 12 offered by Rep. Crowley) to transfer $1.0 million from the ACI to the International Disaster Assistance account. (The Rep. Crowley amendment would have transferred $10 million.)

The two amendments **defeated** were:

- Amendment 26, offered by Rep. Lee, to transfer $60 million to the Child Survival and Health Programs fund, where it was to be available for HIV/AIDS programs. Of the $60 million, $38 million would be taken from the ACI. Failed 188-240.

- Amendment 27, offered by Rep. McGovern, to reduce ACI funding by $100 million, and transfer half of that funding to the infectious diseases account to combat tuberculosis and the other half to the child survival and maternal health account. (In a floor speech, Rep. McGovern stated that the intent of the amendment was that the full $100 million should be cut from funding for the Colombian military.) Failed 179-249.

The two amendments **withdrawn** were:

- Amendment 47 offered by Rep. Jackson-Lee to transfer $100 million from the ACI to the Child Survival and Health Programs Fund. Withdrawn by unanimous consent.
- Amendment 11 offered by Mr. Conyers to prohibit the use of funds provided as part of Plan Colombia and the ACI for aerial fumigation to eradicate illicit crops in Colombia. Withdrawn by unanimous consent.

On July 19, during the first day of consideration of H.R. 2506, two amendments regarding Colombia were offered and withdrawn after points of order were raised.

- Rep. Souder offered and withdrew Amendment 35 to earmark $27 million of International Narcotics Control and Law Enforcement funds for the purchase of two Buffalo transport/supply aircraft for the Colombian National Police, $12 million for the purchase of six Huey II patrol helicopters for the Colombian Navy, and $5 million for assistance in purchasing operating fuel for drug interdiction along Colombia's north coast and its on rivers. In effect, this would supplement funding for Andean regional counter-drug efforts that would be made available through the ACI.
- Rep. Delahunt offered and withdrew Amendment 17 to require quarterly reports from the Secretary of State on the implementation of the Colombian national security legislation passed by the Colombian Congress on June 20, 2001. According to Rep. Delahunt, that legislation "contains ambiguous provisions that could threaten civilian oversight of the military in Colombia and place at risk the progress that has been made toward reforming the military..."

Senate Action

The Senate Appropriations Committee marked up its version of the Foreign Operations Appropriations bill on July 26, and reported out H.R. 2506, with an amendment in the nature of a substitute (S.Rept. 107-58) on September 4, 2001, reducing ACI funding by $164 million, and imposing conditions on the safety of aerial fumigation programs in Colombia, and requiring reports on human rights conditions in the country. The Senate passed H.R. 2506 on October 24, 2001, after defeating on a point of order an amendment to fund the ACI and the ARI at the level requested by the President, and approving two amendments that transferred $20 million from the ACI to other programs. As passed by the Senate, the bill provides $698 for the ARI, of which $547 is for the ACI, a reduction of $184 million from the President's request, and includes Conditions on the safety of aerial fumigation and the implementation of alternative development programs.

Committee Action

In the July 26 mark-up, the Senate Appropriations Committee cut $164 million from the President's requested ACI funding, and earmarked not less than $200 million of the total of $567 million that would remain in that account for direct apportionment to the U.S. Agency for International Development (AID) for economic and social programs. The ACI cut would bring total ARI funding down to $718 million.

The committee bill would condition the release of funds to purchase chemicals used for the aerial coca fumigation program. To release those funds, the Secretary of State, in consultation with the Secretary of the Department of Health and Human Services and with the Surgeon General, would have to determine and report to Congress on the human health and safety effects of the chemicals and the manner of their application. Specifically, the Secretary would have to report that 1) "the chemicals used in the aerial fumigation of coca, [and]...the manner in which they are being applied, do not pose an undue risk to human health or safety;" and 2) that the fumigation "is being carried out according to the health, safety, and usage procedures recommended by the Environmental Protection Agency, the Centers for Disease Control and Prevention, and the manufacturers of the chemicals." The Secretary would also have to report that "effective mechanisms are in place to evaluate the claims of local citizens that their health was harmed or their licit agricultural crops were damaged by such aerial coca fumigation, and provide fair compensation for meritorious claims."

In contrast to House action, the Senate Appropriations Committee incorporated by reference in its bill the Plan Colombia legislation's cap of 500 on the number of U.S. military personnel and 300 on the number of U.S. civilian contractors in Colombia (Section 3204(b) of P.L. 106-246). The Committee also included a Plan Colombia human rights restriction, requiting the immediate return to the United States of any helicopter purchased with ACI funds that "is used to aid or abet the operations of any illegal self-defense groups or illegal security cooperative." Like the House, however, it would waive the restrictions of Section 482(b) of the Foreign Assistance Act of 1961. The Committee would limit by law funding for Department of State administrative expenses to $14.24 million, whereas the House-bill merely recommends that limit.

In the report accompanying the bill (S.Rept. 107-58), the Committee stated that it "recognizes some progress on human rights" in Colombia, but also expressed concern about "the surge in paramilitary violence, persistent reports of cooperation between the military and the paramilitaries, and the impunity of military officers who order or commit atrocities." It stated that the U.S. government should make it a priority to promote "far more aggressive action...by the Colombian Government and the military, to thwart it." Deploring the "ongoing abuses by the FARC," the Committee called on other nations, "particularly Mexico and the Scandinavian countries, to exert greater influence on the FARC to repudiate these tactics and participate seriously in negotiations toward a settlement of the conflict."

The Committee also called for the Secretary to State to submit to the appropriations committee's reports containing information on several areas of human fights and other concerns. The Committee would expect the first report within 60 days of enactment and every 120 days after that.

This report would include information on two human rights topics for which reporting was also required by the Plan Colombia legislation. These are:

- the extent to which the Colombian armed forces have suspended members credibly alleged to have committed gross violations of human rights, and are providing civilian prosecutors and judicial authorities requested information on the nature and cause of suspension; and
- the extent to which the Colombian armed forces are cooperating with civilian authorities, including providing access to witnesses and relevant military information, in prosecuting and punishing in civilian courts those members credibly alleged to have committed gross violations of human rights or aided or abetted paramilitary groups.

Two other human rights topics are also to be included:

- the extent to which the Colombian armed forces are severing links, including intelligence sharing, at the command, battalion, and brigade levels, with paramilitary groups, and executing outstanding arrest warrants for members of such groups; and
- the extent to which attacks against human rights defenders, trade unionists, and government prosecutors, investigators and civilian judicial officials are being investigated, and alleged perpetrators brought to justice.

The report would also be expected to provide information on the actions taken by the United States, Colombia, and other governments to promote and support peace negotiations, and on financial support for Plan Colombia provided by the Colombian government and the international community.

A second report including information on other areas of human rights concerns would be expected only if national security legislation passed by the Colombian Congress on June 20, 2001, were to become law. In that case, the Secretary of State would be expected to submit a report within 90 days of enactment of the security law and 120 days thereafter on incidents of and any rising trend in arbitrary and prolonged incommunicado detention by members of the Colombian armed forces and police; an assessment of the effectiveness of investigations conducted by military personnel under the new security law compared to investigations by civilian authorities; and an analysis of the security law's implications for Colombia's commitments under international treaties.

The Committee also expressed concern in its report about the spillover effects of the Colombian narcotics trade into Bolivia, Ecuador, and Peru.

Floor Action

After considering H.R. 2506 for two days, the Senate approved the measure on October 24, 2001, largely retaining the basic features of the bill relating to the ARI as reported by the Senate Appropriations Committee. Five amendments relating to the ARI were approved, with the last two reducing ACI funding by $20 million; and one amendment, seeking to restore funding cuts, was defeated on a point of order.

The five amendments that were **approved** were:

- Senate Amendment 1929 by Senator Leahy that not less than $101 million of ACI funds be made available for Bolivia, and not less than $35 million of ACI funds be made available for Ecuador.

- Senate Amendment 1942 by Senator Helms that up to two million of ACI funds be made available to support democracy-building activities in Venezuela.
- Senate Amendment 1951 by Senators Feingold and Wellstone that added another condition relating to aerial fumigation upon which the Secretary of State is to report, namely that alternative development programs be in place in areas where fumigation is being implemented.
- Senate Amendment 1960 by Senators Hutchison and Inouye that reduced ACI funding by $10 million, and made those funds available for the prevention, treatment, and control of tuberculosis.
- Senate Amendment 1961 by Senator Bingaman that reduced ACI funding by $10 million, and made those funds available for relief and reconstruction assistance for victims of earthquakes and drought in El Salvador and elsewhere in Central America.

The amendment that was **defeated** on a point of order was Senate Amendment 1950 by Senators Graham, Hagel, and Dodd to increase funding for the Andean Counter-Drug Initiative to $731 million, the mount of the President's request, which would have effectively overridden the Committee-reported cut of $164 million in that portion of the ARI. Proponents of the amendment argued that full support was necessary to assist troubled Colombia and to deal with the flow of drugs to the United States. Opponents argued that extensive assistance was being provided to the region, that needs elsewhere in the world were great, and that evidence of progress was lacking despite the major contribution of resources in recent years. A point of order was raised by Senator Leahy that the amendment was in violation of the Congressional Budget Act for failing to identify offsets for the proposed $164 million increase in funding, and a motion by Senator Graham to waive the requirements of the Budget Act was defeated 27-72, thereby defeating the amendment.

Foreign Relations Authorization, FY2002-FY2003

House Action

The House International Relations Committee reported out H.R. 1646 on May 4, 2001, with four reporting requirements on Colombia and a prohibition on the issuance of visas to illegal armed groups in Colombia. The bill was passed by the House on May 16, 2001, without additions or modifications in that area. The required reports relate to the elimination of Colombian opium, the effects of Plan Colombia on Ecuador, alternative development and resettlement programs, and the Colombianization of counter-narcotics activities.

Committee Action

H.R. 1646 was introduced by Representative Hyde on April 27, 2001, with two reporting requirements concerning the elimination of Colombian opium poppy crops and the effect of Plan Colombia on Ecuador (see below for details). The measure was referred to the House Committee on International Relations. When the Committee marked up the bill on May 2, it adopted by voice vote two amendments offered by Representative Delahunt: the first imposed reporting requirements on Department of State activities and on the "Colombianization" of counter-narcotics activities; the second prohibited the issuance of visas to supporters of

Colombian illegal armed groups (see below for details). The bill was reported out amended (H.Rept. 107-57) by the Committee on May 4.

Floor Action

After floor consideration on May 10 and 16, with no additional amendments on Colombia or the Andean region, H.R. 1646 was approved by the House on May 16, and sent to the Senate on May 17, with the following provisions relating to the Andean Regional Initiative:

- **Reporting Requirement Concerning Elimination of Colombian Opium.** Sec. 204 requires the Secretary of State, through the Bureau of International Narcotics and Law Enforcement, to submit, not later than 60 days after enactment, a report which outlines a comprehensive strategy to address the crisis of heroin in the United States due to opium originating from Colombia, including destruction of opium at its source.

- **Reporting Requirement Concerning Effect of Plan Colombia on Ecuador**. Sec. 211 requires the Secretary of State, through the Bureau of International Narcotics and Law Enforcement, to submit, not later than 60 days after enactment, a report that outlines a comprehensive strategy to address the spillover effect of Plan Colombia on Ecuador.

- **Reporting Requirement on Department of State Activities**. See. 213 (a) requires the Secretary of State to submit within 180 days of enactment, and every 180 days thereafter, a report on State Department funded and authorized activities to promote alternative development, recovery and resettlement of internally displaced persons, judicial reform, the peace process, and human rights. This report would include summaries of activities undertaken during the previous 180 days, estimated timetables for the next period, an explanation of any delays in meeting planned timetables, and an assessment of steps to be taken to correct such delays.

- **Reporting Requirement on the "Colombianization" of U.S. Funded Counter-narcotics Activities.** See. 213 (b) states that U.S. policy "encourages" the transfer of counter-narcotics activities in Colombia now carried out by U.S, businesses under agreements with the State Department to Colombian nationals, "in particular personnel of the Colombian anti-narcotics police, when properly qualified personnel are available." It also requires the Secretary of State to report within 90 days of enactment and subsequently not later than March 1 on the counter-narcotics activities carried out by U.S. businesses trader State Department agreements, The report must include the names of such businesses, the total State Department payments to each business, a statement justifying the agreement, an assessment of risks to personnel safety and potential involvement in hostilities incurred by employees of each such business, and a plan to provide for the transfer of these activities to Colombians.

- **Denial of Visas to Supporters of Colombian Illegal Armed Groups.** Sec. 236 prohibits the issuance of visas to any alien who the Secretary of State determines has willfully provided direct or indirect support to either of the two leftist guerrilla groups (the Revolutionary Armed Forces of Colombia, i.e., the FARC, and the National Liberation Army, i.e., the ELN) or to the rightist United Self-Defense Forces of Colombia (the AUC); or "has willfully conspired to allow, facilitate, or promote the illegal activities of any of those groups. A waiver is provided for cases where a visa "is necessary to support the peace process in Colombia, for urgent humanitarian reasons, for significant public benefit, or to further the national security interests of the United States."

Senate Action

The Senate Foreign Relations Committee approved the Senate version of the Foreign Relations Authorization for FY2002-FY2003 (S. 1401) on August 1, 2001, and reported out the bill on September 4, 2001, with a requirement for a report outlining a strategy to eradicate opium in Colombia.

Committee Action

The Committee on Foreign Relations reported out S. 1401 on September 4, 2001, with a provision in section 606, similar to a provision in the House version of the bill, requiting the Secretary of State to submit to appropriate congressional committees within 60 days after enactment a report that outlines a comprehensive strategy to eradicate all opium at its source in Colombia.

National Defense Authorization Act, FY2002

House Action

The House Armed Services Committee marked up H.R. 2586 on August 1, 2001, and reported out the bill (H.Rept. 107-194) on September 4, 2001, with a provision containing a cap on U.S. military personnel in Colombia, and this was retained when the House approved the bill on September 25, 2001.

Committee Action

As reported by the House Armed Services Committee, the FY2002 defense authorization bill, H.R. 2586, would cap the number of U.S. military personnel on duty in Colombia that could be supported from Department of Defense funding at 500. This provision, Section 1208, would exclude any military personnel in Colombia (1) serving tours of duty of 30 days or less for the purpose of rescuing or retrieving U.S. military or government personnel, (2) serving with the U.S. Embassy in Colombia as an attaché or as part of the security assistance office or Marine Corps security group, (3) participating in natural disaster relief efforts, or (4) traveling through Colombia but not involved in operations there.

Floor and Conference Action

After floor consideration on September 20, 24-25, the House approved H.R. 2586 on September 25, 2001, with the Committee- reported cap on military personnel in Colombia. The Senate bill, S. 1438, had no corresponding provision. This House provision was not retained in the conference version, S. 1438, S.Rept. 107-333, passed by both chambers on December 13,2001.

Andean Trade Preference Act (ATPA)

(For details on this legislation, see the CRS Trade Briefing Book section on the Andean Trade Preference Act, [http ://www.congress/gov/brbk/html/ebtra127.html].)

House Action

On November 16, 2001, the House passed H.R. 3009, the Andean Trade Promotion and Drug Eradication Act, which would offer expanded trade benefits to the Andean region through December 31, 2006.

Committee Action

On October 5, 2001, the House Ways and Means Committee approved and ordered reported H.R. 3009, the Andean Trade Promotion and Drug Eradication Act, that would extend the ATPA through December 31, 2006, and provide duty-free treatment to selected apparel, tuna, and other products previously excluded. The bill would also expand the conditions countries would have to meet to remain eligible for program benefits.

Senate Action

No floor action thus far.

Committee Action

On November 9, 2001, the Senate Committee on Finance reported H.R. 3090, the Economic Security and Recovery Act, which includes in Title V a six-month extension &the ATPA through June 4, 2002. On November 29, that committee approved S. 525, the Andean Trade Preference Extension Act, with similar, but more bruited benefits than the House's H.R. 3009.

Appendix A. Map Showing Andean Regional Initiative Countries

(Colombia, Bolivia, Brazil, Ecuador, Panama, Peru, and Venezuela)

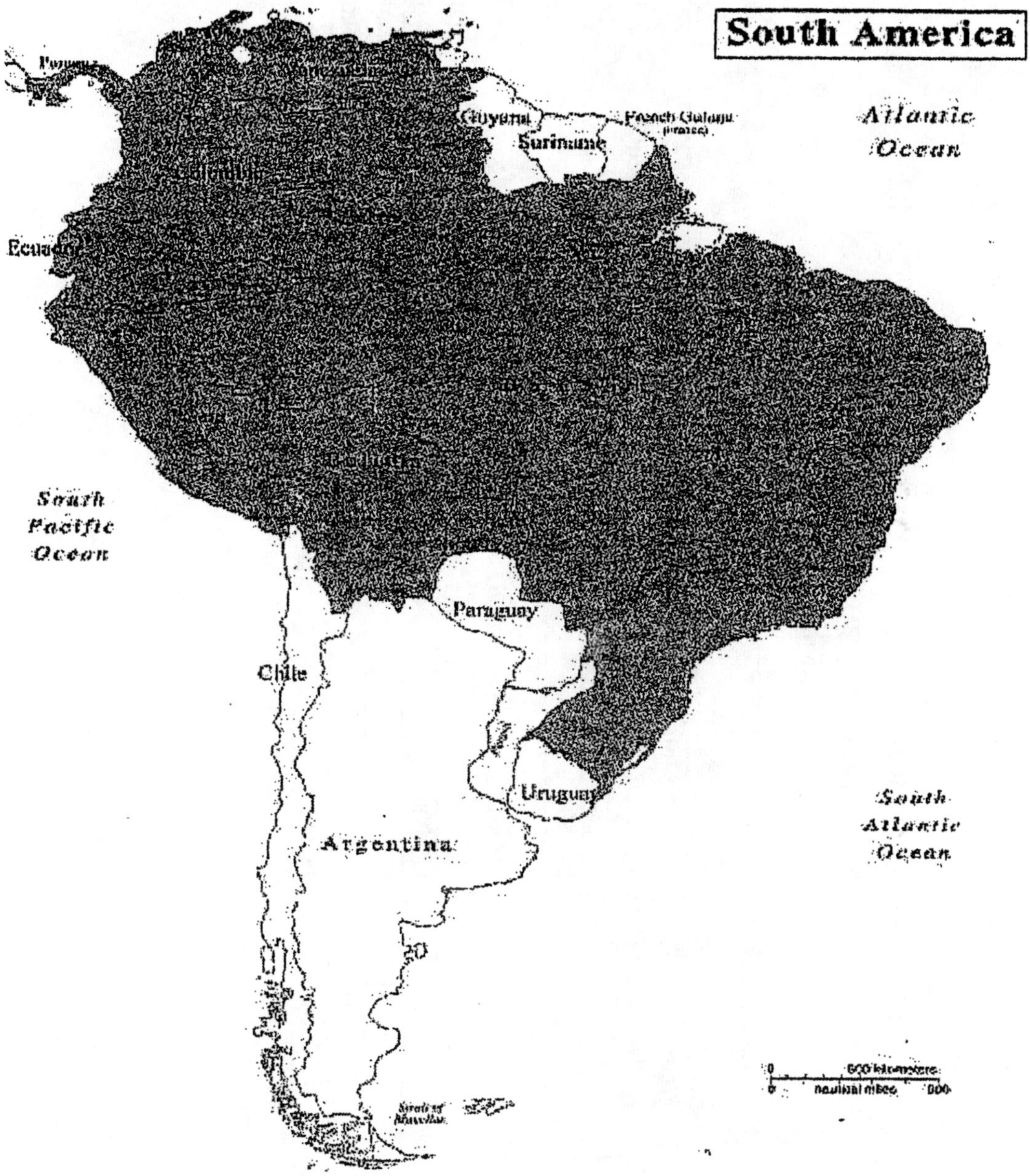

Appendix B. Bush Administration's Proposed FY2002 Andean Regional Initiative(ARI) by Purpose and Functional Accounts

($ millions)

Country	Total ARI	ARI Proposed Funding By Purpose		ARI Proposed Funding By Account				
		Economic/ Social/ Governance	Counter-narcotics and Security	International Narcotics Control (Andean Counter-Drug Initiative)	Development Aid	Child Survival and Diseases	Economic Support Fund	Foreign Military Financing
Columbia	399.00	146.50	252.50	399.00	0	0	0	0
Bolivia	143.48	88.48	55.00	101.00	25.08	6.40	10.00	1.00
Brazil	26.18	11.18	15.00	15.00	3.38	7.80	0	0
Ecuador	76.48	56.48	20.00	39.00	6.48	0	30.00	1.00
Panama	20.50	8.50	12.00	11.00	4.50	0	4.00	1.00
Peru	206.15	128.15	78.00	156.00	28.65	10.50	10.00	1.00
Venezuela	10.50	0.50	10.00	10.00	0	0	0.50	0
Totals	882.29	439.79	442.50	731.00	68.09	24.70	54.50	4.00

Source: ARI Reference Sheet, 150 Account, provided by the Department of State, May 14, 2001.

APPENDIX C. FY2000-FY2001 U.S. ASSISTANCE TO COLUMBIA

(Obligations and authorizations, $ millions)

Category of Foreign Aid or Other Assistance to Columbian Programs	FY2000 Regular Approps.	Plan Columbia (P.L. 106-246) FY2000	FY2001 Regular Approps.	Plan Columbia (P.L. 106-246) FY2001
State Department/INC account[a]	50.0	785.5	48.0	–
State Department INC Air Wing	31.3		28.0	–
Agency for International Development (AID)[a]	4.0	–	4.0	–
International Military Education and Training (IMET)	0.9	–	1.0	–
Foreign Military Financing/Grant		–	–	–
Department of Defense/Section 1004	68.7	4.5	49.8	101.2
Department of Defense/Overlapping Sections 1004/124	1.6	6.0	1.8	0.0
Department of Defense/Section 1033 account projects funded under Section 1033-type authority	7.2	17.4	8.1	13.0
Department of Defense/Section 506 Draw-down authorized	None		None thus far	
Other Section 506 Draw-down (i.e., Departments of Transportation, Justice, State, and the Treasury) authorized				
Totals	163.7	794.6	140.7	114.2
		960.1		254.9
Related Spending: Department of Defense/Section 124	11.1	13.0	14.4	0.0

Note: For detail on Plan Colombia and pre-Plan Colombia funding, see CRS Report RL30541, *Colombia: Plan Colombia Legislation and Assistance (FY2000-FY2001)*

Source: General Accounting Office (GAO-01-26), Department of State, Congressional Budget Justification for Foreign Operations for FY2001; U S Agency for International Development Budget Justification for FY2001, Annex IV; and information provided by Department of State and Department of Defense officials This chart includes direct U S foreign assistance (i e , the categories usually counted as U S foreign aid, which are in italics), as well as the cost of goods and services provided to Colombia from other U S government programs supporting counter-narcotics efforts in Colombia The United States also provides a small amount of DOD Excess Defense Articles (EDA) to Colombia Other funds are spent in Colombia on counter-narcotics and other activities that are considered part of U S programs: for instance, the Drug Enforcement Administration (DEA) spends its own funds on joint operations in Colombia Figures on FY2000 and FY2001 State Department INC funding provided January 10-11, 2001 Figures on DOD Sections 1004, 124, 1004/124, and 1033 funding provided June 29, 2001 DOD Sections 124, 1004, and 1033 funding is taken from regional accounts and the tentative allocations for Colombia can be shifted to respond to developing needs in other areas (Section 124 covers U S operated radar systems in Colombia and elsewhere, and other costs of U S detection and monitoring of drug flights)

[a] FY2000 non-DOD Plan Colombia supplemental funds were all assigned to the State Department INC account; the State Department is transferring them to the other agencies carrying out programs in Colombia with those funds. The AID FY2000 and FY2001 figures are all ESF These AID figures do not include funds provided to AID from INC account

Appendix D. Controversy over Spray Eradication Efforts in Southern Colombia

The following discussion of the controversy over spray eradication (i.e., fumigation) of illegal coca crops in southern Colombia was prepared in response to the controversy over this effort in southern Colombia. This short synopsis of available information on the effects of fumigation of coca crops in Colombia is only meant to provide a summary of various claims; it is not a judgment on their validity.

In its U.S.-supported coca eradication program, the government of Colombia sprays coca crops from aircraft with a mixture of the herbicide glyphosate, manufactured by the U.S. company Monsanto and marketed as "Roundup," and two additives or "adjuvants."[15] According to the State Department (in its report of January 23, 2001, submitted to Congress consistent with the provisions of the Statement of Managers accompanying Title III, Chapter 2 of the Emergency Supplemental Appropriations Act. P.L. 106-246, which provided funding for Plan Colombia), the Environmental Protection Agency (EPA) has found that "the use of glyphosate, as labeled for use in the U.S., is acceptable provided that the regulatory controls required by the EPA - the labeled instructions - are followed." The State Department also claims that the ingredients in the two additives (COSMO FLUX- 411F, a surfactant, and COSMO-iN-D, an anti-foaming additive[16]), both produced in Colombia, are on an EPA list of acceptable chemicals "for use on food crops when the label instructions are followed." This report states an EPA review of "adequate scientific studies" shows that when properly used glyphosate "will not cause adverse effects in humans," and "does not cause risks of concern for birth defects, mutagenic effects, neurotoxic effects, reproductive problems, or cancer." It does, however, state that "splashes" of glyphosate "can cause transient irritation to skin and eyes," although at the same level of irritation as baby shampoo according to one cited study. For its conclusion that there are "no grounds to suggest concern for human health" from the spray mixture used in Colombia, the State Department cited a recent study published in *Regulatory Toxicology and Pharmacology*.[17]

Since spraying began in December 2000 in Colombia's Putumayo province (where it is now indefinitely suspended), however, there have been many allegations that the spray mixture has caused extensive harm to humans, other crops, and • livestock. The ill health effects on thousands of children and adults most commonly reported in the areas of Putumayo fumigation include fever, eye and gastrointestinal irritation, and skin and bronchial irritation and infections. There have also been allegations of increased incidence of brain damage in children in these areas since fumigation was started. In addition, critics claim, many crops

---

[15] The active ingredient in Roundup is isopropylamine salt of N-(phosphonomethyl) glycine, commonly known as glyphosate, Chemical Abstract Registration Number 38641-94-0, EPA Registration Number 000524-004445. "Adjuvant" is a term for an ingredient that facilitates or modifies the action of the principal ingredient.

[16] COSMO FLUX-411F, according to the State Department report, "increases the herbicide penetration through the waxy layer of the coca leaf by allowing ore of the spray to stick to the plant. When more of the spray solution sticks to the plant, the herbicide becomes more effective which means it can be applied in smaller doses." COSMO-IN-D "is used to minimize the foam created by the mixture-circulating pump inside the aircraft spray hopper" in order to avoid the creation of a vacuum within the spray pressure pump which could shut off the spray system during flight.

[17] Gary M. Williams, Robert Kroes, and Ian C. Munro. Safety Evaluation and Risk Assessment of the Herbicide Roundup and its Active Ingredient, Glyphosate, for Humans. *Regulatory Toxicology and Pharmacology*. Vol. 31, No. 2, April 2000. Available through [http://www.ciponline.org/colombia/ 12301.htm] from a hyperlink at the bottom of the text of the State Department's January 23, 2001 report. This publication is the official journal of the International Society of Regulatory Toxicology and Pharmacology.

other than coca have been sprayed, depriving peasants of food crops and other sources of income, and livestock reportedly have suffered ill effects, including hair loss in cattle from moderate exposure, abortion among pregnant cows (possibly due, one source notes, from stampedes caused by the noise of overhead helicopters) and the death of fowl from spraying or drinking contaminated water. (The effects on livestock and fowl are taken from the "Counter-Fact Sheet" of February 9, 2001, prepared by Accion Andina, a non-governmental organization, and posted at [http://usfumigation.org/Literature/FactSheets/ContraDoS/AA-IPS-RAPAL%20Fact%20 Sheet%20-English.htm].) Supporters of aerial fumigation, however, state that negative health and environmental effects can be attributed to drug producers themselves, whom, they claim, also use Roundup to suppress weeds around coca bushes, and who pollute Colombian rivers with chemicals used in processing and refining coca into cocaine in their drug labs.

Some U.S. officials assert that many of the complaints come from those with an interest in continuing coca production, especially as aerial spraying of coca crops has taken place for many years in other areas of Colombia without the outcry that the spraying in Putumayo has produced. However, according to a *Washington Post* article of January 7, 2001, about the spraying in Putumayo: "Until recently, spraying focused almost entirely on remote industrial-sized coca and poppy plantations....Now the planes are targeting more populous farming areas...where coca...is often grown side by side with corn, yucca, pineapple and livestock. Often it shares a plot next to the farmer's tin-roofed shack." ("Aerial Attack Killing More than Coca," by Scott Wilson.) Regarding crop damage, the *Post* reporter stated that his "inspection of fields in the area suggested that food crops have been hit at least as hard as coca." Critics have attributed food crop damage to the side-by-side plantings of legal and illegal crops in Putumayo, but also charge that spray planes fly higher than normal for crop dusting operations elsewhere in order to avoid ground fire, and under unacceptable wind conditions, thus leading to the dispersion of spray beyond intended targets.[18]

Some analysts, however, have noted that complaints of ill effects to humans and annals may not be entirely inconsistent with State Department assertions of safety under controlled circumstances as the health and environmental effects could vary depending on the exact formulation of the spray mix, the manner of its application, and the conditions under which it was used. Some critics have argued that Roundup is not being applied in a manner consistent with U.S. usages and with the manufacturer's recommendations, and that not all issues related to ingredients used in the mixture applied in Colombia have been explored.

- The World Wildlife Fund, in an October 30, 2000 statement, "Comments on Glyphosate," states that existing studies "may not be adequate to assess the impacts resulting from Plan Colombia's actual use of glyphosate (aerial applications, product formulation, frequency and rate of application, etc.), especially given the soils, topography, climatic conditions (temperature, rainfall, etc.) plant and animal species found in Colombia." (Online at: [http://www.ciponline.org/colombia/103001.htm]).

[18] One website's ([http://www.farmsource.com]) discussion of the use of Roundup (accessed through the Monsanto website, [http://www.monsanto.com]) notes that Roundup should "only be applied from aircraft when the potential for drift to adjacent sensitive areas (e.g. residential areas, bodies of water, known habitat for threatened or endangered species, non-target crops) is minimal (e.g. when the wind is blowing away from sensitive areas)." It gives detailed instructions for aerial applications, including the maintenance of an appropriate buffer zone from "any desirable vegetation or crops," i.e., normally some 100 feet, but 500 feet if the wind is blowing up to five miles an hour, and more at greater wind speeds.

- In a February 9, 2001 statement calling for the end of aerial eradication, representatives of three non-governmental organizations claimed that "there is evidence that herbicide concentrations much higher than ones recommended are being applied in Colombia" and that "there are no toxicological studies...regarding the effects of mixing the Cosmoflux-4111F surfactant with pesticides."[19] The statement also noted that Roundup Ultra (which opponents say is the actual variety of Roundup being used in Colombia, although the State Department report cited above does not refer to either trade name) "contains other ingredients besides glyphosate and the two adjuvants." The World Wildlife Fund, in the October 2000 statement cited above, found that studies on the effects of Roundup "focus on the pesticide active ingredient alone, not the combination of inert ingredients actually applied, thereby giving an incomplete assessment of the toxic threat," and asserted that "the inert ingredients mixed with the Roundup to increase its effectiveness can be as, or more, toxic to humans, wildlife and food webs than the pesticide itself." The Monsanto website states that the "new ingredients" in Roundup Ultra are on an EPA approved list (#4B), but the specific "new" ingredients are not named.
- An analysis by agronomist Elsa Nivia, identified as associated with the non-governmental *Red de Accion en Plaguicidas y Alternativas - America Latina*, RAP-AL. PAN-Colombia (Pesticide Action Network), claims that the aerial fumigation of illegal crops in Colombia with Roundup is "very different from the recommended agricultural use in the United States," citing the concentration as 26 times greater than that recommended, with negative effects intensified by the use of Cosmoflux 411F. Even though the authors of the report cited by the State Department had found glyphosate and Roundup to be at most mildly toxic, Ms. Nivia's conclusion from their discussion of the effects of accidental and occupational exposures to higher concentrations, and of the doses that proved lethal in people attempting suicide, is that higher than recommended concentrations or applications could help to explain the severe ill effects reported in the fumigated areas. (See *Las fumigaciones aereas sobre cultivos ilicitos si son peligrosas - Algunas aproximaciones*, by Elsa Nivia. Paper given at a conference on The Wars in Colombia: Drugs, Guns and Oil, held at the University of California at Davis, May 17-19, 2001, accessible through [http://www.usfumigation.org].)

The State Department is funding a study, with design assistance supplied by the Center for Disease Control (CDC) and the EPA, of the health effects of aerial eradication in Putumayo Department. Results are anticipated by late 2001.

---

[19] *Forced Aerial Eradication of Illicit Crops: A Reply to the State Department*, signed by Ricardo Vargas M. of Accion Andina Colombia, Martin Jelsma of Transnational Institute, TNI, and Elsa Nivia of KAPALMIRA. Posted at [http://www.usfumigation.org].

Chapter 6

THE ANDEAN TRADE PREFERENCE ACT

J. F. Hornbeck

ISSUE

Following passage by the 102nd Congress, President George Bush signed into law the Andean Trade Preference Act (ATPA) on December 4, 1991 (P.L. 102-182, Title II), making it part of a multifaceted strategy to counter illicit drug production and trade in Latin America. For ten years, it has provided preferential, mostly duty-free, treatment of selected U.S. imports from Bolivia, Colombia, Ecuador, and Peru. ATPA's goal has been to encourage growth of a more diversified Andean export base, thereby promoting development and providing an incentive for Andean farmers and other workers to pursue economic alternatives to the drug trade. ATPA expires on December 4, 2001.

BACKGROUND

ATPA's trade preference are a small part of a larger Andean counter-narcotics effort; Coca production is the primary target of these efforts and because it is a highly profitable undertaking and particularly enticing for poor areas of the world, a key element of the strategy is supporting the cultivation of alternative cash crops. ATPA's supporters argue that reduced tariffs conceivably play a part of the "alternative development" strategy by providing an additional financial incentive to substitute legal crops (asparagus has been one success story) for coca cultivation. The increase in non-agricultural exports (e.g. copper cathodes), it could be argued, may also reflect, in pan, ATPA's preferential tariff treatment.

Testimony before congressional committees has indicated a desire by groups in the United States and the Andean countries to reauthorize ATPA and consider expanding the tariff preferences to more products and countries. In support of these policy considerations, ATPA has been represented as having a positive effect on drug-crop eradication and crop substitution in the beneficiary countries and providing viable economic alternatives to drug-crop cultivation, production and trafficking.

Others have noted that ATPA's benefits have been quantitatively small. Because many imports are not eligible by law for preferential treatment or enter the United States under other preferential trade arrangements, only 10% of imports from ATPA countries eater the United States exclusively under the ATPA provisions. This has not changed in recent years, suggesting that ATPA's trade effects are unlikely to increase, unless the program's parameters are modified. Because the trade response is retail, so too are ATPA's likely marginal effects On the Andean economies.

Although the trade effects of ATPA have been relatively small, there is some indication that the composition of trade has changed and that, with a few products, a case can be made that ATPA has supported this change. It is possible that the slightly altered composition of U.S. imports from ATPA countries reflects broader change in what Andean countries are producing and that this in turn points to some indirect evidence that resources once used for drug-related activity are being redirected toward ATPA-eligible products. Isolating ATPA's role from other counter-narcotics and economic diversification programs, however, has been a difficult challenge, producing imprecise estimates.

Supporters of ATPA argue that its effects are at least indirectly evident and have proposed at least three program initiatives: 1) reauthorize ATPA to reinforce the U.S. commitment to the alternative development counter-narcotics strategy; 2) extend preferential treatment to other Andean exports to broaden the program effects; and 3) include Venezuela as a beneficiary country.

LEGISLATION 107TH CONGRESS

On October 5, 2001, the House Ways and Means Committee approved an amended extension of ATPA entitled the Andean Trade Promotion and Drug Eradication Act (*H.R. 3009*). It would extend the program through December 31, 2006, and provide duty-free treatment to selected apparel, tuna, and other products previously excluded. It also expands the conditions countries need to meet to become qualified for these benefits.

On March 13, 2001, Senator Graham introduced *S. 525*, the Andean Trade Preference Expansion Act (ATPEA), which would amend the provisions and extend the trade preferences through October 1, 2005. The bill would allow for selected textile and apparel products from one or more of the eligible countries to enter the United States free from duty and quantitative restrictions, similar to benefits provided eligible countries under NAFTA and the Caribbean Basin Trade Partnership Act.

Chapter 7

THE U.S.-CHILE FREE TRADE AGREEMENT

J. F. Hornbeck

ISSUE

On November 29, 2000, then-President Clinton announced that the United States and Chile would negotiate a bilateral free trade agreement (FTA). The terse White House press release emphasized that the FTA would be a joint commitment to pursue fleer trade and investment m the region, would be directly supportive of She effort to complete a Free Trade Area of the Americas (FTAA), and should include labor and environment provisions similar to those in the U.S.-Jordan FTA. President Bush has continued negotiations with Chile in 2001 and there is a widening expectation that an agreement can be reached by the end of, the year or in 2002.

BACKGROUND

Chile has long been interested in expanding trade ties with industrial economies, particularly the United States. It responded enthusiastically to a 1994 invitation to join the North American Free Trade Agreement (NAFTA), but at the time insisted that presidential fast-track trade negotiating authority be in place prior to the commencement of formal negotiations. The Chile accession initiative eventually faded with frustrated efforts to pros fast track, but its policy of pursuing FTAs in the region and around She world continued. Currently, Chile no longer insists on fast track (now trade promotion authority or TPA) being in place to negotiate and is also pursuing FTAs aggressively with the Republic of Korea, Japan, and the European Union, among other countries.

In 1998, She U.S.-Chile Joint Commission on Trade and Investment was created, which eventually spawned the U.S.-Chile FTA initiative. FTA discussions began on December 6, 2000, and negotiators have met almost monthly since then. Many observers expect the agreement can be completed by yearend or in early 2002, the two countries-have agreed to negotiate a comprehensive agreement and have found many areas of "commonality." Progress apparently has been made in the areas of market access (tariff lists were exchanged in July, priority lists followed in September 2001), customs procedures, sanitary and phytosanitary standards, and technical norms and standards.

Key differences have already been identified, however, particularly language covering labor and environmental provisions. Chile has signed FTAs with Canada and Mexico that include NAFTA-like side agreements, which it still prefers. On September 30, 2001, when President Bush signed into law implementing legislation for the U.S.-Jordan FTA, another model was created. Its primary difference involves placing the text of these provisions in the body of the agreement, making labor and environment provisions subject to the full agreement's dispute resolution mechanism. The most controversial aspect of this change is that trade sanctions (rather than a "monetary assessment") could be used as final recourse for dispute settlement. It is unclear whether the Chile-Canada, U.S.-Jordan, or some new or hybrid model for defining environment and labor provisions will emerge in the U.S.-Chile FTA.

A number of other issues remain to be resolved with the Chile FTA. Chile has raised concerns over other U.S. trade policy stands, particularly its frequent reliance on antidumping and countervailing duty action against Chilean industries. The most recent example involves antidumping and countervailing duty petitions filed by red raspberry producers in June 2001. Discussion on investment, intellectual property rights, financial services, and agriculture are also among the more problematic and challenging issues to resolve. Currently, Chile appears reticent to move ahead on some issues of importance to the United States, such as financial services and intellectual property rights, unless some concession is made on U.S. trade remedy practices. Many in the U.S. Congress, however, remain adamant that trade remedy laws not be weakened.

Third party issues have emerged as well, with Brazil having sought to bring Chile into the Southern Common Market (Mercado Comun del Sur - Mercosur) as a full partner. One view from Brazil suggests that because Chile has opted for the U.S. FTA, there is some doubt about the compatibility of also joining Mercosur, perhaps also undermining a one-time emerging strategy for developing a unified South American trade position. Chile argues otherwise, however, that historically it has consistently had an independent trade policy strategy. It views the differential in tariff rates as the main barrier to Chilean accession to Mercosur, a goal it has not abandoned in any case. Chile also believes that there is ample incentive for the United States to negotiate an FTA because the alternative only strengthens Brazil's bargaining position in regional trade negotiations.

Other factors suggest that progress toward an FTA could move relatively quickly. In the U.S., there has been significant momentum in signing other bilateral FTAs, including passage into law of the U.S.-Jordan FTA, and many observers believe that Chile, although small, is a strategically important trading partner. Chile's decision to move toward the United States rather than Mercosur presents an opportunity for deepening relations with a South American country in a region that traditionally has traded heavily with Europe and Asia. U.S. business interests also generally support a trade pact with Chile and have repeatedly expressed frustration over the competitive disadvantage they face from other Chilean bilateral FTAs, especially the one with Canada.

Despite interest in elevating the importance of Chile as a trading partner, it is still a relatively small economy, ranking 32 and 40 in size respectively, for U.S. exports and imports in 2000. Approximately 60% of U.S. exports to Chile are office/electrical equipment and parts (including computers), motor vehicles, and small aircraft. Some 60% of U.S. imports from Chile comprise copper, grapes, fish, lumber, and wine. The U.S. continues to maintain a small and shrinking trade surplus with Chile (see **Table 1** for recent data). Nonetheless, it is conceivable that U.S.-Chilean trade could grow significantly and become a model itself for expanding U.S. ties in South America.

Table 1. U.S.-Chile Merchandise Trade, 1985-2000
($ millions)

Year	U.S. Exports	U.S. Imports	Trade Balance	Trade Turnover
1985	682	745	-63	1,427
1986	823	820	3	1,643
1987	796	981	-185	1,777
1988	1,066	1,181	-115	2,247
1989	1,414	1,292	122	2,706
1990	1,664	1,313	351	2,977
1991	1,839	1,302	537	3,141
1992	2,466	1,388	1,078	3,854
1993	2,599	1,462	1,137	4,061
1994	2,774	1,821	953	4,595
1995	3,615	1,931	1,684	5,546
1996	4,132	2,256	1,876	6,388
1997	4,368	2,293	2,075	6,661
1998	3,979	2,453	1,526	6,432
1999	3,078	2,953	125	6,031
2000	3,455	3,228	227	6,683

Source: U.S. Department of Commerce.
Trade turnover = exports plus imports.

LEGISLATION 107TH CONGRESS

In the Senate, *S. 138*, the Chile-NAFTA Accession Act (Sen. Gramm), and S. 586, the Chile Fast Track Act of 2001 (Sen. Dodd) would authorize the President to enter into an agreement for the accession of Chile to the North American Free Trade Agreement (NAFTA) or for a bilateral free trade agreement between the United States and Chile and have it proceed pursuant to fast-track trade negotiating authority.

Chapter 8

CANADA-U.S. TRADE AND INVESTMENT

Ian F. Fergusson

ISSUE

Canada is the single largest trading partner of the United States, with total merchandise trade (exports and imports) exceeding $408 billion in 2000. Trade has always been a prominent and sometimes contentious part of Canadian-American relations, and the two nations have become bound together increasingly by trade agreements, culminating with the North American Free Trade Agreement in 1994. Although the vast majority of U.S.-Canadian trade and investment takes place smoothly, several disputes remain contentious. Another concern is the growing U.S. merchandise trade deficit with Canada, an imbalance that may give rise to protectionist pressures.

BACKGROUND

The Trade and Investment Relationship

In 2000, U.S. merchandise exports to Canada totaled $179 billion, while imports from Canada reached $229 billion, resulting in a deficit of $50 billion. In bilateral services trade, however, the Untied States recorded a surplus of $6 billion in 1999 (exports of $21 billion and imports of $15 billion). The stock of U.S. direct investment in Canada was $112 billion in 1999, competed with Canadian direct investment in the United States of $80 billion.

The U.S. and Canadian economies are highly integrated. The geographic proximity of the two countries, which share a long land border, has resulted in low transportation costs. A similar cultural and linguistic heritage in English-speaking regions of Canada also facilitates cross-border trade, In fact, since 80% of the Canadian population lives within 100 miles of the U.S. border, trade with the United States is often easier end less expensive than Canadian inter-provincial trade, However, the tightening of border security associated with the recent terrorist attacks on the United States may increase certain costs associated with U.S. Canadian trade.

Trade liberalization over the past 35 years, beginning with the Automotive Agreement of 1965 (which eliminated tariffs on shipments of autos and auto parts between the two countries), through the Canada-U.S. Free Trade Agreement of 1989 (CESTA), and the North American Free Trade Agreement of 1994 (NAFTA), has contributed substantially to economic integration. Under the CUSTA (which was incorporated into NAFTA), bilateral tariffs except for certain agricultural products were phased out during a 10-year period culminating in 1998.

The elimination of tariffs and the reduction of non-tariff barriers have contributed to the process of specialization, as each country is able to produce goods for a larger continent-wide market. Thus, firms are able to improve productivity through increased economies of scale and coordinated production. Such specialization led to increased bilateral trade, much of it in intermediate products. In a 1996 study, it was estimated that about 45% of U. S.-Canadian trade was intra-firm trade, reflecting the substantial integration of the two economies and contributing to increased efficiency and competitiveness of firms on both sides of the border.

The U.S. merchandise trade deficit with Canada increased to $50 billion in 2000 at a rate greatly exceeding the increase in total trade. This growing trade deficit has been attributed to several factors. One reason has been the persistent weakness of the Canadian dollar. Canada generates a disproportionate amount of its foreign exchange through exports of natural resources and primary products, many of which experienced depressed market conditions in the 1990s. Weak demand for Canada's exports has contributed to weak demand, and thus depreciation, of its currency. In turn, the price of Canadian products in U.S. dollars has declined, thus stimulating U.S. imports from Canada. At the same time, the price of U. S. goods in Canadian dollars has increased, thus lowering the demand for U.S. exports in Canada.

The U.S. economy also consistently outperformed the Canadian economy during the 1990s. Canadian real GDP in the five years 1996-2000 grew at an average rate of 3.7% while U.S. real GDP averaged 4.4%. U.S. imports from Canada grew faster than Canadian imports from the United States during this period, as is often the case when a country experiencing relatively high growth rates satisfies increasing domestic demand with higher levels of imports.

Disputes

U.S. agricultural product trade with Canada totaled $16.3 billion in 2000, about 4% of all bilateral merchandise trade. Current agricultural trade disputes center on the U.S. ban imposed on potatoes from Prince Edward Island, a dispute over the marketing practices &the Canadian Wheat Board, and Canada's dairy pricing structure. The management of the Pacific Salmon fishery has also been the source of periodic friction, although the conclusion of an agreement in June 1999 permitting negotiated harvests and conservation of the fishery may alleviate these tensions.

The Softwood Lumber Agreement (SLA) between the United States and Canada expired on April 1, 2001. This agreement, implemented in 1996, set a tariff rate quota on exports of softwood lumber from four Canadian provinces at 14.7 billion board feet per year and set fees for exports in excess of that amount. U.S. lumber producers contend that Canadian provinces subsidize their lumber industry by charging less than market value for lumber harvested (stumpage fees). U.S. timber and environmental groups have also expressed concern about Canadian forestry management and clear-cutting practices. The Canadian government has disputed these allegations and has demanded free trade in lumber. It has asserted that Canadian mills have modernized and are more efficient than U.S. operations.

On April 2, U.S. lumber producers filed countervailing duty and anti-dumping petitions with the International Trade Commission and the Department of Commerce. On April 24, the Department of Commerce initiated anti-dumping and countervailing duty investigations, and on May 16, the International Trade Commission found that there was sufficient indication that the allegedly subsidized imports have caused the U.S. industry material injury. Commerce announced a preliminary subsidy determination of 19.3% on August 10. It also announced the existence of "critical circumstances," a provision of U. S. trade law that allows for the retroactive imposition of this duty if final determinations of subsidy and material injury are made by Commerce and the ITC, respectively. These decisions are expected by December 2001. A preliminary determination in a parallel antidumping proceeding is expected to be announced by the Commerce Department by October 15, 2001.

Canada has long been concerned that its culture is in danger of being overwhelmed by that of the United States, which, in terms of population and GDP, is ten times the size of Canada. Claiming to maintain its cultural identity, Canada has implemented regulations to promote Canadian ownership of film distribution, to encourage Canadian content in radio/TV programming, and to restrict the distribution of foreign magazines. The United States has challenged many of these restrictions, arguing that such laws are disguised protection that denies opportunities to U.S. firms.

Recently, the U.S. film industry has located more of its production of movies and television programs to Canada. This migration has been attributed to many factors including provincial subsidies, the weakness of the Canadian dollar, and the development of the cable movie genre. The Screen Actors Guild has estimated that "runaway film production" cost the U.S. industry 20,000 jobs and $10.3 billion in 1998. Canadians have responded their production facilities are a good value, that many U.S. states offer similar production subsidies, and that Canada consumes much more of the total content production of the two nations than it produces.

LEGISLATION

Congress passed legislation implementing the U.S.-Canada Free Trade Agreement in 1988 (P.L. 100-449) and the North American Free Trade Agreement in 1993 (P.L. 103-182.). Since then, no broad legislation regarding U.S.-Canada trade has been under consideration. In the 107th Congress, resolutions have been introduced expressing the sense of Congress regarding the importation of Canadian lumber (*H.Con.Res. 45*; *H.Con.Res. 54*; *S.Con.Res. 4*).

Chapter 9

SOFTWOOD LUMBER IMPORTS FROM CANADA

Ross W. Gorte

ISSUE

Softwood lumber imports from Canada have been of concern to U.S. lumber producers for many years because of questions about Canadian government timber pricing policies. In 1996, the United States and Canada reached a 5-year agreement on restrictions that expired on March 31, 2001. Resolutions and bills have been introduced in recent Congresses that, if enacted, would have restricted softwood lumber imports from Canada or eliminated the basis for restricting those imports. The Bush Administration will face pressures from proponents and opponents of restrictions, and the 107th Congress may consider legislative proposals on this issue.

BACKGROUND

Concerns about softwood lumber imports from Canada have been raised for many years. In 1981, Congress asked the Department of Commerce to investigate the situation, which found *de minimis* (insignificant) subsidies. Another investigation in 1986 preliminarily found subsidies of 15% of sale values; the expected CVD was supplanted by a Memorandum of Understanding (MOU), with Canada imposing a 15% export tax on softwood lumber. Canada withdrew from the MOU in 1991, arguing that the provinces had responded to the previous concerns. An investigation in 1992 led to a 6.51% duty, but this duty was successfully challenged under the U.S.-Canada Free Trade Agreement. In 1996, the United States and Canada reached the just-expired 5-year softwood lumber agreement – a fee on lumber imports from four Canadian provinces in excess of a specified quota.

Tension between the United States and Canada over softwood lumber trade may be inevitable. Both countries have extensive forest resources, but vastly different population levels and development pressures; vast stretches of Canada are still largely undeveloped, while relatively fewer areas in the United States (outside Alaska) remain relatively pristine. These differences have led to divergent forest policies. In Canada, 90% of the forests are owned by the provincial governments, which have allocated and priced timber to encourage development of the extensive timber reserves. In the United States, 58% of timberlands are privately owned; private markets dominate the allocation and pricing of timber, although U.S. federal and other government-owned forests are regionally important.

U.S. lumber producers assert they have been injured by Canadian subsidies that have given Canadian lumber producers an unfair advantage in selling lumber in the U.S. market. Canadian provincial stumpage fees (for the right to harvest trees) are asserted to be subsidized – priced at less than their market value. The provinces generally use leases and administered fees to allocate and price their timber. Administered fees are unlikely to match market values, but determining whether the fees are significantly below market values, as asserted by U.S. lumber producers, has been controversial, because of differences in tree species, sizes, and grades; in measurement systems; in requirements on harvesters; in environmental protection; and in other factors.

Log export restrictions in British Columbia are also said to be subsidies, because they assure more supply (less competition for timber and thus lower costs) for Canadian producers. Evidence from the U.S. Pacific Northwest, where private logs can be exported but public timber cannot, indicates substantially higher prices for exported logs. However, an August 23 WTO panel report agreed with Canada's charge that U.S. treatment of log export restrictions as subsidies violated WTO agreements.

Injuries to U.S. lumber producers are difficult to establish decisively. Canada's share of the U.S. lumber market has risen substantially, from less than 7% in the early 1950s to more than 35% in the mid-1990s. Under the 1996 agreement, the quantity of imports rose, but the market share was stable. Restrictions have probably put upward pressure on U.S. lumber prices, but the price rise estimated by a group opposed to restrictions would probably have a minor impact on housing costs.

OUTLOOK

The U.S.-Canada softwood lumber agreement terminated on March 31, 2001. No negotiations of an extension or new agreement have occurred. The U.S. Coalition for Fair Lumber Imports has filed antidumping and countervailing duty petitions to restrict Canadian imports. On May 16, the U.S. International Trade Commission issued its preliminary findings of a reasonable indication of injury to the U.S. industry by Canadian lumber imports. On August 17, the Department of Commerce issued its preliminary findings of 19.31% *ad valorem* Canadian subsidies and of critical circumstances. The Bush Administration will face pressure from the U.S. lumber industry and environmentalists to restrict lumber imports, and from U.S. homebuilders and other lumber users to end restrictions. Resolutions have been introduced to support restricting imports and ending restrictions.

Chapter 10

LUMBER IMPORTS FROM CANADA: ISSUES AND EVENTS

Ross W. Gorte and Jeanne Grimmett

SUMMARY

U.S. lumber producers have raised concerns about softwood lumber imports from Canada many years; the current dispute has persisted for at least two decades. Alleged Canadian subsidies (subsidies are a prerequisite for establishing countervailing duties CVDs) were investigated in 1982, 1986, and 1992. No subsidies were found in 1983; however, in 1986, preliminary subsidy findings led to a Memorandum of Understanding (with a 15% Canadian tax on lumber exported to the United States), and to a 6.51% CVD in 1992. The 1992 CVD was challenged under the U.S.-Canada Free Trade Agreement, and was terminated in 1994. A U.S.-Canada Softwood Lumber Agreement (SLA) was reached in 1996 to restrict lumber exports to the United States for 5 years, beginning on April 1, 1996. The SLA expired on March 31, 2001.

U.S. Industry Arguments

The U.S. producers argue that they have been injured by unfair Canadian competition. They argue that the provinces set "stumpage fees" (for the right to harvest trees) administratively at less than their market value. This system, where the provinces own 90% of Canadian timberlands, contrasts with the United States, where 42% of timberlands are publicly owned and where government timber is often sold competitively. These differences in land tenure make comparisons difficult.

In addition, U.S. lumber producers argue that provincial and Canadian federal log export restrictions confer a subsidy to Canadian producers by preventing other producers from getting direct access to Canadian timber. The United States also restricts log exports from federal and state lands, but logs can be exported from the private lands that dominate the U.S. timber market. Canada has challenged U.S. treatment of export restrictions as a subsidy in the WTO, arguing that this is inconsistent with the WTO Agreement on Subsidies and Countervailing Measures.

Finally, U.S. producers argue that they have been injured by imports of Canadian softwood lumber. They point to the steady growth in Canadian exports and market share, from less than 3 billion board feet (BBF) and 7% of U.S. lumber consumption in 1952 to more than 18 BBF annually since t 998 and a market share of more than 33% since 1995. Canadians counter that the U.S. industry has been unable to satisfy the growth in demand. U.S. homebuilders and other lumber users counter that Canadian lumber is needed to satisfy U.S. demands.

Current Issues

Neither an extension of the SLA nor a new agreement is currently being negotiated. In response to petitions, the Department of Commerce initiated countervailing and antidumping investigations on April 30. On May 16, the International Trade Commission issued its preliminary finding that the U.S. industry had probably been injured by lumber imports from Canada. On August 10, the Department issued preliminary findings that Canadian subsidies (and thus the preliminary duty) amounted to 19.31% of sale value, and that critical circumstances existed, allowing the duties to apply retroactively.

On August 23, the WTO panel issued its final report, concluding that U.S. treatment of export restrictions as a subsidy violated the WTO Subsidies and Countervailing Measures Agreement, but not recommending remedial action, since a CVD based on this treatment is not mandatory.

Most Recent Developments

The 1996 U.S.-Canada Softwood Lumber Agreement expired on March 31, 2001. On April 2, the U.S. Coalition for Fair Lumber Imports filed countervailing and antidumping petitions with the relevant U.S. federal agencies, charging that subsidized and below-cost Canadian lumber was being dumped on U.S. markets, harming the U.S. lumber industry. On May 16, the U.S. International Trade Commission issued its preliminary finding a reasonable indication that the U.S. lumber industry was threatened with material injury by softwood lumber imports from Canada. On August 17, the Commerce Department issued preliminary findings that Canadian subsidies' amounted to 19.31% ad valorem (as a percent of lumber values); thus, the Department established a preliminary duty of 19.31%. On August 23, a WTO panel report agreed with Canada's challenge that U.S. treatment of export restraints as a subsidy violated the WTO Agreement on Subsidies and Countervailing Measures, but did not recommend remedial action because a CVD based on this treatment is not mandatory under U.S. trade law.

Background and Analysis

Concerns among U.S. lumber producers about softwood lumber imports from Canada have been raised for decades; the current dispute has persisted for at least 20 years. U.S.

producers argue that they have been harmed by unfair competition, which they assert results from subsidies to Canadian producers, primarily in the form of low provincial stumpage fees (the fees for the right to harvest trees from Province-owned timberlands) and Canadian restrictions on log exports. Canadians defend their system, and U.S. homebuilders and other lumber users advocate unrestricted lumber imports. This issue brief provides a concise historical account of the dispute, summarizes the subsidy and injury evidence, and discusses the current issues and events.

Historical Background

The current dispute began in 1981, when letters from Members of Congress and a petition from the U.S. lumber industry asked the U.S. Department of Commerce (DOC) and the U.S. International Trade Commission (ITC) to investigate lumber imports from Canada for a possible countervailing duty (CVD).[1] The ITC found preliminary evidence of injury to the U.S. industry, but in 1983, the DOC's International Trade Administration (ITA) determined that subsidies were *de minimis* (less than 0.5%), ending the CVD investigation.

In 1986, the U.S. lumber industry filed a petition for another CVD investigation with the DOC and the ITC. A 1985 court ruling on an ITA determination of countervailable benefits on certain imports from Mexico was seen as a favorable precedent for reversing the ITA finding on Canadian lumber subsidies. The ITC again found preliminary evidence of injury to the U.S. industry, and the ITA reversed its 1983 determination, with a preliminary finding that Canadian producers received a subsidy of 15% *ad valorem* (i. e., 15% of lumber market prices). On December 30, 1986, the day before the final ITA subsidy determination, the United States and Canada signed a Memorandum of Understanding (MOU), with Canada imposing a 15% tax on lumber exported to the United States, to be replaced by higher stumpage fees within 5 years. This agreement led the U.S. industry to withdraw its petition.

In September 1991, the Canadian government announced that it would withdraw from the MOU, because most of the provinces had increased their stumpage fees. The U.S. Trade Representative (USTR) responded by beginning a §301 investigation,[2] pending completion of a new CVD investigation by the ITA and the ITC. In March 1992, the ITA issued a preliminary finding of 14.48% ad valorem subsidies, with a final determination in May establishing a 6.51% *ad valorem* subsidies, leading to a 6.51% ad valorem duty. This was confirmed in July with a final ITC finding that the U.S. industry had been injured by Canadian lumber imports.

The Canadian federal government appealed both the ITA and the ITC final findings to binational review panels under the U.S.-Canada Free Trade Agreement (FTA), which was signed on January 2, 1988. In May 1993, the binational subsidy panel remanded the ITA finding for further analysis, and in September, the ITA revised its finding to 11.54% ad valorem subsidies. In December, the binational subsidy panel again remanded the ITA finding

[1] U.S. trade law (19 U.S.C. 1671-1671h) authorizes countervailing duties on imported goods, if the DOC determines that the imports are being subsidized (directly or indirectly) by a foreign country and if the ITC determines that the imports have materially injured a U.S. industry. The duty is set at the calculated level of the subsidies.

[2] Under §301 of the Trade Act of 1974 (19 U.S.C. 24I 1-2420), the USTR can investigate and can respond, with a broad range of feasible actions, to foreign trade practices, which are found to be illegal, unreasonable, or discriminatory, and are burdensome to U.S. interests.

and ordered the ITA to find no subsidies. In January, the ITA complied with the order. Using a provision of the FTA, the USTR requested an Extraordinary Challenge Committee (ECC) to review the binational panel decisions, but the ECC was dismissed in August 1994 for failing to meet FTA standards. In August, the DOC revoked the CVD, and in October, the USTR announced that it would terminate the §301 action.

Two events in September 1994 induced Canada to negotiate restrictions on its lumber exports to the United States. First, the U.S. lumber industry filed a lawsuit challenging the constitutionality of the FTA review process. Second, the Uruguay Round Agreements Act (URAA; P.L. 103-465) explicitly approved the President's "statement of administrative action" (SAA) that had accompanied his proposed legislation; the SAA stated that, because of Canadian practices, lumber imports from Canada could be subject to a CVD. In February 1996, the two nations announced an agreement-in-principle –a fee on Canadian lumber exports to the United States in excess of a specified quota for 5 years – with the final U.S.-Canada Softwood Lumber Agreement (SLA) signed in May and retroactive to April 1, 1996. The SLA was effective through March 31, 2001.

Analysis: Subsidies and Injury

Annual Canadian lumber imports have risen from less than 3 billion board feet (BBF), about 7% of the U.S. market, in the early 1950s to more than 18 BBF, more than a third of the U.S. market, in the late 1990s. U.S. lumber producers argue that subsidies to Canadian producers give them an unfair advantage in supplying the U.S. market and that this has injured U.S. producers. These two issues – subsidies and injury – are the basis in U.S. trade law for determining if a CVD is warranted.

Subsidies: Canadian Stumpage Fees

The U.S. lumber industry has argued that the stumpage fees charged by the Canadian provinces are less than the market price of the timber would be and are therefore a subsidy to Canadian producers. About 90% of the timberlands in the 10 provinces are owned by the provinces. The provinces require management plans for forested areas and allocate the timber harvests through a variety of agreements or leases, often for 5 or more years with renewal options. Stumpage fees for the timber are determined administratively, often with adjustments to reflect changes in market prices for lumber. This contrasts with the U.S. situation, where 42% of the forests are publicly owned and where public timber is typically sold in competitive auctions; thus, much of the timber in the United States is sold by public and private landowners at market prices.[3] The use of administered fees in Canada opens the possibility that the Canadian system results in transfers to the private sector at less than their fair market value, as the U.S. lumber industry has charged. However, comparisons of U.S. and Canadian stumpage fees are often disputed, because of: differences in measurement systems and the imprecision of converting Canadian cubic meters of logs to U.S. board feet of lumber; differences in the diameter, height, quality, mad species mix of U.S. and Canadian

[3] Some argue that U.S. federal agencies are not comparable to traditional, market-oriented private "willing sellers," because they do not make investments or sales based on profitability, as a private landowner presumably would. However, the U.S. federal government owns only 33% of U.S. timberlands, and thus probably has less impact on timber markets than do the Canadian provinces.

forests; differences in management responsibilities imposed on timber buyers (e.g., road construction, reforestation); differences in environmental conditions and policies; and other factors.

Subsidies: Export Restrictions

Export restrictions by British Columbia (BC) were identified as a subsidy to BC lumber producers by the ITA in its 1992 CVD investigation. BC generally prohibits the export of logs from Crown (provincial) lands, to assure domestic production, provide jobs, and encourage economic development. Export restrictions on public timber in the United States indicate substantially higher prices for export logs than for comparable logs sold domestically. Most economists would consider restrictions that reduce domestic prices below the world market price to be subsidies, and the General Agreement on Tariffs and Trade (GATT) generally prohibits export restrictions. In addition, current U.S. trade law allows the DOC to consider an export restraint on a product to be a subsidy if the private parties who would be exporting the product provide the restrained good to domestic purchasers for less than adequate remuneration. Nonetheless, Canada has challenged the ITA treatment of export restrictions as a subsidy, arguing that this treatment is inconsistent with the World Trade Organization (WTO) Agreement on Subsidies and Countervailing Measures. This challenge is discussed more below.

Injury to the U.S. Lumber Industry

Proving injury or threat of injury to U.S. lumber producers is also essential to establishing a CVD. The share of the U.S. softwood lumber market provided by Canadian lumber has grown substantially over the past 50 years. In 1952, lumber imports from Canada were less than 3 BBF, and Canada's market share was less than 7%. In 1998 and 1999, Canadian lumber imports were more than 18 BBF, and Canada's market share has fluctuated between 33% and 35% since 1995. These facts are cited by U.S. producers as evidence that Canadian imports have come at the expense of normal domestic growth in industrial lumber production. U.S. homebuilders and other lumber users counter that Canadian lumber is essential to meeting domestic demand, and argue for unrestricted imports. Despite consistent ITC findings of injury, indisputable proof of injury to U.S. producers is difficult to establish.

Current Issues and Events

Three aspects of this situation are currently the focus of attention in this long-running dispute over the exports of softwood lumber from Canada to the United States.

Expiration of the 1996 Agreement

The SLA expired on March 31, 2001, thus ending the rights and obligations of Canada and the United States regarding lumber products covered by the Agreement. Since neither an extension of the SLA nor a new agreement is currently being negotiated, private and governmental parties are employing and exploring other options regarding the future of U.S.-Canadian lumber trade. On March 28, Commerce Secretary Evans reportedly stated to a group of Senators that he would monitor lumber import levels upon expiration of the SLA, as a step toward a possible "critical circumstances" determination allowing early relief (*Inside US Trade*, April 6, 2001). Canada has dismissed the idea of imposing an export tax on lumber products for the time being; Canadian International Trade Minister Pettigrew reportedly stated in the Canadian House of Commons that the government would not support such a measure unless the four Canadian provinces that export softwood lumber favored it (*International Trade Reporter*, March 22, 2001, p. 476). USTR Zoellick has stated that he may consider the negotiation of an export tax were any unfair trade proceedings to be resolved in favor of U.S. producers (*International Trade Reporter*, March 8, 2001, p. 386). Some industry and consumer groups, as well as some in Congress, have called for the agreement not to be extended or replaced and for instead allowing any trade cases to proceed to conclusion or to be pursued through the World Trade Organization (WTO).

On April 2, the U.S. Coalition for Fair Lumber Imports filed antidumping and CVD petitions. On April 24, the DOC announced that it was initiating the antidumping and CVD investigations, because the petitioners had standing and had shown adequate industry support. The investigations were officially initiated with notices in the Federal Register on April 30, at pages 21328-21332 for the antidumping petition and at pages 21332-21335 for the CVD petition. On May 16, the ITC issued its preliminary determination that there was "a reasonable indication that a U.S. industry is threatened with material injury by reason of imports of softwood lumber from Canada that are allegedly subsidized and sold in the United States at less than fair value" (Investigations Nos. 701-TA-414 and 731-TA-928 (Preliminary)). The DOC published its preliminary determination on Canadian subsidies in the *Federal Register* on August 17, at pages 43186-43216. It found subsidies o f 19.31% *ad valorem* (as a percent of sale value), and established a preliminary duty at that level. DOC also found that critical circumstances exist, allowing retroactive application of the duty.

Canadian WTO Challenges Regarding U.S. Countervailing Duty Law

The DOC recognized the countervailability of export restrictions in its 1992 determination of subsidies involving Canadian softwood lumber and in a 1990 determination of subsidies involving leather from Argentina. In the SAA accompanying the Uruguay Round Agreements Act (H.Doc 103-316, vol. 1, pp. 925-926), and in the DOC's Federal Register explanation of its implementing rule (63 *Federal Register* 65349-65351, Nov. 25; 1998), the Executive Branch confirmed that if it were again to investigate situations and facts similar to those in the two cases just described, U.S. trade law would continue to permit it to reach the same conclusion. Canada has challenged this policy in the WTO, alleging that the U.S. interpretation, as set forth in these documents, is inconsistent with U.S. obligations under the WTO Agreement on Subsidies and Countervailing Measures (SCM). On August 23, the final panel report in the case agreed with Canada, that export restraints do not constitute a financial contribution from the government, and thus do not confer a countervailable subsidy under the SCM Agreement; however, it recommended no remedial action, since U.S. law does not *require* the DOC to treat an export restraint as a subsidy and since there is no current U.S. measure based on such a finding.

In apparent anticipation of possible U.S. antidumping and CVD cases against Canadian softwood lumber imports, Canada filed another WTO complaint against the United States on January 17, 2001, challenging § 129(c)(1) of the URAA, which sets forth procedures for administrative compliance with adverse WTO panel reports involving U.S. antidumping or CVD measures. Arguing that § 129(c)(1) prohibits the United States from refunding estimated duties in trade remedy proceedings that are found to be inconsistent with WTO obligations, Canada alleges that the provision violates portions of the WTO Dispute Settlement Understanding and various WTO antidumping and countervailing duty obligations. Consultation was unsuccessful, and on August 23, a WTO panel was established to examine the complaint.

LEGISLATION

H.Con.Res. 45 (Kolbe)/S.Con.Res. 4 (Nickles)

Express the sense of Congress of the desirability of open trade in softwood lumber between the United States and Canada. H.Con.Res. 45 introduced February 28, 2001; referred to the House Ways and Means Committee. S.Con.Res. 4 introduced January 29, 2001; referred to the Senate Finance Committee.

H.Con.Res. 54 (Chambliss)/S.Con.Res. 8 (Snowe)

Express the sense of Congress that the Administration should resolve problems of unfairly traded Canadian lumber, and should make it the top trade priority. H.Con.Res. 54 introduced March 7, 2001; referred to the House Ways and Means Committee S.Con.Res. 8 introduced February 7, 2001; referred to the Senate Finance Committee.

CHRONOLOGY

08/01 – On August 23, a WTO panel final report held that U.S. treatment of export restraints as subsidies violated WTO agreements. Also, on August 23, a WTO panel was established to examine Canada's complaint that U.S. treatment of duties found to violate WTO agreements also violated WTO agreements.

08/01 – On August 17, the DOC issued its preliminary finding of 19.31% *ad valorem* Canadian subsidies and the existence of critical circumstances.

05/01 – On May 16, the ITC issued its preliminary finding of injury to the U.S. lumber industry by Canadian lumber imports.

04/01 – On April 2, the U.S. Coalition for Fair Lumber Imports filed antidumping and CVD petitions to restrict Canadian softwood imports. On April 24, the DOC announced the initiation of the antidumping and CVD investigations.

03/01 – At midnight on March 31, the 1996 Softwood Lumber Agreement expired.

01/01 – On January 17, Canada requests consultations with United States under WTO Dispute Settlement Understanding, arguing that U.S. procedures for administrative compliance with adverse WTO panel reports violate the Understanding.

09/00 – WTO panel established to assess Canadian objection to U.S. treatment of export restrictions.

05/00 – Canada requests consultations with United States under WTO Dispute Settlement Understanding, arguing U.S. treatment of export restrictions is

	inconsistent with WTO Agreement on Subsidies and Countervailing Measures.
06/99 –	U.S. Customs Service reclassifies rougher-headed lumber and notched studs as softwood lumber subject to SLA.
12/98 –	U.S. Court of International Trade upholds Custom Service ruling that drilled studs are softwood lumber subject to SLA.
06/98 –	U.S. Customs Service issues final decisions reclassifying drilled studs as softwood lumber subject to the SLA.
02/97 –	U.S. Customs Service issues New York Ruling Letter B81564 classifying drilled studs as builders' joinery exempt from the SLA.
05/96 –	USTR and Canada sign Softwood Lumber Agreement (SLA), retroactive to April 1, 1996.
12/94 –	Negotiations begin between the USTR and Canada to restrict lumber imports.
10/94 –	USTR terminates §301 action against Canadian lumber imports.
08/94 –	ECC dismissed and 2/94 binational subsidy panel order affirmed.
01/94 –	Binational subsidy panel orders ITA to find no subsidies; ITA complies.
10/93 –	ITC reanalysis confirms original finding of injury to U.S. industry.
09/93 –	ITA reanalysis confirms and revises final finding to 11.54% *ad valorem* subsidies by Canada.
07/93 –	Binational injury panel remands ITC analysis of injury for further analysis.
05/93 –	Binational subsidy panel remands ITA analysis of subsidies for further analysis.
08/92 –	Canada challenges ITA and ITC findings under the U.S.-Canada Free Trade Agreement (FTA), leading to binational panels to review the ITA finding of subsidies and ITC finding of injury.
07/92 –	ITC issues final finding of injury, confirming the CVD.
05/92 –	ITA issues final finding of subsidies, establishing the CVD at 6.51% *ad valorem*.
10/91 –	USTR initiates §301 action; ITA self-initiates a CVD investigation.
09/91 –	Canada announces it will withdraw from the MOU.
12/86 –	Canada and USTR announce a Memorandum &Understanding (MOU) with a 15% Canadian export tax instead of a CVD.
10/86 –	ITA issues preliminary finding of subsidies, setting a CVD at 15% ad valorem.
05/86 –	U.S. Coalition for Fair Lumber Imports files a CVD petition.
03/83 –	ITA issues preliminary finding of *de minimis* subsidies, ending CVD investigation.
10/82 –	U.S. lumber industry files petition requesting a CVD.
12/81 –	Letters from Members of Congress to USTR requesting a CVD investigation of lumber imports from Canada.

For Additional Reading

1. Benjamin Cashore, *Flights of the Phoenix." Explaining the Durability of the Canada-US Softwood Lumber Dispute* (Orono, ME: Canada-American Center, Dec. 1997).
2. Brink Lindsay, Mark A. Groombridge, and Prakash Lougani, *Nailing the Homeowner: The Economic Impact of Trade Protection of the Softwood Lumber Industry* (Washington, DC: Cato Institute, 2000).
3. FLC Les Reed, *Two Centuries of Softwood Lumber War Between Canada and the United States: A Chronicle of Trade Barriers Viewed in the Context of Saw Timber Depletion* (Montreal, Canada: Free Trade Lumber Council, May 2001).
4. Random Lengths, *What's New This Week? U.S.-Canada Trade Dispute Timeline* (at [http://www.randomlengths.com/newtimeline.html] on May 2, 2000).
5. World Resources Institute, *Canada's Forest at a Crossroads: An Assessment in the Year 2000*, a Global Forest Watch Canada Report (Washington, DC: 2000).

Chapter 11

ASIA PACIFIC ECONOMIC COOPERATION (APEC)

Dick K. Nanto

ISSUE

APEC is the leading organization in the Asia/Pacific that is working cooperatively to reduce trade and investment barriers among its 21 member economies, advance Asia-Pacific economic dynamism, and develop more of a sense of community among its members. U.S. participation in APEC is part of the broader U.S. debate over whether the United States should continue, to pursue free trade and investment relations with Asia Pacific nations and whether and under what conditions the President should be provided fast track trade negotiating (trade promotion) authority that might be used to negotiate free trade agreements with APEC or with individual APEC members.

APEC also is of interest to Congress because 1) it is becoming a vehicle to generate trade initiatives to be considered by the World Trade Organization; 2) the APEC Leaders' Meeting provides an opportunity for the U.S. President to raise and discuss issues with the heads of other APEC commies; 3) any concrete trade or investment measures developed under APEC that require a change in existing U.S. law and cannot be done by presidential proton will need legislative approVe1; and 4) in view of the debate over the North American Free Trade Agreement (NAFTA), to create a free-trade arrangement that includes China, Japan, South Korea, Taiwan, Indonesia, Chile, and other Asian-Pacific nations is likely to be highly controversial.

BACKGROUND

On October 20-21, 2001, the Ninth APEC Leaders' Meeting (summit) was hosted by China in Shanghai. President Bush, Secretary of State Powell, U.S. Trade Representative Zoellick, Commerce Secretary Evans, and other members of the Administration attended. The official theme for APEC 2001 was "Meeting New Challenges in the New Century: Achieving Common Prosperity through Participation and Cooperation," with the sub-themes of (1) sharing the benefits of globalization and the new economy, (2) advancing trade and investment, and (3) promoting sustained economic growth. The war on terrorism and slowing world economic growth, however, dominated discussions.

The leaders' statement on counter-terrorism was the first time APEC dealt explicitly with a non-economic issue. APEC leaders aim reaffirmed the goal of achieving free trade and investment among APEC members and to provide support for a new round of multilateral trade negotiations under the World Trade Organization. The leaders also issued the Shanghai Accord in which they committed themselves to broaden APEC's vision for the future by identifying a conceptual and policy framework to guide APEC in the new century. The Accord included clarifying APEC's roadmap for achieving the free trade and investment goals on schedule with an assessment of overall progress in 2005; promoting the adoption of appropriate trade policies for the New Economy; following up on the APEC Trade Facilitation Principles; pursuing greater transparency in economic governance; and strengthening APEC's implementation mechanism.

At the November 2000 APEC Leaders' Meeting held in Brunei, former President Clinton held bilateral summits with several leaders of APEC countries - including China, Japan, Russia, Singapore, and South Korea. Following the APEC meetings, Clinton traveled to Vietnam. As a part of the bilateral summits, the United States and Singapore announced that they would begin negotiations on a bilateral free trade agreement; the United States, New Zealand, Singapore, Brunei, and Chile agreed in principle to an "open skies" pact (eliminating restrictions on airline flights, prices, and routes among themselves), and the U.S. and China announced that China would ban certain missile-related exports in exchange for a lifting of U.S. sanctions prohibiting Chinese launches of American satellites.

APEC is an association of 21 economies bordering the Pacific Ocean who are working cooperatively to reduce barriers to trade and investment; ease the exchange of goods, services, resources, and technical know-how; and strengthen economic and technical cooperation. APEC began in 1989 as an Australian initiative in recognition of the growing interdependence among Asia-Pacific economies and in response to the free-trade areas, which had developed in Europe and North America. Membership initially consisted of twelve countries but has now grown to twenty-one. They include the United States, Canada, Mexico, Peru, Chile, Japan, Russia, South Korea, China, Taiwan, Hong Kong, Indonesia, Brunei, Malaysia, Singapore, Thailand, Vietnam, the Philippines, Australia, New Zealand, and Papua New Guinea. The United States plays a key leadership role in APEC.

In 1994, in the Bogor Declaration, the leaders of APEC declared their intention to establish free trade and investment in the region by the year 2010 for industrialized members and 2020 for the others. This is being accomplished through concerted actions by individual APEC members, by pursuing trade and investment liberalization and trade facilitation in specific sectors, and by individual members establishing free-trade arrangements with each other.

LEGISLATION

Some trade liberalization under APEC arguably will require fast-track negotiating authority and congressional approval (*H.R. 1446*). U.S. financial support for APEC falls under the State Department's budget (*H.R. 1646*) under Contributions to International Organizations and has been $601,000 per year. Several bills would authorize negotiations to establish free-trade areas with APEC countries. These include *S. 138* and *S. 586* (with Chile), *S. 935* (with Australia), *S. 943* (with New Zealand), *S. 944* (with the Republic of Korea), and *H.R. 1566* (with Singapore, Australia, and New Zealand). *H.Con.Res. 73* requests that during the APEC summit, the President call for the release of all Chinese political prisoners and Chinese ratification of the International Covenant on Civil and Political Rights. *H.ConRes. 194* calls for APEC to allow participation by Taiwan's President Chen Shui-bian in the Shanghai Leader's Meeting.

Chapter 12

VIETNAM TRADE AGREEMENT: APPROVAL AND IMPLEMENTING PROCEDURE

Vladimir N. Pregelj

SUMMARY

The procedure leading to the entry into force of the U.S. trade agreement with Vietnam, including a reciprocal extension of nondiscriminatory treatment, calls for its approval by the enactment of a joint resolution of Congress, considered under a specific fast-track procedure with deadlines for its various stages, with mandatory language and no amendments. After favorable reports on the legislation in both houses, H.J.Res. 51, approving the nondiscriminatory treatment, was enacted on October 16, 2001; the agreement was also ratified by Vietnam on December 4, 2001, and entered into force by exchange of notices of acceptance between the two parties on December 10, 2001. The functional sequence of the legislative and executive steps involved in the implementation of the agreement is described in this report.

BACKGROUND[1]

After protracted negotiations and a one-year delay after its adoption in principle, the United States and Vietnam signed, on July 13, 2000, a comprehensive bilateral trade agreement, The key statutory purpose of the agreement is the restoration of nondiscriminatory tariff treatment[2] ("normal-trade-relations" (NTR), formerly "most- favored-nation" treatment) to U.S. imports from Vietnam, suspended since 1951. Hence, the agreement contains a provision reciprocally extending the NTR treatment and certain other provisions required by law for trade agreements with non-market economy (NME) countries. In addition, it contains

[1] For detailed background information on the U.S.-Vietnam trade agreement, see CRS Report RL30416, *The Vietnam-U.S. Bilateral Trade Agreement,* by Mark E. Manyin.

[2] Although the internationally adopted term "most-favored-nation treatment" has been replaced, in all current and future U.S. statutes, under Set, on 5003 of P.L. 105-206, by the term "normal trade relations" or a similar expression, its functional equivalent-nondiscriminatory treatment been retained in the relevant legislation, while the term "most-favored-nation treatment" remains in universal international use.

comprehensive specific commitments by Vietnam in matters of market access (e.g., reduced tariff rates on imports from the United States), intellectual property rights, trade in services, and investment, such as the United States already has in force as a matter of general trade policy. To enter into force, the agreement must be approved by the enactment of a joint resolution of Congress.

Restoration of NTR treatment to Vietnam as an NME country is also contingent on Vietnam's compliance with the freedom-of-emigration requirement of the Jackson-Vanik amendment (Section 402) of the Trade Act of 1974.[3] In the case of Vietnam, such compliance is achieved by an annual Presidential waiver of full compliance under specified statutory conditions; such waiver may be disapproved by the enactment of a joint resolution of Congress. The President has issued such waivers for Vietnam since mid-1998, but in no instance has a disapproval resolution, if introduced, been passed by Congress, allowing the waiver to continue in force.

IMPLEMENTING PROCEDURE

The statutory requirements and legislative procedure leading to the enactment and entry into force of a trade agreement with a non-market economy (NME) country, including Vietnam, are set out in detail in Sections 151, 404, 405, and 407 of the Trade Act of 1974 (P.L. 93-618), as amended. Section 151 has been enacted as an exercise of the rulemaking power of either house and supersedes its other rules to the extent that they are inconsistent with it. Its provisions can be changed by either house with respect to its own procedure at any time, in the same manner and to the same extent as any other rule of that house (Section 151(a); 19 U.S.C. 2191(a)).

All alphanumerical statutory references cited in this report are to sections of the Trade Act of 1974. While care has been taken to reflect accurately the meaning of the statutes, consulting the actual language of any statute is recommended in case of any ambiguity.

Functionally, the consideration and enactment of the approval resolution and the implementation of the agreement follow a specific expedited ("fast-track") procedure explained below. Additional information, based on past practice of implementing trade agreements with NME countries in general, but applicable also to Vietnam, is provided in footnotes

(1) Enactment Necessary

The agreement can take effect only if approved by enactment of a joint resolution (Section 405(c)); 19 U.S.C.2435(c)).

(2) Transmittal of the Agreement by the President to Congress

The text of the bilateral trade agreement with Vietnam must be transmitted by the President to both houses of Congress, together with a proclamation[4] extending

[3] For detail on the Jackson-Vanik amendment, see CRS Report 98-545 E, *Jackson-Vanik Amendment*: A Survey, by Vladimir N. Pregelj.

[4] Although the proclamation is issued at the time of transmittal of the agreement to Congress, its entry into force is specifically delayed to the date of the exchange of notices of acceptance of the agreement by its two parties

nondiscriminatory treatment to Vietnam and stating his reasons for it (Section 407(a); 19 U.S.C. 2437). While there is no statutory deadline for the transmittal of the proclamation and the agreement to Congress after its signing, the law requires that the transmittal take place "promptly" after the proclamation is issued.[5]

(3) Mandatory Introduction of Approval Resolution

On the day the trade agreement is transmitted to the Congress (or, if the respective house is not in session on that day, the first subsequent day on which it is in session), a joint resolution of approval (Sec. 151(b)(3); 19 U.S.C. 2191(b)(3)) must be introduced (by request) in each house by its majority leader for himself and the minority leader, or by their designees (See. 151(c)(2); 19 U.S.C. 2191(c)(2)).[6]

(4) Language of Approval Resolution

The language of the resolution is prescribed by law (Sec. 151(b)(3); 19 U.S.C. 2191(b)(3)) to read, in this particular instance, after the resolving clause: "That the Congress approves the extension of nondiscriminatory treatment with respect to the products of Vietnam transmitted by the President to the Congress on June 8, 2001".[7]

(5) Committee Referral

The resolution is referred in the House to the Committee on Ways and Means and in the Senate to the Committee on Finance (Sec. 151(c)(2); 19 U.S.C. 2191(c)(2)).

(6) Amendments Prohibited

No amendment to the resolution, and no motion, or unanimous-consent request, to suspend the no-amendment rule, is in order in either house (Sec. 151(d); 19 U.S.C. 2191(d)).

(7) Committee Consideration in the House[8]

If the Ways and Means Committee has not reported the resolution within 45 day[9] after its introduction, the Committee is automatically discharged from further consideration of the resolution, and the resolution is placed on the appropriate calendar (Sec. 151(e)(1); 19 U.S.C. 2191(e)(1)).

---

[5] Trade agreement with Vietnam and other required documents were transmitted by the President to Congress on June 8, 2001. They have been published as House Document 107-85.

[6] S.J.Res. 16 and H.J.Res. 51 to approve the trade agreement with Vietnam were introduced, respectively, on June 11 and 12, 2001.

[7] Although the language of the approval resolution mentions only nondiscriminatory treatment, other relevant statutes make it clear that the enactment of such resolution is required for the approval of any agreement containing the extension of nondiscriminatory treatment.

[8] Committee consideration in the House as described in the body of this report, differs from that in the Senate (see item (9). This is due to the treatment, in this report, of the approval resolution as a "revenue" measure (an "implementing revenue resolution", which it is widely presumed to be, since it would affect-adversely- customs revenues due to the significantly lower NTR tariff rates assessed on imports from Vietnam after the agreement enters into force (cf. See. 151(b)(2)); 19 U.S.C. 2191(b)(2); but see also footnote 11). As such, the resolution is required by the U.S. Constitution to originate in the House.. This origination provision, however, does not mean that a companion resolution may not be introduced and considered in the Senate, but only that the measure eventually passed by both houses and submitted to the President for signature, has to be a House measure.

[9] In computing the number of days in either house, any day on which that house is not in session is excluded (See. 151(c)(3); 19 U.S.C. 2193(e)(3)). - H.J.Res. 51 was reported favorably on September 5, 2001 (H.Rept. 107-189).

(8) Floor Consideration in the House

(a) A motion to proceed to the consideration of the approval resolution is highly privileged and non-debatable; an amendment to the motion, or a motion to reconsider the vote whereby the motion is agreed or disagreed to, is not in order (Sec. 151(f)(1); 19 U.S.C. 2191(f)(1)).

(b) Debate on the resolution is limited to 20 hours[10], divided equally between the supporters and opponents of the resolution; a motion further to limit debate is not debatable; a motion to recommit the resolution, or to reconsider the vote whereby the resolution is agreed or disagreed to, is not in order (Sec. 151(f)(2); 19 U.S.C. 2191(f)(2)).

(c) Motions to postpone the consideration of the resolution and motions to proceed to the consideration of other business are decided without debate (Sec. 151(f)(3); 19 U.S.C. 2191(f)(3)).

(d) All appeals from the decisions of the Chair relating to the application of the rules of the House of Representatives to the approval resolution are decided without debate (Sec. 151(f)(4); 19 U.S.C. 2191(f)(4)).

(e) In all other respects, consideration of the approval resolution is governed by the rules of the House of Representatives applicable to other measures in similar circumstances (Sec. 151(f)(5); 19 U.S.C. 2191(f)(5)).

(f) The vote (by simple magnify) on the final passage of the approval resolution must be taken on or before the 15th day[11] after the Ways and Means Committee has reported the resolution, or has been discharged from its bather consideration (Sec. 151(e)(1); 19 U.S.C. 2191(e)(1)).

(9) Committee Consideration in the Senate[12]

An approval resolution adopted by the House of Representatives and received in the Senate is referred to the Finance Committee (Sec. 151(c)(2) and (e)(2); 19 U.S.C 2191(c)(2) and (e)(2)).[13] If the Finance Committee has not reported the resolution within 15 days after its receipt from the House or 45,days[14] after the introduction of its own corresponding resolution (whichever is later), the Committee is automatically discharged from further consideration of the resolution, and the resolution is placed on the appropriate calendar (Sec. 151(e)(1); 19 U.S.C. 2191(e)(1)).

(10) Floor Consideration in the Senate

(a) A motion to proceed to the consideration of the approval resolution is privileged and non-debatable; an amendment to the motion, or a motion to reconsider the vote whereby the motion is agreed or disagreed to, is not in order (Sec. 151(g)(1); 19 U.S.C. 2191(g)(1)).

---

[10] This statutory deadline has in past practice often been reduced by floor actor.

[11] Computed as in footnote 9. – H.J.Res. 51 passed House September 6, 2001.

[12] This item describes the procedure for enacting "revenue" joint resolutions approving trade agreements with non-market economy countries. Ambiguity in the applicable statutory language, however, has engendered a controversy as to whether they are to be considered as "revenue" or "non-revenue" measures, which may eventually have to be resolved by a parliamentarian ruling.

[13] Although a joint resolution of approval must be introduced in both houses (see item (3)), Section 151 contains no specific provisions regarding the consideration of a Senate "revenue" approval resolution (situation presumed in the procedure as described in this report). The reason for this omission appears to be in that a "revenue" measure can be enacted only as a House measure (see footnote 8).

[14] Both computed as in footnote 9. - S.J.Res. 16 was reported favorably July 27, 2001 (S.Rept. 107-49).

(b) Debate on the approval resolution and on all debatable motions and appeals connected with it is limited to 20 hours, equally divided between, and controlled by, the majority leader and the minority leader, or their designee, (Sec. 151(g)(2); 19 U.S.C. 2191(g)(2)).

(c) Debate on any debatable motion or appeal is limited to one hour, equally divided between, and controlled by, the mover and the manager of the resolution, except that if the manager of the resolution is in favor of any such motion or appeal, the time in opposition is controlled by the minority leader or his designee; such leaders may, from time under their control on the passage of the resolution, allot additional time to any Senator during the consideration of any debatable motion or appeal (Sec. 151(g)(3); 19 U.S.C. 2191(g)(3)).

(d) A motion further to limit debate on the approval resolution is not debatable; a motion to recommit it is not in order (See. 151(g)(4); 19 U.S.C. 2191(g)(4)).

(e) The vote (by simple majority) on the final passage of the approval resolution must be taken on or before the 15th day[15] after the Finance Committee has reported the resolution, or has been discharged from its limber consideration (See. 151(e)(2); 19 16 2191(e)(2)).

(f) Although, unlike in the case of the House procedure,[16] this is not specifically mentioned in Section 151, the Rules of the Senate govern the consideration of the approval resolution in the Senate in all aspects not specifically addressed in Section 151.

(g) If prior to the passage of its own approval resolution, the Senate receives the approval resolution already passed by the House, it continues the legislative procedure on its own resolution, but the vote on the final passage is on the House resolution.

(11) President's Implementing Authority

(a) After the joint resolution approving the trade agreement with Vietnam is passed by both houses and signed by the President, it becomes public law, in effect, authorizing the President to put into effect the already issued proclamation[17] implementing the agreement extending nondiscriminatory treatment to Vietnam (Secs. 404(a) and 405(c); 19 U.S.C. 2434(0 and 2435(c)).

(b) Application of non-discriminatory treatment is limited to the term during which the agreement remains in remains (See. 404(b); 19 U.S.C 2434(b)) (see also footnote 19 and text which it accompanies).

(c) The President may at any time suspend or withdraw nondiscriminatory treatment of Vietnam (Sec. 404(c); 19 U.S.C. 2434(c)) and thereby subject all imports from that country to column 2 tariff rates (i.e., full rather than NTR rates).

(12) Approval by Vietnam

The agreement also must be approved by Vietnam.[18]

(13) Entry into Force

After the joint resolution of approval is enacted and the agreement is approved by Vietnam, the proclamation (see item (2) becomes effective, the agreement enters into force, and non-discriminatory treatment is extended to Vietnam on the date of exchange of written

---

[15] Computed as in footnote 8. - H.J.Res. St passed House October 3, 2001.

[16] See item (8)(e).

[17] See footnote 4. - Pres. Proc. 7449 (June 8, 2001; 66 F.R. 31375).

[18] A resolution approving the agreement was adopted by Vietnam's National Assembly on November 28 and signed by Vietnam's President on December 4, 2001.

notices of acceptance of the agreement by the United States and Vietnam. A notice of the effective date of the agreement is published by the U.S. Trade Representative in the Federal Register.[19]

(14) Maintenance in Force

According to its own terms (Article 8 of Chapter VII - General Articles), the agreement with Vietnam remains in force for a period of three years and is automatically renewable for successive three-year terms unless either party to it, at least 30 clays before the expiration of the then current term, gives notice of its intent to terminate the agreement. If either party ceases to have domestic legal authority to carry out its obligations under the agreement, it may suspend the application of the agreement, or, with the agreement of the other party, any part of the agreement.[20]

In addition, Section 405(b)(1) (19 U.S.C. 2435(b)(1)) limits the life of trade agreements restoring nondiscriminatory treatment to NME countries to an initial term of three years. Agreements may be renewable for additional three-year terms if a satisfactory balance of trade concessions has been maintained during the life of the agreement and the President determines that actual or foreseeable U.S. reductions of trade barriers resulting from multilateral negotiations are satisfactorily reciprocated by the other country.[21]

---

[19] Notices of acceptance were exchanged on December 10, 2001 (66 F.R. 65019).

[20] One such circumstance would arise if Vietnam's waiver under the Jackson-Vanik amendment (see p. 1-2) were no longer in force either by the President's failure to renew it annually or through the enactment of a joint resolution disapproving its annual extension. Enactment of such resolution (H.J.Res. 55) to disapprove the extension of Vietnam's waiver, introduced on June 1, 2001 (but defeated in the House on July 26, 2001) would have prevented the extension of nondiscriminatory treatment to Vietnam or, if already in force, nullified it.

[21] The latter provision reflects the fact that, by being granted nondiscriminatory treatment by the United States, an NME country would benefit from U.S. concessions extended to third countries, without itself, theoretically, having to extend any concessions specifically to the United States; it would merely have to apply to the United States the same concessions that it has granted to third countries. In the case of Vietnam, however, the bilateral agreement does provide for comprehensive U.S.-specific concessions in addition to those applicable merely on MFN basis.

Chapter 13

THE VIETNAM-U.S. BILATERAL TRADE AGREEMENT

Mark E. Manyin

BACKGROUND

On July 13, 2000, after nearly five years of bargaining, the U.S. and Vietnam announced they had signed a bilateral trade agreement (BTA).[1] On June 8, 2001, President Bush submitted the agreement, which requires congressional approval, to Congress. Following President Bush's transmission, joint resolutions (H.J.Res. 51 and S.J.Res 16) were introduced in both chambers, and referred to the House Ways and Means Committee and the Senate Finance Committee. On September 6, 2001, the House approved the agreement by voice vote. The Senate passed the agreement, by a vote of 88-12, on October 3, 2001 (Roll Call 291). On October 16, 2001, President Bush signed the agreement into law (P.L. 107-52). Vietnam's National Assembly ratified the BTA on November 28, 2001, and Vietnamese President Tran Duc Luong is expected to sign it soon. The agreement will not go into effect until the United States and Vietnam exchange written notices of acceptance. Vietnam has not yet approved the agreement.

The BTA is a major step toward fully normalizing U.S.-Vietnam commercial relations, as it restores reciprocal most-favored-nation (MFN, also known as normal trade relations [NTR]) treatment between the two countries, and commits Vietnam to undertake a wide range of market-oriented economic reforms.[2] Extending MFN treatment to Vietnam will significantly reduce U.S. tariffs on most imports from Vietnam.

---

[1] The text of the agreement- along With a separate Annex on Services and two separate letters on investment- may be found on the home page of the United States Trade Representative [http://www.ustr.gov] and on the home page of the United States-Vietnam Trade Council [http://www.usvtc.org]. The White House has prepared a "fact sheet" on the BTA. It may be found at: [http://www.usinfo.state.gov/regionaI/ea/vietnam/ whtrd713.htm].

[2] In 1998, legislation was enacted to replace the term "most-favored-nation" treatment in existing and future legislation with the term "normal trade relations" (NTR). The former term is used in this report for reasons of historical continuity and because of its continued use in international trade relations, including in U.S. bilateral trade agreements. See CRS Issue Brief IB93107, *Most-Favored-Nation (Normal-Trade-Relations) Policy of the United States*, by Vladimir N. Pregelj.

CONGRESS' ROLE IN THE NORMALIZATION OF U.S.-VIETNAM TRADE RELATIONS[3]

Following the victory of communist North Vietnam over U.S.-backed South Vietnam in 1975, the United States ended virtually all economic interchange with unified Vietnam. The commercial restrictions included not only those that previously had been imposed only on North Vietnam (see the following section), but also a halt to bilateral humanitarian aid, opposition to financial aid from international financial institutions (such as the World Bank), a ban on U.S. travel to Vietnam and an embargo on bilateral trade.

Washington and Hanoi gradually began to normalize relations in the early 1990s, following improvements on the issues of Vietnam's activities in Cambodia and prisoners of war (POWs) and missing-in-action (MIA) personnel in Vietnam.[4] In 1994, President Clinton ordered lifting of the trade embargo against Vietnam. The following year, the two countries established ambassadorial-level diplomatic relations. In 1998, President Clinton granted Vietnam its first waiver from the requirements of the so-called Jackson-Vanik amendment (contained in the Trade Act of 1974, Title IV, section 402), which prohibit the President from normalizing commercial relations with selected socialist and formerly socialist countries if they do not meet certain requirements regarding freedom of emigration. Presidential waivers were also granted to Vietnam in 1999, 2000, and 2001. Congress may reject the annual waiver by passing a joint disapproval resolution. Each time waivers have been granted to Vietnam, the House has defeated disapproval resolutions (See **Figure 1**.) As explained below, until the U.S.-Vietnam BTA goes into effect the waiver does not change Vietnam's current, non-MFN trade status with the United States. Instead, it allows the U.S. Overseas Private Investment Corporation (OPIC) and the U.S. Export-Import Bank to support U.S. businesses exporting to and/or operating in Vietnam.

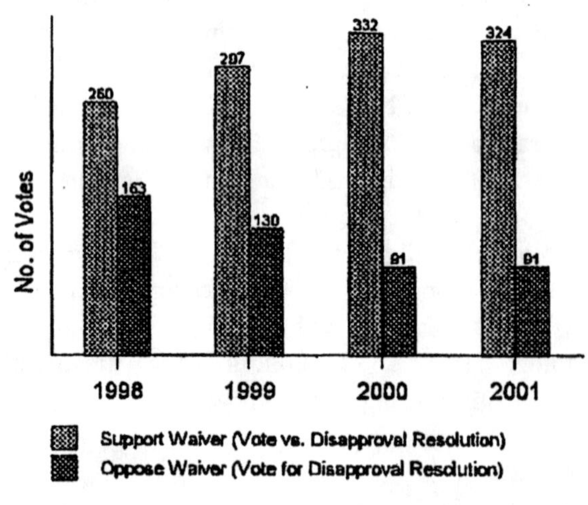

Figure 1. House Votes on Vietnam's Jackson-Vanik Waiver, 1998-2000

[3] Vladimir Pregelj, CRS Specialist in International Trade and Finance, provided assistance with this station.

[4] For a more detailed account of the history of U.S.-Vietnam normalization, see CRS Issue Brief IB98033, *The Vietnam-U.S. Normalization Process*, by Mark Manyin.

Restoration of Temporary MFN Status to Vietnam

The U.S. denied MFN treatment communist-controlled areas of Vietnam in August of 1951. At that time, under Section 5 of the Trade Agreements Extension Act of 1951, MFN tariff rates were suspended for all countries of the Sino-Soviet bloc.[5] When communist North Vietnamese forces unified the country in 1975, MFN status was suspended for the entire country.

In 1974, the U.S. issued strict conditions for restoring MFN status to those non-market economies (NMEs) subject to Section 5 suspension (in practice, the new conditions applied to virtually all countries of the former Sino-Soviet bloc). Under Title IV of the Trade Act of 1974, MFN treatment may be restored to NME countries after two requirements have been met:

a) The President issues a determination that the country is not in violation of the freedom-of-emigration requirements of the Jackson-Vanik amendment.[6] To date, Vietnam has not been found to be in full compliance with Jackson-Vanik requirements. Alternatively, subject to certain conditions, the President may waive these requirements, as Presidents Clinton and Bush have done since 1998. Jackson-Vanik waivers must be renewed annually, and Congress may reject them by passing a joint disapproval resolution.
b) The completion of a bilateral trade agreement that contains certain required provisions, including a reciprocal MFN clause. Such an agreement would require approval by the Congress (and by the Vietnamese National Assembly). Once the BTA is approved, the President can extend temporary MFN tariff treatment to Vietnam. The MFN treatment would be temporary because it is contingent upon Vietnam meeting the requirements described in the previous paragraphs - i.e. either obtaining a Presidential determination or a Presidential waiver, both of which are valid only for one year and are subject to congressional review.[7] This is the same process through which Congress has reviewed China's temporary MFN status.

---

[5] Section 5 of the Trade Agreements Extension Act of 1951 (65 Star. 73), which Congress passed in response to the outbreak of the Korean War, required the President to suspend the application of MFN tariff rates to the Soviet Union and all countries or areas under the control of international communism. Yugoslavia, anon-Soviet bloc country, was the one exception. For more on the history of the U.S.'s MFN policy, see CRS Issue Brief IB93107, *Normal-Trade-Relations (Most-Favored-Nation) Policy of the United States*, by Vladimir Pregelj. Currently, the U.S. denies MFN treatment to only six countries - Afghanistan, Cuba, Laos, North Korea, Vietnam, and Yugoslavia (Serbia and Montenegro).

[6] After the issuance of a determination of full compliance with the Jackson-Vanik amendment's freedom-of-emigration requirements, the President must issue semiannual reports to Congress arguing that the relevant country is not in violation of the freedom-of-emigration requirements. The President's end-of-year report is subject to congressional disapproval by joint resolution.

[7] Note that Vietnam's MFN treatment would be temporary regardless of whether it received a Jackson-Vanik waiver or a Presidential report that Vietnam is in full-compliance with the Jackson-Vanik amendment, in the ease of the latter, the President's annual year-end report would be subject to congressional review, and therefore could be rejected by a joint disapproval resolution.

Congressional Procedures for Considering a U.S.-Vietnam BTA[8]

To go into effect, Title IV bilateral trade agreements must be approved by a joint resolution of Congress. Once the President transmits the agreement to Congress, a resolution must be introduced in both Houses. The resolutions are subject to special expedited procedures, under which amendments are not permitted in either chamber.

Additionally, there are deadlines of 45 session-days for committee consideration (by the House Ways and Means and the Senate Finance Committees), and 15 session-days for floor debate in both chambers. Because the approval resolutions are revenue measures, the Senate must vote on a House-passed resolution, and Congress would have a maximum of 90 session-days to act on the resolution: 45 days for consideration by the House Ways and Means Committee; followed by 15 days for floor debate in the House; followed by 15 days for consideration of the House-passed resolution in the Senate Finance Committee; followed by 15 days for floor debate in the Senate.

As with most trade agreements with non-market economies, the U.S.-Vietnam BTA would remain in effect for a 3-year period and would be extended automatically unless renounced by either party. Additionally, each extension would require a presidential determination that Vietnam is satisfactorily extending reciprocal MFN treatment to U.S. exports.

After the BTA: Extending Permanent MFN Treatment to Vietnam

Following the BTA, the next step toward normalizing U.S.-Vietnam commercial ties would be restoring permanent MFN status (also known as permanent NTR or PNTR status) to Vietnam, a process that would require Congress to "graduate" Vietnam from the group of non-market economies that are denied unconditional MFN treatment. This would be done by terminating the application of the relevant Title IV provisions to Vietnam, as has been done for several countries, including Bulgaria, the Czech Republic, Slovakia, Hungary, and Romania. In May 2000, the House voted to give permanent MFN status to China once it joins the World Trade Organization.

Vietnam and the World Trade Organization (WTO)

Vietnam applied to join the WTO in 1995. Many observers believe that Vietnam is a number of years away from meeting the requirements for WTO membership. In March 2001, Vietnam's Trade Minister expressed his government's goal of acceding to the WTO by 2004. As a practical matter, countries seeking to enter the WTO must obtain the consent of all WTO member countries. Typically, these bilateral negotiations focus on tariff concessions and other market access issues that will govern bilateral trade relations after the applicant becomes a member. Thus, at some point in the future, Vietnam and the U.S. are likely to engage in another set of negotiations about the changes Vietnam must make to its trade regime before

---

[8] For more on this topic, see CRS Report RS20717, *Vietnam Trade Agreement: Approval and Implementing Procedure*, by Vladimir Pregelj.

the U.S. will support Vietnam's application for WTO membership. Upon completion of this agreement, it is likely that the U.S. president will ask Congress to extend permanent MFN treatment to Vietnam, much as President Clinton did after completing WTO accession negotiations with China in November 1999.[9]

Table 1. Vietnam's Path to Commercial Normalization with the United States

Step	Action
Step 1. Removing the U.S. trade embargo	In February 1994, President Clinton ordered the embargo on Vietnam lifted.
Step 2. Granting an annual waiver of Jackson-Vanik restrictions on OPIC and Ex-Im Bank operations in the country.[10]	President Clinton issued waivers for Vietnam in 1998, 1999, and 2000, as did President Bush in 2001. Each time, disapproval resolutions were defeated in the House.
Step 3. Signing bilateral trade agreement, subject to Congressional approval, that includes an extension on conditional MFN treatment.	An agreement was signed in July 2000. It was approved by Congress and signed into law by the President in 2001. Vietnam has yet to ratify the agreement.
Step 4. Restoring permanent MFN status by passing a law "graduating" Vietnam from its status as a non-MFN country.	Presumably, this step will be taken if and when Vietnam joins the World Trade Organization (WTO).

U.S. and Vietnamese Interests in a Bilateral Trade Agreement

U.S. Interests in a Bilateral BTA

U.S.-Vietnam trade and investment flows are extremely low. Although Vietnam is the world's 13th most populous country, with nearly 80 million people, for the past several years annual U.S. exports have hovered in the $200-$300 million range (see Table 2 below), a figure roughly equivalent to three days' worth of exports to Japan, and roughly one-fifth the amount the U.S. exported to South Vietnam in 1970.[11] Major U.S. exports to Vietnam include aircraft, fertilizer, telecommunications equipment, and general machinery. Cumulative

[9] If Vietnam acceded to the WTO before the U.S. extended to it permanent MFN status, its WTO membership could place the U.S. in violation of the WTO requirement that unconditional MFN treatment be applied to all WTO members. The U.S. could avoid this by invoking the WTO's non-application article (Article XIII) prior to Vietnam's accession to the WTO. Thus, if Vietnam were to join the WTO, Hanoi's accession would not in and of itself alter the status of U.S.-Vietnam trade relations, which would continue to be governed by Title IV of the Trade Act of 1974, as well as the U.S.-Vietnam BTA. However, the U.S. would not be guaranteed all the benefits of Vietnam's accession to the WTO, including the use of the WTO's dispute resolution mechanism to deal with U.S.-Vietnam trade disputes.

[10] Alternatively, as described earlier, this step could be taken through a Presidential determination that Vietnam is in full compliance with the Jackson-Vanik amendment's freedom-of-emigration requirements. Along with China and Belarus, Vietnam has not been certified to be in full compliance with the Jackson-Vanik requirements.

[11] In 1970, the United States exported $342 million to South Vietnam. Adjusted for inflation, this amount equals approximately $1.5 billion today.

foreign direct investment (FDI) by U.S. companies in Vietnam is also low, valued at about $1 billion, making the United States the ninth-largest source of investment in Vietnam.

Table 2. U.S.-Vietnam Trade, 1994-2000
(millions of dollars)

	U.S. Imports from Vietnam	U.S. Exports from Vietnam	Trade Balance
1994	50.45	172.22	121.77
1995	198.97	252.86	53.89
1996	319.04	616.05	297.01
1997	388.19	277.79	-110.40
1998	553.41	274.22	-279.19
1999	601.90	277.30	-324.60
2000	827.40	330.50	-496.90
Major Imports from Vietnam		Shrimp, footwear, coffee, petrol products, cashews	
Major Exports to Vietnam		Industrial & office machinery, footwear parts, telecommunications equipment, fertilizer, cotton	

Source: U.S. Department of Commerce. Data are merchandise trade on a custom basis.

To boost U.S. exports and investment, U.S. negotiations demanded that Vietnam provide more comprehensive and derailed concessions in the areas of services, investment, and market access than had been obtained in previous bilateral trade pacts with other Jackson-Vanik countries. As discussed in the following section, it appears the U.S. successfully obtained moat of them negotiating objectives.

Following the signing of the agreement, Clinton Administration officials and business representatives were careful not to argue that the BTA will significantly boost U.S, exports dad investment to Vietnam in the short term. Rather, they stressed that U.S. exporters and investors will benefit most in the medium to long-term, as Vietnam continues market-oriented reforms, becomes more dev eloped and in, grated into the global economy, and as Vietnam phases in more and more of the BTA's requirements. Moreover, exports to and investment in Vietnam arc expected to increase as Hanoi and other members of the Association of Southeast Asian Nations (ASEAN) - a 10-country, 500-million person market - follow through on commitments to reduce trade barriers by 2006. Ultimately, U.S. trade and investment opportunities in the future will depend on a) Hanoi's implementation of the BTA; b) Vietnam's progress on moving toward a more market-oriented economy; and c) Vietnam's rate of economic growth.

In the short- to medium-term, the BTA will require Vietnam to improve the climate for foreign investors. U. S. businesses in Vietnam will receive legal protections that are unavailable today. More sectors will be open to U.S. multinationals. Additionally, the BTA will help make the Vietnamese business environment more predictable and transparent. Currently, a frequent complaint from foreign executives in Vietnam is the lengthy delay in obtaining investment licenses from the government. To make matters more difficult, foreign investors often are not aware of all the regulatory requirements for obtaining licenses, leading to complaints of arbitrary treatment by local and central government authorities.

Many of the agreement's proponents also contend that the bilateral trade pact will nudge Vietnam toward a more democratic society by committing the government to enact market-oriented reforms, weakening the government's tight political controls, solidifying the rule of law, integrating Vietnamese enterprises more fully into the global economy, and economically empowering individuals. BTA proponents also point out that the agreement will help to bring Vietnam closer to compliance with WTO rules, facilitating Hanoi's eventual WTO accession. Once Vietnam joins the WTO, its trade policies will be subject to even greater international scrutiny and disciplines. Strategically, BTA backers argue that the U.S.-Vietnam BTA, together with BTAs recently completed with Cambodia and Laos, will promote regional stability by smoothing the integration of Indochina into the regional and global community.[12]

Arguments Against the BTA

The agreement's critics argue that Vietnam's government is likely to fall short on implementing the agreement and/or is likely to erect new, hidden barriers to imports and foreign investment, while low-cost Vietnamese exports - particularly textiles - to the U.S. will increase. Some U.S. trade unions have criticized the pact's lack of provisions on minimum labor standards and environmental protection. Vowing to fight the agreement in Congress, AFL-CIO President John Sweeney in July 2000 argued that "it [the BTA] is missing what we've been championing - core labor standards, human rights and environmental protection." Textile manufacturers and other groups have said they will lobby Congress and the Administration for changes to safeguard their industries from low-priced Vietnamese imports.[13]

Many observers, including labor groups, also oppose the pact on human rights grounds, arguing that human rights considerations should take priority over trade ties and/or that Hanoi's ruling elite would capture most of the gains from increased globalization. Indeed, on the same day the House approved the BTA, it also passed the Vietnam Human Rights Act, (H.R. 2833, by a vote of 410 - 1), which would ban increases (over FY2001 levels) in non-humanitarian aid to the Vietnamese government if the President does not certify that Vietnam is making "substantial progress" in human rights. The act allows the President to waive the cap on aid increases. In its most recent annual review of Vietnam's human rights situation, the U.S. State Department reported that Hanoi continues, "to repress basic political and some religious freedoms and to commit numerous abuses," notably "not tolerating most types of public dissent."[14]

---

[12] Testimony of Ambassador Charlene Barshevsky before the Senate Foreign Relations Subcommittees on International Economic Policy and Asia-Pacific Affairs, August 4, 1999. Note that Congress has approved the U.S.-Cambodia BTA, which is now in force, but has yet to approve the agreement with Laos.

[13] "U.S. Labor Vows Fight Against Vietnam Trade Pact," *ABCnews.com*, accessed July 17, 2000; see also "Clouds Part Over Vietnam's Bumpy Road to Reform," *Reuters*, July 18, 2000.

[14] U.S. Department of State *2000 Report on Human Rights Practices in Vietnam*, released February 26, 2000, available at [http://www.state.gov/g/drl/rls/hrrpt/2000/].

Vietnam's Interests in a BTA

After recording impressive growth for much of the 1990s following Hanoi's launch of the *doi moi* (economic renovation) reforms, Vietnam's economy has slowed since the 1997-99 Asian financial crisis, which originated in nearby Thailand. Annual economic growth declined from a peak of 9.5% in 1995 to 4.8% in 1999 and 6% in 2000. Foreign direct investment - a major stimulus for the country's growth - dwindled from over $8 billion in 1996 to $600 million in 1999, the lowest level since 1992.[15]

It is likely that the deterioration in Vietnam's economic fortunes played a major role in jump-starting the BTA talks with the U.S. in the spring of 1999, as a significant portion of Vietnam's leadership came to see increased U. S. investment and MFN access to the U.S. market as major ways for Vietnam to reverse its declining growth rates. As of December 2000, the United States was only the ninth largest source of foreign investment in Vietnam and absorbed less than 5% of Vietnam's exports. The bilateral trade agreement presumably will increase these levels considerably by conferring to Vietnamese exporters the same tariff rates that are applied to other MFN-recipient countries. The World Bank has estimated that Vietnam's exports to the U.S. will rise to $1.3 billion - more than 60% over 2000 levels - in the first year of MFN status, as U.S. tariff rates on Vietnamese exports would fall from their non-MFN average of 40% to less than 3%.[16]

Obtaining MFN status is likely to dramatically transform the product mix of Vietnam's exports to the U.S. Since the trade embargo was lifted in 1994, most of Vietnam's exports to the U.S. have been in items that either receive duty-free treatment (zero tariffs) or that have identical tariffs for MFN and non-MFN countries. In the short term, the BTA is likely to increase Vietnam's exports of labor-intensive manufacturing with large differences between the MFN and non-MFN tariff rates. Judging by Vietnam's leading exports to the European Union and Japan (see **Figure 2**), exports of the following items are likely to increase substantially: garments, leather products, footwear, household plastic products and processed foods.[17]

---

[15] For more on Vietnam's economic situation, see CRS Report 98-551, *Vietnam: Economic Reforms and Commercial Relations with the United States*, by Raymond J. Ahearn, and CRS issue Brief IB98033, *Vietnam-U.S. Relations*, by Mark Manyin.

[16] Fukase, Emiko, and Will Martin, *The Effects of the United States Granting Most-Favored- Nation (MFN) Status to Vietnam*, (Washington, DC: World Bank Development and Research Group, 1999). In a 1998 report, the World Bank estimated that half of the projected increase in exports to the U.S. will consist of clothing items. The rest is likely to consist of manufactures and processed agricultural goods. See World Bank, *Rising to the Challenge*, 1998, available at [http://www.worldbank.org.vn/rep 1/rep001.htm].

[17] EUROSTAT Internal and External Trade of the EU Database; *2000 Japan Statistical Yearbook*; *AsiaPulse*, [http://sg.dailynews.yahoo.com/headlines/asia/], accessed on August 18, 2000.

Figure 2. Imports from Vietnam, Selected Countries & Products, 1999

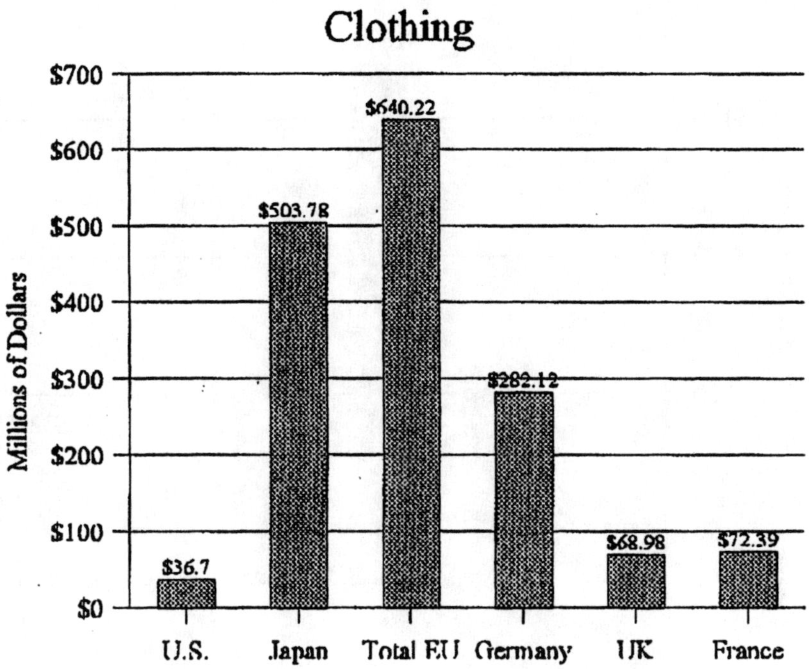

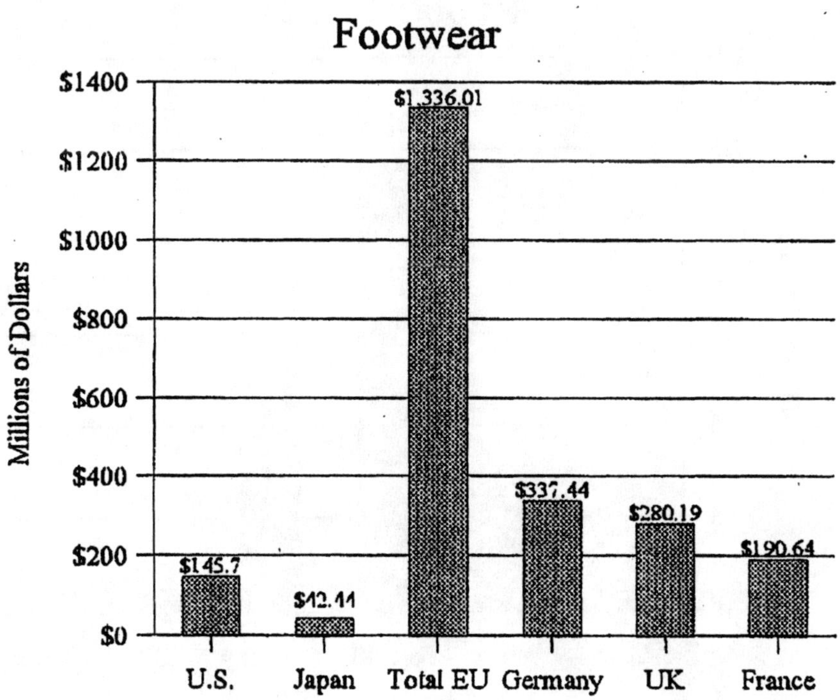

Leather Goods
Millions of Dollars
$200
$150
$100
$50
$0
$2
$51.63
$169.61
$57.35
$15.5
$33.48
U.S.
Japan
Total EU
Germany
UK
France

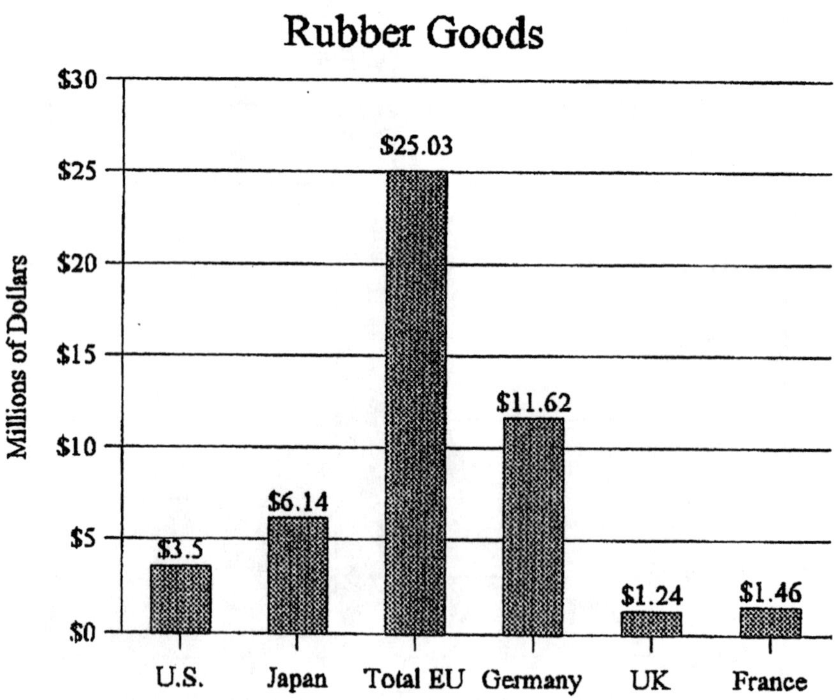
Rubber Goods
Millions of Dollars
$30
$25
$20
$15
$10
$5
$0
$3.5
$6.14
$25.03
$11.62
$1.24
$1.46
U.S.
Japan
Total EU
Germany
UK
France

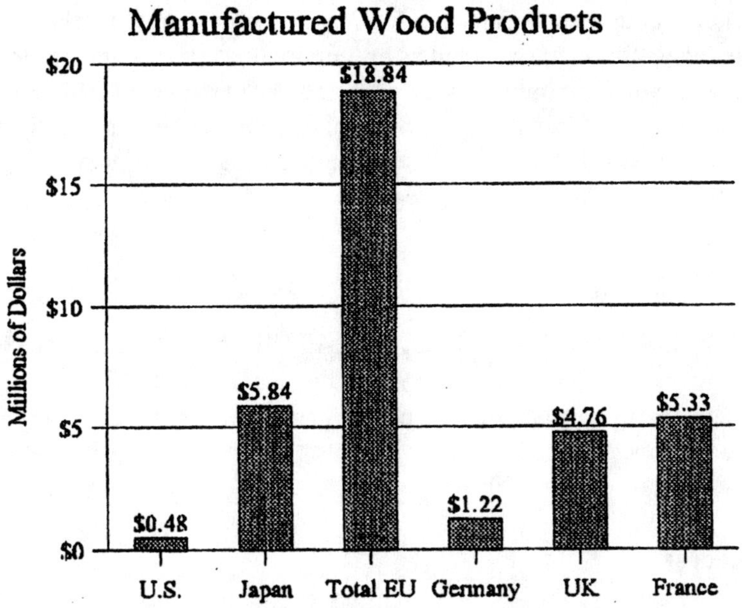

Figure 2. Imports from Vietnam, Selected Countries & Products, 1999

(**Source:** U.S. International Trade Commission, EUROSTAT, and Japan Tariff Association)

Vietnam's Clothing Exports

In particular, Vietnam's clothing exports are expected to increase dramatically. Vietnam currently exports few apparel products to the U.S. - less than $40 million in 1999 -because of the higher, non-MFN, tariff rates it faces. In contrast, Vietnamese garment exports to Japan and the 15 countries of the European Union in 1999 totaled more than $500 million and $640 million, respectively (see Figure 2). Based on the experience of Cambodia, which was granted MFN status by the United States in 1996, the World Bank estimates Vietnamese apparel exports will increase nearly tenfold - to $384 million- in the first year after receiving MFN status.[18]

The BTA agreement contains no provisions on Vietnamese textile exports to the U.S., but the safeguard provision would allow the U.S. to impose quotas on textile imports in the event of a surge of imports. In private, U.S. and Vietnamese officials have said they expect to begin negotiating a bilateral textile agreement, which presumably would set quotas for Vietnamese textile exports, soon after a Congressional vote on the BTA. Some Members of Congress have called for the Bush Administration to publicly commit to negotiating a textile agreement, and have pressed for a commitment that such an agreement would include provisions that would link the size of Vietnam's quotas to progress in its labor rights.[19]

Passing a trade agreement would also bring Vietnam one step closer to receiving U.S. trade benefits under the generalized system of preferences (GSP), which allows many imports

[18] Fukase and Martin, *The Effects of the United States Granting Most-Favored-Nation (MFN) Status to Vietnam*, p. 12.
[19] *Inside U.S. Trade*, May 25, 2001.

from less-developed countries to enter the U.S. market duty-free.[20] Furthermore, Vietnamese officials see the bilateral trade agreement as an important stepping-stone to joining the WTO, providing them with non-discriminatory access to all WTO members. Not only do they regard the BTA as necessary to obtaining U.S. support for Vietnam's application for WTO membership, but they also see the processes of negotiating and implementing the agreement as useful for raising Vietnam's legal, regulatory, and economic systems to the WTO's standards.

Overview of Vietnam-U.S. Bilateral Trade Agreement[21]

The trade agreement consists of four parts: market access; trade in services, intellectual property rights, and investment.

1) Market Access

Vietnam has agreed to take the following steps to open its markets:

- Guarantee most-favored-nation (MFN) treatment to U.S. goods;
- Treat imports the same as domestically produced products (also known as "national treatment");
- Eliminate quotas on all imports over a period of 3 to 7 years;
- Make its government procurement process more transparent;
- Allow for the first time U.S. companies and U.S.-invested companies to import and export most products (to be phased in 3-6 years). (Presently, foreign companies have to rely on licensed Vietnamese importers, most of which are state-owned enterprises.)
- Ensure that state enterprises comply with WTO rules;
- Adhere to WTO rules in applying customs, import licensing, technical standards, and sanitary and phytosanitary measures.

Tariff Concessions

The U.S.-Vietnam BTA is unique in that, in contrast to previously negotiated bilateral trade agreements between the U.S. and Jackson-Vanik countries, it includes specific commitments by Vietnam to reduce tariffs on approximately 250 products, about four-fifths of which are agricultural goods. Typically, the cuts range from 33% to 50% and are to be phased in over a three-year period. Vietnam's tariffs are not considered to be extremely high for a developing country (the U.S. Foreign Commercial Service estimates that Vietnam's average tariff line is 15%-20%).

---

[20] Under Section 502 of the Trade Act of 1974, to be eligible for GSP treatment, Communist countries, in addition to meeting other conditions required of recipient developing countries, must receive MFN treatment, and belong to the WTO and the IMF. Paragraph 1:3:8 of the Vietnam-U.S. BTA states that "the United States shall consider Vietnam's eligibility for the Generalized System of Preferences."

[21] In addition to the text of the agreement itself, this section borrows from "Vietnam Trade Agreement: Summary of Key Provisions," *Reuters*, July 13, 2000.

Also in the area of market access, the agreement includes a **safeguard** provision that would allow either side to raise tariffs temporarily if it encounters a surge of imports.

2) Intellectual Property Rights

Vietnam has pledged to phase in the World Trade Organization Agreement on Trade-Related Intellectual Property Rights (TRIPs) over 18 months. The bilateral TRIPs agreement goes above and beyond the WTO's TRIPs agreement by including Vietnamese commitments to protect satellite signals within 30 months.

3) Trade in Services

In the area of services, Vietnam has committed to uphold WTO rules such as MFN, national treatment, and disciplines on domestic regulation. Additionally, Vietnam has agreed to allow U.S. companies and individuals to invest in markets in a wide range of service sectors, including accounting, advertising, banking, computer, distribution, education, insurance, legal and telecommunications. Most sector-specific commitments are phased in over three to five years. Vietnam's commitments in three of the largest U.S. service sectors – banking, insurance, and telecommunications – are highlighted below.

Banking Services

Vietnam agreed to the following liberalization measures: For the first nine years after the agreement goes into effect, U.S. banks may form joint ventures with Vietnamese partners, with U.S. equity between 30% and 49%. After nine years, 100% subsidiaries are permitted.

Insurance

Under the BTA, for "mandatory" insurance sectors (such as automobile and construction-related insurance), after three years Vietnam will allow U.S. companies to form joint ventures, with no limit on the U.S. equity share. After six years, 100% subsidiaries are permitted. For life insurance and other "non-mandatory" insurance sectors, after three years joint ventures are permitted, with a limit of 50% U.S. equity. After five years, 100% subsidiaries are allowed.

Telecommunications

Under the BTA, for higher-end telecommunications services (such as Interact, e-mail, and voice mail services), Vietnam will permit joint ventures after two years, with a 50% cap on U.S. equity participation. Interact services have a three-year phase in period. For basic telecommunications services (such as facsimile, cellular mobile, and satellite services), joint ventures are permitted after four years, with U.S. companies limited to a 49% stake. For local, long distance, and international voice telephone services, joint ventures are permitted after six years, with a 49% cap on U.S. ownership. Vietnam agreed that it will consider increasing the U.S. equity limits when the agreement is reviewed in three years.

4) Investment

Regarding investment, the U.S.-Vietnam trade agreement includes guarantees of MFN treatment, national treatment, transparency, and protection against expropriation. Additionally, Vietnam pledged to implement the following changes in its investment regime:

- Investment screening: Currently, foreign businesses must obtain government approval to invest in Vietnam. Under the BTA, investment screening will be phased out for most sectors within two, six, or nine years, depending on the sector involved.
- Profit repatriation: Presently, Vietnamese enterprises have greater freedom than foreign multinationals to convert their Vietnam-earned profits into hard currency. The State Bank of Vietnam must approve the conversion of currency on behalf of foreign businesses, and the Bank does not give permission to convert currency to foreign-invested companies.[22] Under the BTA, foreign multinationals will receive the same rights for profit repatriation as Vietnamese firms; however, Vietnam's currency is still not fully convertible.
- Capital contribution floors: Currently, the U.S. stake in a joint venture must be at least 30%. This requirement will be eliminated in three years.
- Personnel requirements for joint ventures: Presently, Vietnam requires that certain board members of joint ventures be Vietnamese and requires that certain types of decisions be made by consensus (thereby granting veto power to the Vietnamese board members).
- Under the BTA, within three years Vietnam would allow U.S. multinationals to select top executives without regard to nationality.
- Trade-related investment measures (TRIMs): Vietnam has agreed to eliminate within five years all TRIMs that are inconsistent with the WTO, such as local Content requirements.

5) Transparency

Vietnam has agreed to adopt a fully transparent commercial regime by allowing comment on draft laws and regulations by ensuring that advance public notice is given for all such laws and regulations; by publishing these documents; and by allowing U. S. citizens and corporations the right to appeal rulings.

Vietnam's Implementation of the BTA

It is an open question whether the Vietnamese government has the will or the wherewithal to implement the pervasive reforms required by the U.S.-Vietnam bilateral trade agreement. Implementing the agreement will require cooperation at the local government level, where central control often is weak and corruption is rampant. An unprecedented level

[22] United States Foreign Commercial Service, "Country Commercial Guide: Vietnam," July 15, 1999.

of cooperation among governmental ministries will also be required. Powerful vested interests - particularly the state-owned enterprises and the Vietnamese People's Army - undoubtedly will put pressure on local and central government officials to erect new barriers to foreign competition.

In a sign that the government is determined to push ahead with market liberalization despite the obstacles, Vietnam's trade ministry has already begun preparing draft laws and regulations on reshaping the country's trade regime. In January 2001, the Ministry of Trade issued a directive allowing foreign-invested enterprises to directly export most items.[23] The Trade Ministry also has finalized regulations to cancel most import-export licensing requirements for virtually all Vietnamese and foreign firms.[24] Additionally, all ministries have been ordered to identify all laws and regulations that must be changed in order to implement the trade agreement.[25]

Comparison with the 1999 "Agreement in Principle"

In July 1999 the U.S. and Vietnam announced an "agreement in principle" on a BTA, but for nearly a year Vietnam delayed finalizing the deal because of intense divisions among the Vietnamese Communist Party (VCP) leadership (see the following section for an analysis of the reasons for Vietnam's hesitation). The Clinton Administration did not release the full terms of the July 1999 agreement in principle. According to one negotiator, the only significant differences between the final BTA and the 1999 agreement lie in the area of trade in services (Chapter III and Annex G), specifically in the area of telecommunications.[26]

Telecommunications

In general, the 1999 agreement in principle would have allowed U.S. companies the right to obtain a majority (51%) stake in certain Vietnamese telecommunications sectors after a certain number of years (often referred to as the "phase-in" period). Following the November 1999 U.S.-China agreement on China's WTO accession - which granted U.S. companies the right to a 49% maximum stake in Chinese telecommunications enterprises - the Vietnamese negotiators demanded that they receive similar equity caps. The U.S. agreed to this concession, but in exchange received significantly shorter phase-in periods. Vietnam also agreed to consider increasing the U.S. equity limits when the agreement is reviewed in three years.

Two telecommunications sectors, wireless and basic voice services, illustrate the differences between the 1999 and 2000 documents. In wireless telecommunications, under the 1999 agreement Vietnam would have allowed U.S. companies the right to set up joint ventures after three years, with a 51% maximum stake for U.S. companies. Under the 2000 BTA, Vietnam is to grant U.S. companies the right to set up wireless joint ventures after two years (three years for internet services), with a 50% cap on U.S. equity participation.

---

23 "Trade Amendments Set to Assist Foreign Companies," *Vietnam Investment Review*, January 8, 2001.

24 "With an Eye on WTO, Vietnam to Relax Trade," *Australian Financial Review*, February 14, 2001. The Ministry reportedly is awaiting final governmental approval of these regulatory changes.

25 Memo from the Office of the Vietnamese Prime Minister, "Re: Preparatory Tasks After the U.S. and Vietnam Agreement," November 21, 2000.

26 July 2000 interview with U.S. government official.

In the area of basic voice telecommunication services (local, long distance and international phone service), press reports indicate that the 1999 agreement would have phased-in a right to invest after 11 years, with a 51% maximum stake for U.S. companies. Under the 2000 BTA, Vietnam is to allow U.S. companies to set up joint ventures after six years, with a 49% cap on U.S. ownership.

Insurance

According to press reports, under the 1999 agreement Vietnam would have permitted U.S. companies to invest in its insurance sector in two to six years. The phase-in period varied by insurance sector. Details are unavailable on foreign equity caps.[27] Under the July 2000 BTA, Vietnam is to grant U.S. companies the right to set up 50-50 joint ventures in its insurance sector after three years, and wholly, owned (100% stake) ventures after five years.

Market Access

The final BTA includes commitments by Vietnam to reduce tariffs on approximately 250 products, about four-fifths of which are agricultural goods. 1999 press reports implied that the agreement in principle contained 330 tariff items scheduled for tariff reduction. A U.S. official involved in negotiating the agreement, however, has argued that this number is incorrect, stating that the tariff changes in Annex E of the final BTA are essentially the same as those agreed upon in 1999.

Comparison with Past BTAs

In negotiating bilateral trade deals with Jackson-Vanik countries, U.S. negotiators generally have tried to break new ground with each successive agreement. As one indication of that policy, the 1979 agreement China was less than 10 pages, while the far more comprehensive U.S.-Vietnam BTA is more than ten times that length. The Vietnam-U.S. BTA goes beyond past agreements in its more detailed commitments in the areas of services and investment. Furthermore, Vietnam's tariff concessions represent a new development. Previous Jackson-Vanik BTAs contained few or no market access commitments because in those negotiations the U.S. proposed to carry out tariff discussions at a future date, not as part of the final BTA itself.[28]

VIETNAM'S AMBIVALENCE TOWARD ECONOMIC INTEGRATION

Though the U.S. and Vietnam reached an agreement in principle on the BTA in July 1999, for nearly a year Vietnam delayed signing the deal. What were the reasons for Vietnam's hesitancy?

---

[27] "USTR Lays Out Key Issues to be Resolved in U.S.-Vietnam Trade Deal," *Inside U.S. Trade*, July 30, 1999.

[28] November 1999 interview by the author with trade policy expert Craig VanGrasstek, President VanGrasstek Communications.

Internal Factors

Consensus-Based Decision-Making

Vietnam's official reason for the delay was that it needed time to vet the agreement among decision-makers in Vietnam. Vietnam's consensus-style of decision-making and the weakness of the country's current leadership probably extended this vetting process: The BTA is the most extensive agreement Vietnam has ever negotiated, and the assent of virtually all officials involved in implementing the deal was required before Hanoi would take such a radical step. Furthermore, the weakness of the country's current top leaders-VCP General Secretary Le Kha Phieu, Prime Minister Phan Van Khai, and President Tran Duc Luong - made it difficult for them to forge a consensus on such a controversial issue.[29]

Questions from Vietnamese Conservatives

Ever since the Vietnamese Communist Party's (VCP) 8th Party Congress in 1996, disagreements between reformers and conservatives in Vietnam's 19-member Politburo - the country's supreme ruling body - have paralyzed economic decision-making. As the bilateral trade agreement with the U.S. requires Vietnam to jump-start its reforms and deepen its integration into the global economy, it is not surprising that the Politburo also has been divided over whether to finalize the deal.

The conservatives fear that economic reform will undermine the "socialist foundations" of the country's economic and political systems, and thereby erode the VCP's legitimacy and monopoly on power. They also fear that Vietnam's sovereignty will be eroded by increasing Vietnam's economic dependence on the West and by increasing Vietnam's vulnerability to regional economic downturns such as the 1997-99 Asian financial crisis. Among their specific concerns, conservatives worry that shifting to a more market-oriented economy will force the Politburo to curtail subsidies to the country's state-owned enterprises, the backbone of the socialist economic system. Many conservatives are understandably worried that further rationalization will raise unemployment rates, which already exceed 10%, according to some estimates. Social and political pressures on the Party have already been heightened in recent years by peasant uprisings and widespread accusations of government corruption. High-level U.S. pressure on Vietnam for its human rights record, applied during Secretary of State Madeleine Albright's September 1999 trip to Vietnam, is said to have further rankled conservative forces opposed to the trade agreement.

In January 2000, a group of reform-minded leaders were transferred to key economic and political posts. These moves, combined with the BTA signing, the unveiling of a new Enterprise Law, the passage of new amendments to the Foreign Investment Law, and the opening of Vietnam's first stock market on July 20, 2000, may be signs that Hanoi's policy logjam is breaking up in the reformers' favor.

Opposition from Vested Interests

Parochial interests also may have played a role in Vietnam's deliberations. According to many sources, Vietnam's military leaders have been among the staunchest opponents of the BTA. Many argue that the military- known as the People's Army of Vietnam - is worried that

---

[29] Zachary Abuza, "Leadership Transition in Vietnam since the Eighth Party Congress: The Unfinished Congress," *Asian Survey*, (December 1998).

the trade deal would threaten its vast commercial interests. According to one estimate, the business enterprises of the People's Army of Vietnam generated over $600 million in revenue in 1998, a figure equivalent to nearly 60% of the entire military budget.[30] Evidence of the military's influence can be seen in Vietnam's bargaining position on telecommunications liberalization during the BTA negotiations. Hanoi demanded an eleven-year phase-in period for FDI liberalization in cable communications, a sector in which the People's Army has invested heavily since 1995. In contrast, Vietnam's negotiators were willing to accept a four-year phase in for cellular communications, an area in which the Ministry of Defense has few investments.[31]

External Factors. Balancing China and the U.S.

Yet another hypothesis is that Hanoi was concerned that a trade deal with the United States would antagonize China. Beijing and Hanoi recently have strengthened their ties, and conservative elements in Hanoi may be wary of upsetting Beijing by appearing too closely aligned with the U.S. In particular, the Vietnamese leadership may have wished to avoid jeopardizing negotiations with China over a land-border treaty, negotiations that were not concluded until December 1999. There are also reports that Chinese leaders warned the Vietnamese not to conclude the BTA before Beijing had finalized its own WTO accession negotiations with the U.S., talks that were concluded in November 1999. However, some analysts and Administration officials reject this reasoning as a stalling tactic by the Vietnamese, who are said to often use the Chinese as an excuse for delaying foreign policy moves about which they are uncertain. As one observer has pointed out, Chinese opposition did not prevent Vietnam from joining the Association of Southeast Asian Nations (ASEAN) in 1995.[32]

Most observers agree that, apart from the issue of unsubstantiated Chinese pressure, the China factor played a positive role in spurring the Vietnamese to move forward, due to Hanoi's fears of increased economic competition with Beijing following China's likely accession to the WTO in 2000 or 2001.

---

[30] Huw Watkin, "Proud Military Slips into Decline as Aid Dries Up," *South China Morning Post*, July 7, 1999, and Huw Watkin, "Military Puts Boot in as Treaty with US Seen Growing Threat to Business Empire," *South China Morning Post*, September 14, 1999.

[31] Zachary Abuza, "The Polities of Globalization: Explaining Vietnam's Rejection of the U.S. Trade Deal," (Boston, MA: Simmons College, 2000), p.20.

[32] Abuza, "The Politics of Globalization," p.21-22.

Chapter 14

CHINA AND THE WORLD TRADE ORGANIZATION

Wayne M. Morrison
Specialist in International Trade and Finance
Foreign Affairs, Defense, and Trade Division

SUMMARY

China has sought over the past several years to become a member of the World Trade Organization (WTO), the international agency that administers multilateral trade rules. China's WTO membership (as well as that of Taiwan's) was formally approved at the WTO Ministerial Conference in Doha, Qatar in November 2001. On December 11, 2001, China officially became a WTO member. WTO membership will require China to significantly liberalize its trade and investment regimes, which could produce significant new commercial opportunities for U.S. businesses. A mare concern for Congress is to ensure that China fully complies with its WTO commitments. This report will be updated as events warrant.

After 15 years of bilateral and multilateral negotiations, China formally entered the WTO on December 11, 2001. The negotiations on China's accession to the WTO focused on many Chinese practices that distort flows of trade to and from China, such as tariffs and non-tariff barriers, restrictions on foreign investment, lack of national treatment for foreign firm, inadequate protection of intellectual property rights (IPR), and Wade-distorting government subsidies. Membership in: the WTO will require China to change many laws, institutions, and polities to bring them into conformity with international trade rules.

THE WTO ACCESSION PROCESS

The rules for joining the WTO are stated in the Agreement Establishing the WTO, which was signed on April 15, 1995, as part of the Final Act implementing the results of the Uruguay Round of multilateral trade negotiations. The Agreement provides that any state or separate customs territory may accede to the WTO on terms to be agreed between it and the WTO. It further provides that decisions on accession shall be taken by the Ministerial

Conference (the highest authority in the WTO), which shall approve an agreement on the terms of accession by two-thirds majority.[1]

Negotiations over the terms of accession typically proceed on two fronts – multilateral consultations in a Working Party composed of all interested WTO members and bilateral negotiations between the applicant and each major trading partner. The Working Party focuses on the general rules and principles of the applicant's protocol: it seeks to ensure that the applicant will accept the normal obligations and responsibilities of WTO membership and sets schedules for complying with various WTO agreements. The bilateral meetings, on the other hand, focus on tariff concessions and other market access issues that will govern bilateral trade relations after the applicant becomes a member, and will apply on an MFN basis to all other WTO members.

An applicant becomes a member by persuading first the Working Party and then the full WTO to approve an accession package, which consists of a protocol that lists the commitments undertaken by the applicant concerning WTO rules, a Working Party report elaborating on those commitments, and a schedule of bilateral market access commitments for trade in goods and services. Chinese officials negotiated to develop such a package with the Working Party in Geneva and with 37 WTO members.

China's Interest in WTO Membership

China made its accession to the WTO a major priority for a number of reasons. First, it would represent international recognition of China's growing economic power. Second, it would enable China to play a major role in the development of new international rules on trade in the WTO. Third, it would give China access to the dispute resolution process in the WTO, reducing the threat of unilaterally imposed restrictions on Chinese exports. Fourth, it would make it easier for reformers in China to push for liberalization policies if they could argue that such steps are necessary to fulfill China's international obligations. Finally, Chinese leaders hoped WTO membership would induce file United States to grant China permanent normal trade relations (PNTR), or most-favored-nation (MFN), status, thus ending the annual trade status renewal process and subsequent congressional debate over U.S.-China relations.

The Role and Interest of the United States

The United States played a central role in China's WTO accession process. U.S. trade officials insisted that China's entry into the WTO had to be based on "commercially meaningful terms" that would require China to significantly reduce trade and investment barriers within a relatively short period of time. For many U.S. firms, China remains a difficult market to penetrate, due mainly to Chinese government policies designed to protect

[1] While WTO decisions on important matters such as accessions formally require a two-thirds majority, in practice, the WTO has relied on confines to reach important decisions.

and promote domestic industries.[2] These policies attempt to encourage imports of products that are deemed beneficial to China's economic development, such as-high technology, and machinery and raw materials used by export-oriented industries. Goods and services not considered to be of high priority, or which compete directly with domestic Chinese firms, often face an extensive array of trade barriers. Such barriers often force foreign firms to invest in China in order to gain market access, although they face a variety of restrictions in doing so as well. U.S. officials blame such policies for the surging U.S. trade deficit with China, which reached nearly $84 billion in 2000.

Many U.S. trade analysts viewed China's WTO accession process as an opportunity for gaining substantially greater access to China's market. China has been one of the world's fastest growing economies over the past several years (real GDP growth averaged 9.5% annually from 1979 to 2000), and many trade analysts argue that China could become a potentially large market for a wide variety of U.S. goods arid services if greater market access were afforded. Accession to the WTO would require China to lower its trade barriers, afford "national treatment" to foreign firms, make its trade laws more transparent, and subject its trade regime to review by the WTO dispute resolution process. Other U.S. proponents of China's WTO membership contended that it will advance the cause of human rights in China by enhancing the rule of law there for business activities, diminishing the central government's control over the economy, and promoting the expansion of the private sector in China.

THE U.S.-CHINA WTO AGREEMENT

U.S. and Chinese officials reached a bilateral agreement relating to China's WTO bid on November 15, 1999.[3] The agreement would commit China to reduce tariffs and remove non-tariff barriers (some upon accession and others over specified phase-in periods). The full text of the agreement was released by the Clinton Administration on March 14, 2000. Some of the major commitments China agreed to include the following:

- Provide full trading and distribution rights (including the ability to provide services auxiliary to distribution) for U.S. firms in China.
- Cut average tariffs on agricultural products from an overall average of 22% to 17.5%; tariffs for U.S. priority agricultural products (such as beef, grapes, wine, cheese, poultry, and pork), would fall from 31% to 14%). Overall industrial tariffs would fall from an average of 24.6% to 9.4%; tariffs on U.S. priority industrialproducts would fall to 7.1%. Tariffs on information technology products would be fall from an average of 13.3 % to zero.
- Establish a tariff-rate quota system for imports of agricultural bulk commodities (such as wheat, corn, cotton, barley, and rice), i.e., imports up to a specified quota level would be assessed a low tariff (1-3%), while imports above a certain level

[2] U.S. exports to China in 2000 were $16.3 billion (a 23.9% increase over 1999 levels), making China the 11th largest U.S. export market.

[3] These measures were included in the final WTO China accession agreement.

would be assessed a much higher tariff rate. In addition, private trade in agricultural products would be permitted for the first time.

- Phase out quotas and other quantitative restrictions (some upon accession, many within two years).
- Eliminate unscientifically based sanitary and phytosanitary restrictions on agricultural products, end export subsidies, and reduce domestic subsidies.
- Open service sectors, including distribution, insurance, value-added telecommunications, banking, securities, and professional services. China would expand (over various transitional periods) the Scope of allowed services and gradually remove geographical restrictions on foreign service providers. The amount of permitted foreign ownership in service industries would vary (and in some cases expand over time) from sector to sector.
- Reduce restrictions on auto trade. Tariffs on autos would fall from 80-100% to 25% (tariffs on auto parts reduced to an average rate of 10%) by 2006. Auto quotas would be eliminated by 2005. U.S. financial firms would be allowed to provide financing for the purchase of cars in China.
- Remove various restrictions on foreign investors in China, including technology transfer, local content, and export performance requirements.
- Accept use by the United States of certain safeguard, countervailing, and antidumping provisions to respond to possible import surges of various products from China, such as textiles, that might cause, or threaten to cause, market disruption to a U.S. industry.

CHINA JOINS THE WTO

China completed all of its WTO bilateral agreements on September 13, 2001, when it reached a trade agreement with Mexico, the last of the 37 WTO members that had requested an agreement. China completed negotiations with the WTO Working Party on September 17, 2001, on the terms of its accession.[4] China's WTO membership was formally approved by the WTO on November 10, 2001, and on November 11, China informed the WTO that it had ratified the WTO agreements. As a result, China officially joined the WTO on December 11, 2001.

China's entry into the WTO has important implications for the world trading system. By some estimates, China is the world's third largest economy, after the United States and Japan, and the world's 10th largest trading economy. A World Bank report estimates that China's share of world trade could triple from 3.0% in 1992 to 9.8% by the year 2020, malting China the world's second largest trading nation after the United States.[5] The growing importance of China in the world economy was an important factor in the heightened interest among WTO members in bringing China into the WTO and thereby subjecting its trade regime to multilateral trade rules. China's WTO application was particularly difficult because, in many respects, China is still a developing Country, and yet, its economy and trade are significant. Many WTO members, including the United States, argued that China needed to make

[4] The WTO Working Party handling Taiwan's accession formally rapped up its negotiations on September 18, 2001.
[5] The World Bank, China 2020: China Engaged, 1997, p. 31.

substantial reforms to its trade regime in order to join the WTO, while China insisted it be treated as a developing country, which would have enabled it to implement reforms over a longer period of time. In the end, a compromise agreement was reached that requires China to make immediate and extensive reductions in various trade and investment barriers, but allows it to maintain some level of protection (or a transitionary period of protection) for certain sensitive sectors.

THE ROLE OF CONGRESS

Congress did not play a direct role in the WTO accession process. That is, current U.S. law did not require congressional approval of the November 1999 U.S.-China WTO trade agreement, nor was it needed for the United States to support China's admission to the WTO. However, most trade analysts argued that, in order to ensure that the United States gained the full benefits of China's WTO accession, the U.S. needed to enact legislation granting PNTR treatment to China prior to its accession.[6] According to this view, without such a change in law, the United States would have been forced to invoke Article XIII in the WTO, the non-application clause.[7]

CONGRESSIONAL ACTION ON PNTR

During its negotiations with China over the terms of its WTO accession, the Clinton Administration pledged that, in return for significant market opening commitments on the part of China, it would press Congress to enact PNTR legislation. Once the November 1999 U.S.-China agreement was reached, the Clinton Administration began to push for passage of PNTR legislation.

On May 15, 2000, Representative Bill Archer introduced H.R. 4444, a bill to grant PNTR status to China upon its accession to the WTO (as long as the President certified that the final terms of China's accession were at least equivalent to the November 1999 U.S.-China trade agreement). Several provisions were added by the House to H.R. 4444 in response to various congressional concerns. In addition to the provisions contained in the original version of H.R. 4444, the final bill, which passed in the House on May 24, 2000, the Senate on September 19, 2000, and was signed into law on October 10, 2000 (P.L. 106-286), would:

- establish a special Congressional-Executive commission to monitor, and report on, various aspects of China's policies on human rights, including labor practices and religious freedom;

[6] Under the Jackson-Vanik Amendment (Section 402) to the Trade Act of 1974 (19 U.S.C. 2432), freedom-of-emigration requirements, the United States can and does (on an annual basis) extend normal trade relations (NTR) treatment to China.

[7] Article XIII can be invoked by either a current WTO member or an acceding WTO member if either member does not consent to the application of WTO agreements to each other (such as the granting of "unconditional" MFN status). Analysts believe that the current renewal of China's NTR status is not consistent with WTO rules, and hence the U.S. would have had to invoke Article XIII to avoid violating WTO rules. If the United States (or China) invoked Article XIII, the WTO agreements technically would not apply between the United States and China, and thus China could choose not to apply the WTO agreements to U.S. firms and investors.

- require the U.S. Trade Representative (USTR) to annually issue a report assessing China's compliance with its WTO trade obligations;
- codify the anti-surge mechanism established under the November 1999 U.S.-China trade agreement and establishes procedures for obtaining relief from import surges;
- expand funding for various U.S. government agencies to monitor China's compliance with its WTO trade commitments; and
- set up a special government task force to halt U.S, imports from China of products suspected of using prison labor.

IMPLICATIONS FOR U.S.-CHINA COMMERCIAL RELATIONS

China's accession to the WTO, and a U.S. extension of PNTR status to China (which the President is expected to do shortly), will likely have important ramifications for U.S.-China economic relations. First, Congress will no longer vote annually on China's trade status, which could help bring greater stability and predictability to the trade relationship. Second, the United States (as well as China) will be able to use the WTO dispute resolution process to resolve trade disputes, rather than relying on unilateral threats of trade sanctions. Third, subjecting China's trade regime to multilateral rules means that the United States will no longer have to "go it alone" in trying to get China to open its markets; other WTO members would have an equally strong stake in ensuring China's compliance with its WTO commitments. Finally, China's accession to the WTO will likely improve the business climate in China, leading to greater trade and investment opportunities for U.S. firms. A sizable increase in U.S. exports to China would help reduce tensions over trade issues.

However, many analysts have raised concern over the ability and willingness of the Chinese government to fully implement its WTO commitments once it obtains membership. U.S. trade agreements with China on market access (1992) and IPR protection produced mixed results in terms of compliance; in some instance Chinese removed one barrier, but replaced it with another. Corruption and local protectionism are rampant ha China, and gaining the cooperation of local officials and government bureaucrats that oversee various affected industries could prove difficult in the short run. In addition, economic reforms required under WTO commitments could lead to significant short-term employment disruptions in China; especially among farmers and employees of inefficient state-owned enterprises. Some analysts warn that such disruptions might erode the government's determination to fully implement its WTO commitments, especially if it fears social stability is threatened. Congress will likely press the Bush Administration to ensure China's trade compliance with its WTO commitments. The required annual report by the USTR on China's WTO implementation (due one year after China's WTO entry) could become the focal point of potential Congressional concerns over China's compliance. If U.S. exports fail to increase significantly, and the USTR's report finds serious deficiencies with China's compliance, Congress may press the Administration to file numerous dispute resolution cases against China in the WTO.

Chapter 15

CHINA'S ACCESSION TO THE WTO

Wayne M. Morrison

ISSUE

China is seeking to join the World Trade Organization (WTO), the international agency that administers multilateral trade ruler Part of the WTO accession process involves negotiating bilateral trade agreements with existing WTO members, including the United States. The United States and China reached t bilateral WTO trade agreement on November 15, 1999. In September 2001, China completed all of the multilateral and bilateral trade negotiations required for WTO accession and now awaits formal WTO approval. The 106th Congress passed legislation granting permanent normal trade relations (PNTR) status to China upon its accession to the WTO (P.L. 106-286) The 107th Congress will likely focus on efforts ensure that China Abide by its trade commitments once it joins the WTO.

BACKGROUND

WTO Membership

Negotiations over the terms of accession typically proceed on two fronts – multilateral negotiations in a Working Party composed of all interested WTO members and bilateral negotiations between the applicant and each major trading partner. The Working Party focuses on the general rules and principle of the applicant's protocol: it seeks to ensure that the applicant will accept the normal obligations and responsibilities of WTO membership, such as most favored nation (MFN), or nondiscriminatory, trade treatment; reliance on tariffs, rather than non-tariff barriers, when it is deemed necessary to protect domestic producers; adherence to tariff rates at fixed maximum levels; and national treatment of foreign firms and imported products. The bilateral negotiations, on the other hand, focus on tariff concessions and other market access banes that will govern bilateral trade relations after the applicant becomes a member; these agreements would apply equally and fully to all other WTO members.

An applicant becomes a WTO member by persuading first the Working Party and then the full WTO to approve an accession package, which consists era protocol that lists the commitments undertaken by the applicant concerning WTO rules, a Working Party report elaborating on those commitments, and a schedule of bilateral market access commitments for trade in goods and services. Formally, WTO decisions on important matters such as accessions require a two-thirds majority. In practice, the WTO has relied on consensus to reach important decisions.

The U.S.-China WTO Agreement

On November 15, 1999, the United States and China reached a bilateral trade agreement pertaining to China's WTO accession. That agreement would commit China to reduce tariffs and remove non-tariff barriers (some on accession and others over specified phase-in periods) on a wide variety of goods and services. The Administration made the entire agreement public on March 14, 2000. Under this agreement, China would take the following steps:

- Provide full trading and distribution rights (including the ability to provide services auxiliary to distribution) for U.S. firms in China.
- Cut overall agricultural tariffs for U.S. priority products (including beef, grapes, wine, cheese, poultry, and pork) from 31.5% to 14.5% by 2004. Cut overall average industrial tariffs from 24.6% to 9.4% by 2005 (with even deeper cuts for U.S. "priority industrial products" (such as wood, paper, chemicals, and capital and medical equipment). Cut average tariffs on information technology products from 13.3% to zero by 2005.
- Establish a tariff-rate quota system for imports of agricultural bulk commodities (such as wheat, corn, cotton, barely, and rice), i.e., imports up to a specified quota level would be assessed a low tariff (1-3%), while imports above a certain level would be assessed a much higher tariff rate. In addition, private trade in agricultural products would be permitted for the first time.
- Phase out quotas and other quantitative restrictions (some upon accession, many within two years, and most within five years). Quota levels for many products would expand by 15% each year until the elimination of the quota.
- Eliminate unscientifically based sanitary and phytosanitary restrictions.
- End agricultural export subsidies and reduce domestic subsidies.
- Open service sectors (many of which are currently closed to foreign firms), including distribution, value-added telecommunications, insurance, banking, securities, and professional services (including legal, accountancy, taxation, management consultancy, architecture, engineering, urban planning, medical and dental, and computer-related services). China would expand (over various transitional periods) the scope of allowed services and gradually remove geographically restrictions of foreign service providers. The amount of permitted

foreign ownership in service industries would vary (and in some cases expand over time) from sector to sector.

- Reduce restrictions on auto trade. Tariffs on autos reduced from 80-100% to 25% (tariffs on auto parts reduced to an average rate of 10%) by 2006. Auto quotas would be eliminated by 2005. U.S. financial firms would be allowed to provide financing for the purchase of cars in China.
- Provide fair treatment for foreign-invested firms in China, including the elimination of government policies that require technology transfer, local content, and export performance levels.
- Provide that Chinese state-owned firms make purchases and sales based on commercial considerations and give U.S. firms the opportunity to compete for sales on a non-discriminatory basis.
- Accept the use by the United States of certain safeguard, countervailing, and antidumping provisions (over transitionary periods) to respond to possible surges in U.S. imports from China of various products, such as textiles, that might cause or threaten to cause market disruption to a U.S. industry.

PNTR Legislation in the 106th Congress

The Clinton Administration and many trade analysts argued that, in order to ensure that U.S. exporters and investors gain the full benefits of China's accession to the WTO, legislation to grant permanent normal trade relations (PNTR) status to China had to be enacted (prior to China's accession); currently that status is renewed annually. Such legislation (H.R. 4444.) was passed by the 106th Congress and became law on October 10, 2000 (P.L. 106-286), The Act grants PNTR status to China upon its accession to the WTO, provided that the President first certify that the WTO accession agreement for China is no less favorable than the November 1999 U.S.-China bilateral trade agreement. Other provisions were included to respond to various congressional concerns. The Act:

- established a special congressional-executive commission to monitor and report on various aspects of China's policies on human rights, including labor practices and religious freedom;
- requires the USTR to annually issue a report assessing China's compliance with its WTO trade obligations;
- codified the anti-surge mechanism established under the November 1999 U.S.-China trade agreement and establish procedures for obtaining relief from import surges;
- authorized increased funding for U.S. government agencies to monitor and seek enforcement of China's compliance with its WTO trade commitments;
- mandated the establishment of a special government task force to halt U. S. imports from China of products suspected of using prison labor; and
- authorized funding for programs to promote the rule of law in China.

Outlook for China's WTO Accession

In September 2001, China completed its multilateral negotiations with the WTO Working Party handling its accession application and reached a trade agreement with Mexico, the last of the original 37 WTO members that requested a bilateral trade agreement with China. China's WTO membership (as well as that of Taiwan's) will likely be formally approved at the next WTO Ministerial Conference in Doha, Qatar in November 2001. China can then officially join the WTO 30 days after it has formally adopted the WTO trade agreements. This indicates that China will likely join the WTO by early 2002.

LEGISLATION

The 107th Congress will likely press the Bush Administration to ensure China's compliance with its WTO commitments (if and when it accedes). The required annual report by the USTR on China's WTO implementation could become the focal point of potential congressional concerns over China's compliance. If U.S. exports fail to increase significantly and the USTR's report finds serious problems with China's compliance, Congress may press the Administration to file dispute resolution cases against China in the WTO.

Chapter 16

CHINA-U.S. TRADE ISSUES

Wayne M. Morrison

SUMMARY

U.S.-China economic ties have expanded substantially over the past several years; total U.S.-China trade rose from $5 billion in 1980 to an estimated $122 billion in 2001; China is now the fourth-largest U.S. trading partner. Yet, U.S.-China commercial relations have been strained by a number of issues, including a surging U.S. trade deficit with China (which hit nearly $85 billion in 2001), China's restrictive trade and investment practices, and its failure to provide adequate protection for U.S. intellectual property rights (IPR).

During the 1990s, the United States actively pressed China to liberalize its trade regime and improve protection of U.S. IPR. Under the threat of U.S, trade sanctions, China signed bilateral trade agreements with the United States on market access (1992) and IPR protection (1992 and 1995). These agreements produced mixed results: market access and IPR protection have significantly improved in China, but U.S. firms continue to face numerous trade barriers, and IPR piracy remains a serious problem in China.

In recent years, the United States has sought to use China's application to join the World Trade Organization (WTO) as a means to gain greater market access in China. The United States insisted that China could join the WTO only if it substantially cut trade and investment barriers. After many years of tough negotiation, China's WTO membership was formally approved by the WTO on November 10, 2001, and on December 11, 2001, it formally became a WTO member.

China's entry into the WTO will require it to significantly reform its trade regime by eliminating or reducing an extensive array of tariff and non-tariff barriers on goods, services, and foreign investment. The removal of these barriers could result in significant new opportunities for U.S. exporters.

In order to ensure that the WTO agreements would fully apply between the United States and China (once China joined the WTO), the 106th Congress passed legislation (H.R. 4444, P.L. 106-286) authorizing the President to grant China permanent normal trade relations (PNTR) status after it joined the WTO (the President extended PNTR status to China on December 27, 2001). The Act also requires the U.S. Trade Representative (USTR) to annually issue a report assessing China's compliance with its WTO trade obligations. Finally, the Act and established a special Congressional-Executive Commission to examine China's human rights policies.

In recent years, the United States has sought to use China's application to join the World Trade Organization (WTO) as a means to gain greater market access in China. The United States insisted that China could join the WTO only if it substantially cut trade and investment barriers. After many years of tough negotiations, China's WTO membership was formally approved by the WTO on November 10, 2001, and on December 11,
The 107th Congress will likely press the Bush Administration to closely monitor China's compliance with its WTO commitments. A number of issues regarding China's compliance have already arisen. The required annual report by the USTR on China's WTO implementation will likely become the focal point of potential congressional concerns over China's compliance.

MOST RECENT DEVELOPMENTS

On December 27, 2001, President Bush issued a proclamation extended PNTR status to China, effective January 1, 2002.

On December 11, 2001, China formally joined the WTO.

On November 10 2001, President Bush certified that China's WTO accession agreement satisfied the conditions set by Congress for extending PNTR status to China.

BACKGROUND AND ANALYSIS

U.S. Trade with China

U.S.-China trade rose rapidly after the two nations established diplomatic relations (January 1979), signed a bilateral trade agreement (July 1979), and provided mutual MFN treatment beginning in 1980. Total trade (exports plus imports) between the two nations rose from \$4.8 billion in 1980 to an estimated \$122.4 billion in 2001 – making China the 4th largest U.S. trading partner (see **Table 1**). The U.S. trade deficit with China has grown significantly in recent years, due largely to a surge in U.S. imports of Chinese goods relative to U.S. exports to China. That deficit has rose from \$3.5 billion in 1988 to \$83.8 billion in 2000. China is now the largest deficit trading partner of the United States.

U.S. trade data for January-November 2001 indicate that the U.S. trade deficit with China in 2001 was likely slightly above 2000 levels, at about \$85 billion. The sharp slowdown in the rate of growth in the U.S.-China trade imbalance was due mainly to a sharp decline in the rate of growth in U.S. demand for Chinese imports, caused mainly by the slowdown in the U.S. economy that has occurred since early 2001.

Table 1. U.S. Merchandise Trade with China: 1988-2001
($ in billions)

Year	U.S. Exports	U.S. Imports	U.S. Trade Balance
1988	5.0	8.5	-3.5
1989	5.8	12.0	-6.2
1990	4.8	15.2	-10.4
1991	6.3	19.0	-12.7
1992	7.5	25.7	-18.2
1993	8.8	31.5	-22.8
1994	9.3	38.8	-29.5
1995	11.7	45.6	-33.8
1996	12.0	51.5	-39.5
1997	12.8	62.6	-49.7
1998	14.3	71.2	-56.9
1999	13.1	81.2	-68.7
2000	16.3	100.1	-83.8
2001 (estimate)	18.9	103.5	-84.6

Source: U.S. Department of Commerce. Data for 2001 are estimates based on partial year data.

Major U.S. Exports to China

U.S. exports to China in 2000 totaled $16.3 billion, accounting for 2.1% of total U.S. exports to the world; and making China the 11th largest market for U.S. exports (see **Table 2**). The top five U.S. exports to China in 2000 (2001 data are not yet available) were electrical machinery, transport equipment (mainly aircraft and parts), office machines (e.g., computers), oilseeds, and general industrial machinery and equipment. Together, these five commodities accounted for about 42% of total U.S. exports to China in 2000. U.S. exports to China in 2000 were nearly 24% higher than 1999 levels. Much of that increase was accounted for by a surge in U.S. exports of oilseeds and computers.

Many trade analysts argue that China could prove to be a significant market for U.S. exports in the future. China is one of the world's fastest growing economies and rapid economic growth is likely to continue in the near future, provided that economic reforms are continued. China's goal of modernizing its infrastructure and upgrading its industries is predicted to generate substantial demand for foreign goods and services. Chinese officials predict that such needs will generate $1.5 trillion in increased imports from 1999-2005.

Table 2. Top 5 U.S. Exports to China: 1996-2000
($ in millions)

SITC Commodity Groupings	1996	1997	1998	1999	2000	1999/2000 % Change
Total All Commodities	11,978	12,805	14,258	13,118	16,253	23.9
Electrical machinery, apparatus and appliances, and parts	583	741	1,014	1,381	1,747	26.5
Transport equipment (mainly aircraft and parts)	1,725	2,129	3,605	2,326	1,698	-27.0
Office machines and automatic data processing machines	266	344	879	843	1,498	77.8
Oilseeds	422	419	288	354	1,020	188.0
General industrial machinery & equipment and parts	755	767	674	685	839	22.4
Total Top 5	3,771	4,400	6,460	5,589	6,802	21.7

Commodities sorted by top exports in 2000.
Source: U.S. Department of Commerce.

According to a U.S. Department of Commerce report: "China's unmet infrastructural needs are staggering. Foreign capital, expertise, and equipment will have to be brought in if China is to build all the ports, roads, bridges, airports, power plants, telecommunications networks and rail lines that it needs." Finally, economic growth has substantially improved the purchasing power of Chinese citizens, especially those living in urban areas along the east coast of China. It is projected that by the year 2005, China will have more than 230 million middle-income consumers (i.e., those earning $1,000 or more annually), whose combined retail spending will exceed $900 billion. If achieved, this would likely make China the world's largest market for consumer goods and services and a major market for luxury goods.

Major U.S. Imports from China

China is a relatively large source of many U.S. imports, especially labor-intensive products. In 2000, imports from China totaled $100.1 billion, accounting for 8.0% of total U.S. imports, and making China the 4th largest supplier of U.S. imports. U.S. imports from China in 2000 rose by 22.3% over 1999 levels. The top five U.S. imports from China in 2000 were miscellaneous manufactured articles (such as toys, games, etc.); office machines; telecommunications equipment, sound recording, and reproducing equipment (such as telephone answering machines, radios, tape recorders and players, televisions, VCRs, etc.); footwear; and electrical machinery (see Table 3). Together, imports of these five commodities accounted for nearly 59% of total U.S. imports from China in 2000.

Table 3. Top 5 U.S. imports From China: 1996-2000
($ in millions)

SITC Commodity Groupings	1996	1997	1998	1999	2000	1999/2000 % Change
Total All Commodities	51,495	62,552	71,156	81,786	100,063	22.3
Miscellaneous manufactured articles (e.g., toys, games, etc.)	11,857	14,176	15,543	17,273	19,441	33.2
Office machines and automatic data processing machines	3,579	5,044	6,360	8,259	11,000	33.2
Telecommunication & sound record & reproduce app. & equip.	4,552	5,220	6,546	7,502	9,935	32.4
Footwear	6,392	7,415	8,008	8,434	9,195	9.0
Electrical machinery, apparatus and appliances, and parts	3,903	4,922	5,776	7,062	9,119	29.1
Total Top 5	30,282	36,777	42,534	48,529	58,690	20.9

Commodities sorted by top 5 imports in 2000.
Source: U.S. Department of Commerce.

CHINA'S ECONOMY

China's economic reforms and open investment policies (which were begun in 1978) have contributed to a surge in economic growth. From 1979 to 2000, China's real GDP grew at an average annual rate of 9.4%, making it one of the world's fastest growing economies; real GDP grew by 7.2% in 2000. Many economists predict that, if China continues to implement economic reforms, its annual real GDP growth will likely average at least 7% over the next two decades, enabling China to double the size of its economy every 10 years.

China has quickly become a major recipient of foreign direct investment (FDI), a key factor in its rapid economic growth. Much of that investment has gone into export-oriented production facilities. Annual utilized FDI in China grew from $636 million in 1983 to about $47 billion in 2001. There are now 390,000 foreign-invested firms in China; the cumulative level of FDI in China at the end of 2001 totaled $395.5 billion. A significant share of FDI in China has come from overseas Chinese, especially Hong Kong and Taiwan. The United States is the second largest investor in China. Major U.S. corporate investors in China include Motorola, Atlantic Richfield, Coca Cola, Amoco, United Technologies, Pepsi Cola, Lucent Technologies, General Electric, General Motors, and Ford Motor Company.

China has quickly become a major world trading power. Total Chinese trade (exports plus imports) rose from $21 billion in 1978 to $509 billion in 2001. Chinese exports in 2001 were $266 billion, imports were $244 billion, producing a $22 billion trade surplus. Large foreign investment and the surging exports have enabled China to accumulate a significant level of foreign exchange reserves, which reached $203 billion in October 2001.

MAJOR U.S.-CHINA TRADE ISSUES

While China's economic reforms and rapid economic growth have expanded U.S.-China commercial relations in recent years, disputes have arisen over a wide variety of issues, including, China's failure to provide adequate protection of U.S. intellectual property rights (IPR), the widespread and pervasive use by China of trade and investment barriers, China's alleged use of prison labor for various exported products to the United States, and the conditions for China's accession to the World Trade Organization (WTO).

Violations of U.S. Intellectual Property Rights

Section 182 of the Trade Act of 1974 as amended (also known as "Special 301"), requires the USTR to identify "priority foreign countries" that fail to provide adequate and effective protection of U.S. intellectual property rights (IPR), such as patents, copyrights, trademarks, and trade secrets, or deny fair and equitable market access to U.S. firms that rely on IPR protection. The USTR is directed to seek negotiations with the priority foreign countries to end such violations and, if necessary, to impose trade sanctions if such negotiations fail to produce an agreement.

In April 1991, China (along with India and Thailand) was named as a "priority foreign country" under Special 301. The USTR began a Section 301 investigation in May 1991, claiming China's laws failed to provide adequate protection of patents, copyrights, and trade secrets. In November 1991, the USTR threatened to impose $1.5 billion in trade sanctions if an IPR agreement was not reached by January 1992. Last-minute negotiations yielded an agreement on January 16, 1992. China promised to strengthen its patent, copyright, and trade secret laws, and to improve protection of U.S. intellectual property, especially computer software, sound recordings, chemicals, and pharmaceuticals.

In June 1994, the USTR again designated China as a Special 301 "priority foreign country," because it had failed to enforce recently enacted IPR laws. In particular, the USTR cited the establishment of several factories in China producing pirated compact and laser disks, as an example of China's "egregious" violation of U.S. IPR. In addition, the USTR stated that trade barriers had restricted access to China's market for U.S. movies, videos, and sound recordings, and that such restrictions encouraged piracy of such products in China. On February 4, 1995, the USTR announced that insufficient progress had been made in talks with Chinese officials and issued a list of Chinese products, with an estimated value of $1.1 billion, which would be subject to 100% import tariffs. However, a preliminary agreement was reached on February 26, 1995, and a formal agreement was signed on March 11, 1995. The new agreement pledged China to substantially beef up its IPR enforcement regime and to remove various import and investment barriers to IPR-related products. Specifically, China agreed to:

Take immediate steps to stem IPR piracy in China over the course of the next 3 months by taking action against large-scale producers and distributors of pirated materials, and prohibiting the export of pirated products.

Establish mechanisms to ensure long-term enforcement of IPR laws, such as banning the use of pirated materials by the Chinese government, establishing a coordinated IPR enforcement policy among each level of government, beefing up IPR enforcement agencies, creating an effective customs enforcement system, establishing a title verification system in China to ensure that U.S. audio visual works are protected against unauthorized use, reforming China's judicial system to ensure that U.S. firms can obtain access to effective judicial relief, establishing a system of maintaining statistics concerning China's enforcement efforts and meeting with U.S. officials on a regular basis to discuss those efforts, improving transparency in Chinese laws concerning IPR, and strictly enforcing IPR laws.

Provide greater market access to U.S. products by removing import quotas on U.S. audio visual products, allowing U.S. record companies to market their entire works in China (subject to Chinese censorship concerns), and allowing U.S. intellectual property-related industries to enter into joint production arrangements with Chinese firms in certain cities.

Several U.S. firms charged that IPR piracy in China worsened in 1995, despite the 1995 IPR agreement, and pressed the USTR to take tougher action against China. The International Intellectual Property Alliance (IIPA), an association of major U.S. copyright-based industries, estimated that IPR piracy by Chinese firms cost U.S. firms $2.3 billion in lost trade during 1995.

On April 30, 1996, the USTR again designated China as a Special 301 "priority foreign country" for not fully complying with the February 1995 IPR agreement. According to the USTR, while China had cracked down on piracy at the retail level (launching raids and destroying millions of pirated CDs and hundreds of thousands of pirated books, sound recordings, and computer software), it had failed to take effective action against an estimated 30 or so factories in China that were mass-producing and exporting pirated products. U.S. officials called on the Chinese government to close such factories, prosecute violators, and destroy equipment used in the production of pirated products. Further, the USTR stated that China failed to establish an effective border enforcement mechanism within its customs service to prevent the export of pirated products. Finally, The USTR indicated that China failed to provide sufficient market access to U.S. firms, due to high tariffs, quotas, and regulatory restrictions. Shortly after, the USTR indicated it would impose U.S. sanctions on $2 billion worth of Chinese products by June 17, 1996, unless China took more effective action to fully implement the IPR agreement. On June 17, 1996, USTR Charlene Barshefsky announced that the United States was satisfied that China was taking steps to fulfill the 1995 IPR agreement. Barshefsley cited the Chinese government's recent closing of 15 plants producing illegal CDs and China's pledge to extend a period of focused enforcement of anti-piracy regulations against regions of particularly rampant piracy, such as Guangdong Province. The Chinese government also promised to improve border enforcement to halt exports of pirated products as well as illegal imports of presses used to manufacture CDs. Further, the Chinese government reaffirmed its pledge to open up its market to imports of IPR-related products. Finally, Chinese officials promised to improve monitoring and verification efforts to ensure that products made by Chinese CD plants and publishing houses are properly licensed.

The USTR has stated that China has made great strides in improving its IPR protection regime, noting that it has passed several new IPR-related laws, closed or fined 74 assembly operations for illegal production lines, seized millions of illegal audio-visual products, curtailed exports of pirated products, expanded training of judges and law enforcement officials on IPR protection, and has expanded legitimate licensing of film and music production in China. In April 1999, the USTR announced that the Chinese government had issued a new high-level directive to all Chinese government entities directing that they use only legitimate computer software, a move described by the USTR as a "milestone in China's efforts to increase intellectual property protection."

The USTR notes, however, that IPR piracy remains a serious problem in China, especially illegal reproduction of software, retail piracy, and trademark counterfeiting. Chinese enforcement agencies and judicial system often lack the resources needed to vigorously enforce IPR laws; convicted IPR offenders generally face minor penalties. In addition, while market access for IPR-related products has improved, high tariffs, quotas, and other barriers continue to hamper U.S. exports; such trade barriers are believed to be partly responsible for illegal IPR-related smuggling and counterfeiting in China. The IIPA estimated that IPR piracy in China cost U.S. firms $1.7 billion in lost sales in 1999—an improvement over 1998 losses, which were estimated at $2.6 billion.

Major Chinese Trade Barriers

For many U.S. firms, China remains a difficult market to penetrate, due largely to Chinese government policies, which attempt to protect and promote domestic industries. Chinese trade policies generally attempt to encourage imports of products, which are deemed beneficial to China's economic development and growth (and which are generally are not produced in China), such as high technology, as well as machinery and raw materials used in the manufacture of products for export. In many cases, preferential trade policies are used to encourage these priority imports. Goods and services not considered to be high priority, or which compete directly with domestic Chinese firms, often face an extensive array of tariff and non-tariff barriers. Such policies make it difficult to export products directly to China. As a result, many U.S. firms have established production facilities in China to gain access to the China market. However, foreign-invested firms in China face a wide variety of barriers as well. U.S. government officials maintain that China's restrictive trade and investment policies are a leading cause of the surging U.S.-China trade imbalance. Major Chinese barriers of concern include:

- *High tariffs*. The simple average Chinese tariff rate is currently 15% (down from an average rate of 42% in 1992), but tariffs on selected items, such as autos and various agricultural products, can rise to 100% or more.
- *Pervasive non-tariff barriers* are arbitrarily used to control the level of certain imports into China, including quotas, import licenses, registration and certification requirements, and restrictive technical and sanitary standards (especially in respect to agricultural products).

- *Non-transparent trade rules and regulations*. China's trade laws and regulations are often secretly formulated, unpublished, unevenly enforced, and may vary across provinces, making it difficult for exporters to determine what rules and regulations apply to their products. In addition, foreign firms find it difficult to gain access to government trade rule-making agencies to appeal new trade rules and regulations.
- *Trading rights*. China restricts the number and types of entities in China that are allowed to import products into China, which limits the ability of both Chinese and foreign firms in China to obtain imported products. Foreign companies are not permitted to directly engage in trade in China. In addition, trading rights for many agricultural products are given exclusively to Chinese state trading companies, which are directed to import only if there is a domestic shortfall of certain products.
- *Distribution rights*. Most foreign companies are prohibited from selling their products directly to Chinese consumers.
- *Investment restrictions*. Chinese officials pressure foreign investors to agree to contract provisions, which stipulate technology transfers, exporting a certain share of production, and commitments on local content. Other problems faced by foreign firms in China include the denial of national treatment (i.e., foreign firms are treated less favorably than domestic firms), foreign exchange controls, distribution mad marketing restrictions, and the lack of rule of law.

In October 1991, the Bush Administration initiated a Section 301 case against four significant unfair trading practices affecting U.S. exports to China: tariff and non-tariff barriers to certain products, restrictive import license requirements, technical barriers to trade (such as discriminatory standards for agricultural products), and non-transparency in Chinese trade laws. The Section 301 case was the most sweeping market access investigation in the USTR's history; it was essentially aimed at reforming China's entire trade regime.

On August 21, 1992, the USTR determined that negotiations had failed to resolve the trade dispute and threatened to impose $3.9 billion in U.S. trade sanctions unless an agreement was reached by October 10, 1992. The proposed sanctions were (at that time) the highest level ever issued by the USTR under a Section 301 case. On October 10, 1992, the United States and China reached an agreement settling the Section 301 case. China pledged to reduce or eliminate a wide variety of trade barriers over the next five years (according to specific timetables), including tariffs, quotas, import controls, import licenses, and import substitution laws. In addition, China agreed to make its trade regime more transparent by publishing trade laws and regulations. Finally, China agreed to eliminate scientific standards and testing barriers to agricultural imports.

The market access agreement was supposed to have been fully implemented by the end of 1997. USTR officials noted that China made significant reforms to its trade regime as specified under the trade agreement. However, in some cases, China eliminated certain trade barriers, only to impose new barriers (such as certification requirements for certain products). In addition, China failed to fully eliminate discriminatory sanitary regulations on several imported food products. Finally, while China began to more regularly publish its trade laws and regulations, lack of transparency remained a problem for many foreign firms. For example, China has not published many of its quota levels.

Prison Labor Exports

Some analysts charge that the use of forced labor is widespread and a long-standing practice in China and that such labor is used to produce exports, a large portion of which may be targeted to the United States. The importation from any country of commodities produced through the use of forced labor is prohibited by U.S. law, although obtaining proof of actual violations for specific imported products is often extremely difficult.

On August 7, 1992, the United States and China signed a Memorandum of Understanding (MOU) to ensure that prison labor products were not exported to the United States. However, U.S. disputes with China over its implementation of the MOU led to the signing of a "statement of cooperation" (SOC) on March 14, 1994, which included provisions which clarify procedures for U.S. officials to gain access to Chinese production facilities suspected of exporting prison labor products. President Clinton's May 1994 report to Congress on renewing China's MFN status stated that China had generally abided by the agreements on prison labor. However, the U.S. Department of State's *China Country Report on Human Rights Practices for 1998* states that: "Although the signing of the SOC initially helped foster a more productive relationship between the U.S. Customs and Chinese authorities, cooperation overall has been inadequate." According to the 2000 State Department Human Rights report, during 1999, the U.S. Customs Service unsuccessfully pursued several standing requests to visit eight sites suspected of exporting prison labor products (one of which dated back to 1992, and several dating back to 1994), and renewed requests (several dating back to 1994) for the Chinese Ministry of Justice to investigate seven factories and three penal facilities for evidence of prison labor exports. The Justice Ministry did not respond to any of these requests. On February 28, 2001, U.S. Customs announced that it had seized and destroyed 24 million binder clips (valued at $2 million) that were documented as having been made in China using prison labor.

China and the World Trade Organization

Negotiations for China's accession to the General Agreement on Tariffs and Trade (GATT), and now WTO (the successor organization to the GATT), have gone on for 15 years. Chinese leaders have stated that gaining entry into the World Trade Organization (WTO) is a major Chinese priority. They believe that WTO membership would enable China to gain full nondiscriminatory treatment in its trade relations with WTO members (especially the United States) and provide it access to the multilateral trade dispute resolution process. Supporters of China's WTO membership argue that it would bring China's trade regime in line with other WTO members and would result in a significant reduction of Chinese trade barriers. Negotiations on China's WTO membership are being held on two fronts: multilateral negotiations in a Working Party composed of all interested WTO members and bilateral negotiations between China and individual WTO members. At issue have been the specific steps China would be required to take to gain accession to the WTO.

Background on U.S.-China WTO Talks

China and the United States reportedly made significant progress towards resolving major differences in their bilateral WTO negotiations during Chinese Premier Zhu Rongji's meeting with President Clinton on April 8, 1999. According to U.S. officials, China offered to cut tariffs significantly and remove non-tariff barriers on U.S. trade in agriculture, industrial goods, and services, and to eliminate various restrictions on foreign investment, Wading rights, and distribution for U.S. firms in China. Separately, China agreed to eliminate unjustified sanitary and phytosanitary (SPS) bans on wheat, citrus, and beef immediately.

Although the Clinton Administration stated that China's market access offer would bring China into the WTO at above existing WTO standards on issues and sectors of major concern to the U.S., it concluded that an agreement could not be finalized until certain outstanding issues could be resolved, namely market access in China for banking, securities, and audio visual services, and safeguard provisions on potential import surges. However, the United States and China did reach an agreement (the Bilateral Agricultural Cooperation Agreement) under which China agreed to remove technical barriers to trade (such SPS restrictions) on U.S. meat, citrus, and wheat exports to China.

On April 13, 1999, the two sides agreed to intensify negotiations towards reaching a final agreement. However, following the accidental NATO bombing of the Chinese embassy in Belgrade on May 7, 1999, China suspended the WTO talks (as well as its implementation of the bilateral agreements on wheat, citrus, and beef). These talks were officially resumed on September 11, 1999, during a meeting between President Clinton and Chinese President Jiang Zemin in New Zealand.

The U.S.-China WTO Agreement

On November 15, 1999, U.S. and Chinese officials announced that a bilateral agreement relating to China's WTO bid was reached. The Clinton Administration released the full text of the agreement on March 14, 2000. Under the agreement, China promised that after gaining WTO membership it would take the following steps (some on accession and others over specified phase-in periods):

- Provide full trading and distribution rights (including the ability to provide services auxiliary to distribution) for U.S. firms in China.
- Cut average tariffs for U.S. priority agriculture products (beef, grapes, wine, cheese, poultry, and pork) from 31.5% to 14.5% by 2004. Overall, industrial tariffs would fall from an average of 24.6% to 9.4% by 2005 (tariffs on U.S. "priority products," such as wood, paper, chemicals, and capital and medical equipment, would fall even further). Tariffs on information technology products, such as computers, semiconductors, and telecommunications equipment, would be cut from an average level of 13.3% to zero by 2005.
- Establish a tariff-rate quota system for imports of agricultural bulk commodities (such as wheat, corn, cotton, barley, and rice), i.e., imports up to a specified quota level would be assessed a low tariff (1-3%), while imports above a certain level would be assessed a much higher tariff rate. Private trade in agricultural products would be permitted for the first time.

- Phase out quotas and other quantitative restrictions (some upon accession, many within two years, and most within five years). Quota levels for many products would expand by 15% each year until the elimination of the quota.
- Eliminate unscientifically based SPS restrictions on agricultural products and end export subsidies.
- Open service sectors (many of which are currently closed to foreign firms), including distribution, value-added telecommunications, insurance, banking, securities, and professional services (including legal, accountancy, taxation, management consultancy, architecture, engineering, urban planning, medical and dental, and computer-related services). China would expand (over various transitional periods) the scope of allowed services and gradually remove geographical restrictions on foreign service providers. The amount of permitted foreign ownership in service industries would vary (and in some cases expand over time) from sector to sector.
- Reduce restrictions on auto trade. Tariffs on autos would fall from 80-100% to 25% (tariffs on auto parts reduced to an average rate of 10%) by 2006. Auto quotas would be eliminated by 2005. U.S. financial firms would be allowed to provide financing for the purchase of cars in China.
- Provide fair treatment for foreign firms operating in China by removing government rules requiring technology transfer, local content, and export performance conditions.
- Provide that Chinese state-owned firms make purchases and sales based on commercial considerations and give U.S. firms the opportunity to compete for sales on a non-discriminatory basis.
- Accept the use by the United States of certain safeguard, countervailing, and antidumping provisions (over transitionary periods) to respond to possible surges in U.S. imports from China of various products, such as textiles, that might cause or threaten to cause market disruption to a U.S. industry.

China Joins the WTO

On September 13, 2001, China concluded a WTO bilateral trade agreement with Mexico, the last of the original 37 WTO members that had requested such an accord. On September 17, 2001, the WTO Working Party handling China's WTO application announced that it had resolved all outstanding issues regarding China's WTO accession. On November 10, 2001, China's WTO membership was formally approved at the WTO Ministerial Conference in Doha, Qatar on November 10, 2001 (Taiwan's WTO membership was approved the next day). On November 11, 2001, China notified the WTO that it had formally ratified the WTO agreements, which enabled China to enter the WTO on December 11, 2001.

Major aspects of China's WTO accession agreement include the following:

- China will bind all tariffs. The average tariff for industrial goods will fall to 8.9% (and range from 0 to 47%) and to 15% for agriculture (and range from 0 to 65%). Most tariff cuts will be made by 2004; all cuts will occur by 2010.
- China will limit subsidies for agricultural production to 8.5% and will not maintain export subsidies on agricultural exports.
- Within three years of accession, China will grant full trade and distribution rights to foreign enterprises (with some exceptions, such as for certain agricultural products, minerals, and fuels).

- China will provide non-discriminatory treatment to all WTO members. Foreign firms will be treated no less favorably than Chinese farms for trade purposes. Duel pricing practices will be eliminated as well as differences in the treatment of goods produced in China for the domestic market as oppose to those goods produced for export. Price controls will not be used to provide protection to Chinese firms.
- China will fully implement the Trade-Related Aspects of Intellectual Property Rights (TRIPs) Agreement upon accession.
- A 12-year safeguard mechanism will be available to other WTO members in cases where a surge in Chinese exports cause or threaten to cause market disruption to domestic producers.
- China's banking system will be fully open to foreign financial institutions within five years. Joint ventures in insurance and telecommunication will be permitted (with various degrees of foreign ownership allowed).

The Relationship between China's NTR Status and WTO Accession

Under current U.S. law, China's normal trade relations (NTR) status (formally referred to in U.S. law as most-favored-nation, or MFN, status) is renewed on an annual basis, based on the freedom-of-emigration requirements under the so-called Jackson-Vanik amendment, and subject to possible congressional disapproval through passage and enactment of a joint resolution. From 1980 (when NTR status was restored to China after being suspended in 1951) to 1989, the renewal of China's NTR status was relatively non-controversial and was relatively unopposed by Congress. However, congressional concern over the Tiananmen Square incident in 1989 and subsequent crackdown on human rights led many Members to support legislation terminating the extension of China's NTR status or to condition that status on additional requirements, mainly dealing with human fights. Although none of these measures were enacted, many Members sought to use the annual renewal of China's NTR status as a focal point to express concerns, as well as to pressure the executive branch, over a wide range of Chinese trade (e.g., trade barriers and failure to protect IPR) and non-trade (e.g., human rights, prison labor, Taiwan security, and weapons proliferation) issues. Several members opposed such linkage, arguing that it had little effect on Chinese policies and that the often rancorous congressional debate over China's trade status undermined long-term U.S.-Chinese relations and added uncertainty to the trade relationship.

During its negotiations with China over the terms of its WTO accession, the Clinton Administration pledged that, in return for significant market opening commitments on the part of China, it would press the Congress to enact PNTR legislation. Once a satisfactory bilateral agreement was reached with China in November 1999, the Clinton Administration began to push for PNTR legislation.

The Clinton Administration and its supporters argued that China would get into the WTO with or without congressional approval of PNTR status for China, and that failure to pass such legislation would prevent the United States and China from having an official trade relationship in the WTO. As a result, it was contended, U.S. firms would be excluded from the trade concessions made by China to gain entry into the WTO, while U.S. competitors in the WTO would be able to take full advantage of new business opportunities in China, and the United States would be unable to use the WTO dispute resolution process to resolve trade disputes with China. The Clinton Administration further maintained that China's accession to the WTO would promote U.S. economic and strategic interests, namely by inducing China to deepen market reforms, promote the rule of law, reduce the government's role in the economy, and further integrate China into the world economy, malting it a more reliable and stable partner. Finally, the Administration contended that congressional rejection of PNTR would be viewed by the Chinese as an attempt to isolate China economically; such a move would seriously damage U.S.-China commercial relations and undermine the political position of economic reformers in China.

Despite these arguments and strong lobbying by various U.S. business interests, passage of China PNTR was highly uncertain when Congress began consideration of legislation in May 2000. Many Members raised concerns over the effects China' s WTO membership would have on U.S. import sensitive industries, while others expressed reservations over giving up what they perceived as leverage over China's human rights policies. The Clinton Administration and congressional supporters of PNTR legislation sought to craft a compromise that would gain support of undecided members without alienating members who wanted a "clean" PNTR bill.

H.R. 4444, as originally introduced by Representative Bill Archer, would have granted PNTR status to China upon its accession to the WTO as long as the President certified that the terms of its accession were at least equivalent to the November 1999 U.S.-China trade agreement. Several provisions were added by the House to H.R. 4444 in response to various congressional concerns. In addition to the provisions contained in the original version of H.R. 4444, the final bill (which passed in the House on May 24, 2000, and in the Senate on September 19, 2000, and signed into law on October 10, 2000):

- established a special Congressional-Executive commission to monitor, and report on, various aspects of China's policies on human rights, including labor practices and religious freedom;
- requires the USTR to issue a report annually assessing China's compliance with its WTO trade obligations;
- codified the anti-surge mechanism established under the November 1999 U.S.-China trade agreement and establishes procedures for obtaining relief from import surges;
- authorized additional funding for various U.S. government agencies to monitor and seek enforcement of China's compliance with its WTO trade commitments;
- set up a special government task force to halt U.S. imports from China of products suspected of using prison labor; and
- authorized funding for programs to promote the development of the rule of law in China.

On November 10, 2001, President Bush certified that the terms of China's WTO accession agreement were at least equivalent to the November 1999 U.S.-China trade agreement, and on December 27, 2001, he issued a proclamation extending PNTR status to China, effective January 1, 2002.

Outlook for U.S.-China Trade Relations

China's entry into the WTO and a U.S. extension of PNTR to China are likely to have important ramifications for U.S.-China economic relations. First, Congress will no longer vote annually on China's trade status, which could help bring greater stability and predictability to the relationship than has been the case over the past several years. Second, the United States (as well as China) will be able to use the WTO dispute resolution process to resolve trade disputes. Many analysts believe China would more likely comply with a ruling from a multilateral institution than from a threat of unilateral U.S. sanctions. Third, subjecting China's trade regime to multilateral rules and agreements will mean that the United States would no longer have to "go it alone" in trying to get China to open its markets; other WTO members would have an equally strong stake in ensuring China's compliance with its WTO commitments. Finally, China's accession to the WTO will likely improve the business climate in China, leading to greater trade and investment opportunities for U.S. firms. A sizable increase in U.S. exports to China would help reduce tensions over trade issues.

Many analysts have raised concern over the ability of the Chinese government to fully implement its WTO commitments once it obtains membership. Corruption and local protectionism are rampant in China, and gaining the cooperation of local officials and government bureaucrats that oversee various affected industries could prove difficult in the short run. In addition, economic reforms required under WTO commitments could lead to significant employment disruptions, especially among farmers and employees of inefficient state-owned enterprises. Some analysts warn that such disruptions might erode the government's determination to fully implement its WTO commitments, especially if it fears social stability is threatened. A number of disputes have already arisen. For example, in June 2001, China announced it would soon implement new rules on bio-engineered foods. China did not provide details of these rules and reportedly tightened inspection and quarantine procedures, which led to a disruption in U.S. soybean exports to China. President Bush raised the issue with Chinese President Jiang Zemin in October 2001, which led China to agree to the interim use of U.S. and foreign certificates until China implements its new biotechnology regulations. Some analysts charge that China is attempting to limit soybean imports in order to protect its domestic producers. Another dispute occurred in November 2001, when the Chinese government reportedly developed new rules on tariff rate quotas on certain agricultural products that the U.S. charged were discriminatory and violated WTO rules because they created two categories of quota licenses to China.

Congress will likely continue to play an active role in U.S.-China commercial relations. For example, it will likely press the Bush Administration to ensure China's trade compliance with its WTO commitments after its accession. The required annual report by the USTR on China's WTO implementation will likely become the focal point of potential Congressional concerns over China's compliance. If U.S. exports fail to increase significantly, and the USTR's report finds serious problems with China's compliance, Congress may press the Administration to file dispute resolution cases against China in the WTO.

Congressional Members concerned with China's human rights conditions will likely focus their attention on the Congressional-Executive commission on China, which will monitor China's human rights policies and maintain a "victim's list" of citizens suffering from various abuses. The commission will issue annual reports to Congress, including findings and recommendations. The House International Relations Committee will be required to hold hearings on the content of the report. Members may seek to use this process to focus attention on China's human rights abuses, and possibly to develop legislative responses to such abuses. The Chinese government would likely respond negatively to the findings of the commission (and any subsequent action by Congress); it has tended to treat pressure over its human rights policies as interference in its internal affairs.

Chapter 17

U.S.-CHINA TRADE AND COMMERCIAL RELATIONS

Wayne M. Morrison

ISSUE

China's trade reforms and rapid economic growth have made it an increasingly important U.S. trade partner. However, U.S.-Chinese commercial relations have experienced friction over a variety of issues, including a growing trade imbalance, Chinese trade barriers, the lack of protection for U.S. intellectual property rights (IPR), and the terms for China's accession to the World Trade Organization (WTO).

BACKGROUND

U.S.-China Merchandise Trade

Total trade between the two nations has boomed, rising from $4.8 billion in 1980 to $116.4 billion in 2000; China is currently the fourth largest U.S. trading palmer. China in 2000 was the 4th largest supplier of U.S. imports and the 11th largest buyer of U.S. exports. U.S. imports from China have surged in recent years relative to U.S. exports to China. As a result, the U.S. trade deficit with China grew from $10.4 billion in 1990 to $83.8 billion in 2000 (see: Table 1). The U.S. trade deficit with China is now larger than that of any other U.S. trading partner, including Japan.

Table 1. U.S. Merchandise Trade with China: 1990-2000
($ Billions)

Year	U.S. Exports	U.S. Imports	U.S. Trade Balance
1990	4.8	15.2	-10.4
1991	6.3	19.0	-12.7
1992	7.5	25.7	-18.2
1993	8.8	31.5	-22.8
1994	9.3	38.8	-29.5
1995	11.7	45.6	-33.8
1996	12.0	51.5	-39.5
1997	12.8	62.6	-49.7
1998	14.3	71.2	-56.9
1999	13.1	81.8	-68.7
2000	16.3	100.0	-83.8

Source: U.S. Department of Commerce.

The United States is the second largest overall foreign direct investor (FDI) in China after Hong Kong. The cumulative value of U.S. FDI in China from 1979 to 2000 was $30.0 billion, accounting for 8.6% of total billion, in China. U.S. FDI in China in 2000 was $4.4 billion, accounting for 10.7% of FDI in that year.

The United States is China's largest export market, and the importance of that market has grown sharply in recent years. Based on U.S. data on Chinese exports to the United States (Chinese data on its exports to the Urged States do not include exports that are transshipped through Hong Kong, and thus sharply differ with U.S. data which include transshipped exports), and Chinese data on its total exports, it is estimated that Chinese exports to the United States as a percentage of total Chinese exports grew from 15% in 1986 to 40% in 2000.

Chinese Trade Barriers and Failure to Protect U.S. Intellectual Property Rights

U.S. trade officials have argued that China's restrictive trade policies are a major cause of the burgeoning U.S. trade deficit with China. For many U.S. firms, China remains a difficult market to penetrate, due largely to Chinese government policies, which attempt to protect and promote domestic industries. Chinese trade policies generally attempt to encourage imports of products that are deemed beneficial to China's economic development and growth (and that are generally are not produced in China), such as high technology, as well as machinery and raw materials used in the manufacture of products for export.

Goods and services not considered to be high priority, or which compete directly with domestic Chinese firms, often face an extensive array of barriers, including high tariffs, pervasive non-tariff barriers (such as quotas, import licenses, registration requirements, and restrictive technical and sanitary standards), lack of protection for IPR, non-transparent trade rules and regulations, and lack of trade and distribution rights. Such policies make it difficult to export products directly to China. As a result, many U.S. firms have established production facilities in China to gain access to the China market, although their Chinese facilities face a wide variety of barriers as well, including, domestic content and technology transfer requirements, investment restrictions, and inadequate protection of IPR. Lack of IPR protection and enforcement measures in China, especially in regards to illegal reproduction of software, retail piracy, and trademark counterfeiting was estimated to cost U.S. firms $2.1 billion in lost sales in 1999.

U.S. concerns over Chinese trade barriers and poor IPR enforcement led the United States on a number of occasions to threaten to impose trade sanctions against China. As a result, China agreed in 1992 to remove non-tariff barriers to certain products, eliminate scientific standards and testing barriers to agricultural imports, and to make its trade regime more transparent. In addition, China agreed in 1992, 1995, and 1996 to take specified steps to improve its IPR enforcement regime. U.S. officials have noted that these agreements have led to greater market access and IPR protection in China, but that compliance with these agreements has been mixed.

China and the World Trade Organization (WTO)

China is seeking to join the WTO, the multilateral organization that sets rules for most trade. U.S. negotiators have sought to use China's WTO accession process to address U.S. concerns over market access and IPR protection in China. U.S. officials have insisted that China should be admitted to the WTO only under "commercially viable terms" that would require it to dismantle most aspects of its protectionist trade regime and abide by multilateral trade rules. They argue that a meaningful reduction in China's trade barriers could make China a significant market for U.S. agricultural products, industrial goods, and services.

On November 15, 1999, the United States and China signed a bilateral agreement on China's WTO bid. China agreed to cut tariffs on agriculture and industrial goods, eliminate various non-tariff barriers (such as quotas), open various service sectors to foreign firms, remove trading rights restrictions, provide distribution rights to foreign firms, remove various investment restrictions and requirements, and accept provisions that would allow the United States to respond to surges in imports from China if they harmed U.S. domestic industries, such as textiles.

In September 2001, China completed its multilateral negotiations with the WTO Working Party handling its accession application and reached a trade agreement with Mexico, the last of the original 37 WTO members that requested a bilateral trade agreement with China. China's WTO membership (as well as that of Taiwan's) will likely be formally approved at the next WTO Ministerial Conference in Doha, Qatar in November 2001. China can then officially join the WTO 30 days after it has formally adopted the WTO trade agreements.

Because China has not yet gained accession to the WTO, President Bush had to issue a waiver (which he did on June 1, 2001) under the Jackson-Vanik amendment in order to extend China's normal trade relations (NTR) status for an additional year.

LEGISLATION

Legislative action on China during the 106th Congress mainly focused on whether to extend PNTR treatment to China. The House passed such legislation (*H.R. 4444*) on May 24, 2000, while the Senate passed the bill on September 19, 2000. The President signed the bill into law on October 10, 2000 (P.L. 106-286). The Act would extend permanent NTR status to China upon its accession to the WTO, subject to a presidential determination that the terms of China's WTO accession are no less favorable than those contained in the November 1999, U.S.-China bilateral trade agreement. The Act also establishes a congressional-executive commission to monitor China's human rights policies, codifies the import surge provisions of the November 1999, U. S-China trade agreement, and requires the USTR to report annually on China's compliance with its WTO commitments.

Three bills in the 107th Congress would affect U.S.-China commercial relations

- H.J.Res. 50 (Rohrabacher) would disapprove the President's June 2001 waiver to extend China's NTR status. On July 12, 2001, the House Ways and Means Committee voted to adversely report out the measure. On July 19, 2001, the measure failed to pass the House (by of vote of 169 to 259).
- H.R. 1467 (Hunter) would terminate China's NTR status.
- H.R. 1497 (Murtha) would revoke the President's authority to extend PNTR to China.

Chapter 18

China and U.S. Agriculture

Charles E. Hanrahan

Issue

The size of China's market for U.S. agricultural products and future prospects for growth in demand make China's accession to the World Trade Organization (WTO) an important issue for U.S. agriculture. U.S. agricultural exports to Chins were an estimated $2.2 billion in fiscal year 2001, making it the United States' sixth largest market for farm products. An additional $1.2 billion of U.S. farm products were shipped to Hong Kong in 2001. Improved economic growth in China has brought U.S. agricultural exports to near the $2.4 billion reached in 1995. In the long run, if growth is strong, as many economists expect, China's 1.3 billion population, and its burgeoning middle class, suggest an enormous potential as a market for U.S. agricultural products.

Background

U.S.-China bilateral negotiations in 1999 over the latter's accession to the WTO resulted in China's agreement, when it becomes a member of the WTO, to make substantial reductions in agricultural tariffs and to establish global market access quote, that should expand trade for several U.S. agricultural products, including soybean products, wheat, rice, corn, barley, and cotton. In addition, China agreed to end its sanitary and phytosanitary barriers (SPS) to U.S. wheat, meat, and citrus exports.

During the 106th Congress, President Clinton requested and Congress passed legislation (*S. 2277; H.R. 4444/P.L. 106-286*) to accord Chins permanent normal trade relations (PNTR) status. This legislation, which extends to China the same low tariffs applied to other member countries of the WTO, will help ensure that the United States can take advantage of market openings for agriculture and other sectors when China enters the WTO. In debate over PNTR, many U.S. agricultural organizations, particularly those representing commercial farmers and agribusinesses, argued that PNTR along with China's accession to the WTO would (according to USDA estimates) potentially increase U.S. farm exports by $1.6 billion by 2005, and thus raise farm prices and incomes. Failure to grant PNTR, they argued, would have ceded these market opportunities to competitors. PNTR opponents were skeptical about China's willingness to open its markets to competition and to accept WTO rules and disciplines. Opponents raised other issues such as China's questionable human rights policies and labor standards, and U.S. national security concerns.

Once the 106th Congress had acted on PNTR, attention turned to final negotiations on China's WTO accession agreement where differences over agriculture emerged as a major obstacle to completing the accession protocol. China held out for treatment as a developing country when it comes to exemptions from reduction commitments for trade-distorting domestic farm subsidies – that is, domestic support exempted up to 10% of the value of a country's farm production, versus 5% for developed countries. The United States argued that China should be held to the lower 5% exemption because it is such a large actor in world agricultural markets. In early July, the two sides compromised at an 8.5% threshold, with China also agreeing to include input subsidies for poor rural areas that otherwise would have been exempt from the calculation. Agreement has been reached on other outstanding issues, notably the treatment of foreign-owned insurance companies. China's formal admission to the WTO could occur late this year or early in 2002.

LEGISLATION

Congressional committees in the 107th Congress (especially the House Ways and Means, Senate Finance, and House and Senate Agriculture Committees) have indicated that they will closely monitor China's accession to the WTO and its subsequent observance of WTO rules. Because PNTR authority does not take effect until China formally becomes a WTO member, the 107th Congress again confronted the issue of temporarily extending NTR status to China for another year. On July 12, 2001, the House defeated a congressional resolution (*H.J.Res. 50*) to overturn the President's one-year waiver of denial of NTR to China (authority he has under the Jackson-Vanik Amendment to the Trade Act of 1974, *P.L. 93-618*, Section 401). In addition, legislation (*H.R. 1467*) to withdraw PNTR in the wake of a U.S.-Chinese confrontation over a U.S. surveillance flight along China's coast was introduced in the House.

Chapter 19

TRADE: JAPAN

William H. Cooper

ISSUE

U.S.-Japan economic ties bare been burdened by friction for many years, more in some years than in others. The U.S. trade deficit with Japan is a persistent source of that friction as are issues regarding market access in Japan for U.S. exporters. U.S. concerns over Japanese import barriers and over sharp increases in steel imports from Japan have raised tensions. The United States has also been especially wary of Japan's poor economic performance over the last ten years and its effects on the U.S. economy. Throe frictions, at times, threaten the health of the overall U.S.-Japan relationship.

BACKGROUND

Overview

The United States and Japan are the world's two largest economies, accounting for about 40% of the global gross domestic product. The two economies are closely linked through merchandise trade. Japan ranks third as a U.S. export market. It is the leading market for U.S. agricultural exports, such as corn and wheat; for U.S. crude materials, inch as wood; and for U.S.-produced aircraft. Japan is else the second largest supplier of U.S. imports, including cars, consumer electronics, telecommunications equipment, and computers. The United States is Japan's largest export market and import supplier. The two economies are also tied by financial capital flows. Japan is one of the largest sources of foreign portfolio capital (bank deposits, stocks, bonds, and other securities) and of foreign investment (manufacturing plants and real estate) in the United States. Likewise, the United States is the largest source of foreign portfolio and direct investments in Japan.

The U.S. Trade Deficit with Japan, (For many years, the U.S.-Japan economic relationship has been clouded by persistent, large imbalances. As the table below indicates, the U.S. merchandise (exports and imports of goods) trade deficit with Japan hit a record

$81.3 billion in 2000, easily surpassing the previous record set in 1999. Preliminary data for 2001 show the trade deficit declining probably, because the downturn in the U.S. economy has decreased U.S. demand for Japanese imports.

Table 1. U.S. Merchandise Trade with Japan, 1996-2001
($ in billions)

Year	Exports	Imports	Balances
1996	67.5	115.2	-47.2
1997	65.5	121.7	-56.1
1998	57.9	122.0	-64.1
1999	57.5	131.4	-73.9
2000*	31.5	71.3	-39.8
2001*	31.4	65.9	-34.5

Source: U.S. Department of Commerce, Bureau of the Census. Exports are total exports valued on an f.a.s. basis. Imports are general value on a customs basis.
* January-June

Major Market Sector-Specific Disputes

In 1998, the United States experienced a sharp increase in imports of various types of steel products. Among the largest sources of the increases were Japan, Brazil, and Russia. U.S. imports of steel from Japan jumped nearly 162% from 1997 to 1998, according to Commerce Department data. (They declined in 1999 and in 2000.) The increase in steel imports prompted the 107th Congress to seek remedies, and the U.S. steel industry sought relief through U.S. antidumping and countervailing duty programs. Japan has filed complaints in the World Trade Organization (WTO) over some of the U.S. antidumping measures.

A U.S.-Japan bilateral agreement on trade in autos and auto parts expired at the end of 2000, as did an agreement on flat glass at the end of 1999. The agreements were negotiated to improve market access for U.S. exporters by reducing regulations and other barriers. U.S. industry has maintained that market access had not improved significantly and that the agreements should be renewed, while Japan opposed renewal. The United States and Japan have agreed to establish a forum for discussions on auto trade. Outstanding disputes linger on insurance and some other sector trade issues.

Along with bilateral negotiations, the United States and Japan also work together in other multilateral and regional fora. Both are pillars of the *World Trade Organization (WTO) and of the Asian-Pacific Economic Cooperation (APEC)* forum.

Japan's Economic Performance

Japan's economy has been anemic at best since the beginning of the 1990s. Japan showed only modest growth in 2000 and may be in recession in 2001, suggesting that it has yet to attain economic recovery. The economic problems have caused Japan to suffer its worst rate of unemployment in postwar history (5.0% as &July 2001). Ten government fiscal stimulus packages and a loose monetary policy have failed to ensure economic recovery.

Japan has also undertaken some economic restructuring, including reducing government regulations. The United States has insisted that Japan needs to do more and has been pressing Japan to cut regulations in sectors in which U.S. exporters and investors would be expected to be competitive: telecommunications, retail trade, medical devices and pharmaceuticals, housing, and legal services.

LEGISLATION

The surge in steel imports from Japan and other countries led the 106th Congress to consider changes in U.S. trade remedy laws. The 106th Congress passed and President Clinton signed the "Continuing Dumping and Subsidy Act of 2000" (P.L. 106-387.). The law requires antidumping duties and countervailing duties to be distributed to firms injured by dumping and subsidies. Japan and other countries have challenged the WTO legality of the measure. The steel industry is pressing for more action in the 107th Congress.

Chapter 20

SINGAPORE-U.S. FREE TRADE AGREEMENT

Dick K. Nanto

ISSUE

In November 2000, the United States and Singapore announced the launch of negotiations for a U.S.-Singapore Free Trade Agreement (FTA). The FTA would be the fifth such agreement the United States has signed and the first with an Asian country. It is to be modeled after the recently signed U.S.-Jordan FTA and would eliminate tariffs on all goods over time, cover substantially all services sectors, help to develop electronic commerce, protect intellectual property rights, include safeguards and dispute settlement mechanisms, as may contain provisions on labor and the environment. The Bush Administration has indicated that it would support the proposed FTA with Singapore, although it is not likely to favor inclusion of certain labor or environmental provisions.

On May 25, 2001, the U.S. and Singapore completed their third round of negotiations (the first under the Bush Administration). Ralph F. Ives, Assistant U.S. Trade Representative for Asia-Pacific and APEC Affairs led the U.S. delegation. The two sides discussed a comprehensive range of issues, including trade in goods, customs and rules of origin, trade in services, financial services, telecommunications, e-commerce, investment, textiles, intellectual property rights, and dispute settlement. During the negotiations, further progress was reportedly achieved on understanding each other's views and enlarging the areas of their convergence. The negotiators produced a document of consolidated texts but indicated that much work remains. The fourth round of negotiations were held in London from July 16-20 and are to continue on September 17-21, 2001.

The U.S.-Singapore FTA is of interest to the Congress because (1) it will require Congressional approval according to normal legislative procedures; (2) if implemented, it will continue the trend toward greater trade liberalization and globalization; (3) it may contain controversial environmental and/or labor conditions; and (4) it may affect trade flows that would, in turn, affect U.S. businesses, particularly import-competing industries such as textiles and apparel.

BACKGROUND

Singapore is a city-state located in Southeast Asia at the southern tip of Malaysia with a population of 3.5 million, an area roughly 3.5 times the size of the District of Columbia, and gross domestic product of about $100 billion.

This FTA would both develop and strengthen trading relationships with Singapore and bring the two countries a step closer to the realization of APEC's (Asia Pacific Economic Cooperation forum} goal of free trade and investment among the 21 APEC member economies by the year 2010 (for the developed country members). This FTA initiative also results partly from the failure to launch a new round of multilateral trade negotiations under the World Trade Organization (WTO).

Singapore is America's largest trading partner in Southeast Asia with two-way merchandise trade of $37.0 billion and U.S. deficit of $1.4 billion in merchandise trade. Singapore is the 10th largest export market for the United States with $17.8 billion in merchandise exports in 2000. It is the 12th largest source for goods imported into the United States with $19.2 billion in 2000.

Singapore already has 99% free trade. Only alcoholic beverages are subject to import tariffs. Singapore already has signed a free trade agreement with New Zealand and also has begun discussions on such arrangements with Australia, Japan, Mexico, Canada, Chile, and the European Free Trade Association (EFTA).

LEGISLATION

In the 107th Congress, *H.R. 1566* (Leach) was introduced that would urge the President to initiate consultations with the Governments of Singapore, Australia, and New Zealand to determine the feasibility and desirability of negotiations to create a free trade area between the United States and those countries.

The negotiation of free trade agreements is related to debate over granting the President Trade Promotion Authority (TPA). (For legislation on TPA, see the *TPA* entry in this briefing book.)

Chapter 21

JORDAN-U.S. FREE TRADE AGREEMENT (FTA)

Mary Jane Bolle

ISSUE

On June 6, 2000, then President Bill Clinton and King Abdullah II announced that the United States and Jordan would commence negotiations for a bilateral free trade agreement (FTA), eventually leading to reciprocal duty-free trade in goods. The U.S.-Jordan FTA was signed in Washington on October 24, 2000, and the Clinton Administration submitted the agreement to Congress on January 6, 2001. According to the agreement, the FTAs entry into force is "subject to the completion of necessary domestic legal procedures by each Party." The Jordanian parliament reportedly endorsed the FTA by a vote of acclamation on May 9, 2001. On July 26, both the Senate Finance Committee (*S. 643,* Baucus) and the House Ways and Means Committee (*H.R. 2603* Thomas), by voice votes, approved legislation to implement the agreement. The House approved *H.R. 2603* by a voice vote on July 31, 2001, end the Senate approved *H.R. 2603* by a voice vote on September 24, 2001.

BACKGROUND

Trade in Goods and Services

The FTA provides for a 10-year transitional period during which duties on almost all goods (with the exception of tobacco and tobacco-related products) will be phased-out, leading to duty-free trade in goods between the United States and Jordan. The duties on many goods will be phased-out prior to the end of the 10-year transitional period. The FTA also provides for a liberalization of bilateral trade in services. The United States and Jordan undertook specific market-opening commitments in various services sectors, such as business, communications, construction and distribution, education, environment, finance, health, tourism, recreation, and transportation.

In the 106th Congress, the concept of a U.S.-Jordan FTA received widespread bipartisan support. Between March and May 2000, over 45 Members of Congress sent then President

Clinton letters urging him to enter into negotiations for an FTA with Jordan as soon as possible. In these letters, Members provided several interrelated rationales for supporting a U.S.-Jordan FTA: 1) it would strengthen bilateral relations and express the United States' appreciation for Jordan's role in furthering the Middle East peace process and actively cooperating in international counter-terrorism activities; 2) it would promote economic growth in Jordan and regional economic cooperation, thereby enhancing stability and security in Jordan and the Middle East; and 3) it would assist in further promoting economic reform and liberalization in Jordan.

Total U.S.-Jordanian bilateral trade totaled approximately $375 million in 2000, making Jordan the United States' 98th largest trading partner. This level of trade is considered by many to be relatively inconsequential in comparison with total U.S. trade flows. Therefore, many observers believe that the significance of the agreement lies more in geopolitical terms, as well as in the precedent set by including environmental and labor provisions in the main body of the agreement.

Environment and Labor

The U.S.-Jordan FTA contains provisions on environmental and labor standards within the main body of the agreement. In the FTA, the United States and Jordan recognize the principle that it is "inappropriate to encourage trade by relaxing domestic environmental [and labor] laws." Accordingly, the FTA states that neither country should derogate from their existing environmental and labor standards. Although the FTA does not commit either side to modify its existing environmental and labor laws, either country "shall be entitled to take any appropriate and commensurate measures" if the dispute settlement mechanism stipulated in the FTA does not resolve a dispute, presumably including environmental or labor disputes.

The inclusion of environmental and labor provisions has proven to be the most controversial aspect of the U.S.-Jordan FTA, and, as the first FTA to include these provisions in the main body of the agreement, has come to be viewed by some as a model or template for future U.S. free trade agreements. Some observers have argued that environmental and labor issues do not belong in free trade agreements and could actually have a deleterious effect on bilateral trade flows. Other observers have contended that the inclusion of environmental and labor provisions reflects positively on a new commitment to a more comprehensive trade policy agenda that takes into account concerns about potential social ramifications of free trade. Still others have stressed that the provisions in the FTA do not go far enough to protect environmental and labor standards since they only urge the Parties not to relax existing legislation.

The U.S.-Jordan FTA has led some Members of Congress to address the issue &whether or not environmental and labor provisions should be included in this FTA or any future FTA that the United States may negotiate. Some Members of Congress, such as Senate Finance Committee Ranking Member Charles Grassley, have argued that the environmental and labor provisions in the U.S.-Jordan FTA should be viewed uniquely and not as a model for future trade agreements. Other Members of Congress, such as House Minority Leader Richard Gephardt, have expressed pleasure at the inclusion of environmental and labor provisions in the U.S.-Jordan FTA and view them as a precedent for future FTAs.

Approval of the implementing legislation on July 26 came after the Jordanian ambassador and U.S. Trade Representative Robert Zoellick exchanged identical letters pledging to resolve any differences that might arise between the two countries without recourse to formal dispute settlement procedures and without blocking trade.

LEGISLATION

Then President Clinton submitted the U.S.-Jordan FTA to the 107th Congress on January 6, 2001. The Senate Finance Committee held a hearing on the FTA on March 20, 2001.

Senator Max Baucus introduced a bill to implement the U.S.-Jordan FTA (*S. 643*) on March 28, 2001, which was referred to the Senate Finance Committee. The committee held a mark-up session for the bill on July 17 during which it approved an amendment in the nature of a substitute offered by Senator Baucus correcting various technical and typographical errors spotted in the original bill. The committee also rejected an amendment offered by Senator Phil Gramm that would have restricted the scope &the dispute resolution mechanism in the treaty to deal with labor and environmental issues. On July 26, the Senate Finance Committee approved *S. 643* by a voice vote.

On April 4, 2001, Representative Sander Levin introduced in the House a similar bill (*H.R. 1484*), which was referred to the House Ways and Means and Judiciary Committees. On July 26, the House Ways and Means Committee approved *H.R. 2603* (Thomas), an amendment offered by the Chairman in the nature of a substitute, by a voice vote. The House approved H.R. 2603 by a voice vote on July 31, 2001, and the Senate approved *H.R. 2603* by a voice vote on September 24, 2001.

Chapter 22

SYRIA: PROSPECTS FOR TRADE NORMALIZATION

Alfred B. Prados

ISSUE

The United States times a basic policy dilemma concerning Syria that complicates attempts to normalize trade relations between the two countries. Should the United States continue to ban aid to Syria and restrict trade as long as Syria supports several groups that the United States regards as terrorist organizations? Or should the United States ease or remove these sanctions, because Syria apparently has not been directly involved in terrorism since 1986, and Syrian support seems crucial to the success of Arab-Israeli peace negotiations? Congress is considering *H.R. 4811*, the Foreign Operations, Appropriation bill for FY2001, which continues to ban direct and indirect assistance to Syria.

BACKGROUND

Syria received limited amounts of U.S. aid prior to 1967 and again in the mid-to-late 1970s. In 1979, under the provisions of the Export Administration Act [*P.L. 96-72*], the State Department named Syria as a country supportive of international terrorism. The inclusion of Syria on the terrorism list led to the termination of U.S. aid programs for Syria, phase-out of remaining aid funds in FY1981, and imposition of various trade restrictions. In recent years, the State Department has said that there is no evidence of direct Syrian involvement in terrorist acts since 1986, when Syrian intelligence was implicated in an abortive airline bombing attempt; however, the Department notes that Syria continues to provide safe haven and support for several Palestinian and Lebanese groups that have engaged in terrorism, such as the Hamas and Hizballah organizations. In its most recent report on international terrorism, the State Department adds that in August 1999 the Syrian Government directed the leaders of some terrorist organizations based in Damascus to refrain from military activities and limit their actions to the political realm. During the same month, however, a State Department official said the Administration had no plans to remove Syria from the terrorism list.

At present, an array of legislative provisions and executive directives continue to prohibit U.S. aid to Syria and restrict bilateral trade. Many of these bans and restrictions are based on Syria's designation as a country that supports international terrorism. Other bans and restrictions result from unpaid obligations to the United States on Syria's part; Syria's continued enforcement of the Arab boycott against Israel, and specific legislative provisions that prohibit aid to Syria and other named countries. For example, annual foreign operations appropriations acts have banned direct aid to Syria beginning with FY1982 and have brained indirect aid to Syria beginning with FY1987. Until recently, Syria was also denied foreign assistance pursuant to U.S. narcotics legislation; however, in 1997, President Clinton informed Congress of his decision to remove Syria from a list of drug producers or traffickers. The President's action had no direct effect, because the same sanctions remained applicable to Syria under other legislative provisions.

A detailed listing of statutes that ban aid and restrict trade to Syria appears in *CRS Report RL30644 Syria: Sanctions and Aid.* Principal examples of these statutes include the following:

- Section 620A of the Foreign Assistance Act of 1961, as amended, bans U.S. foreign assistance to countries on the terrorism list; Section 40(a) of the Arms Export Control Act bans provision of military aid or munitions to such countries.
- Several other laws require U.S. representatives to vote against or otherwise oppose loans by international lending institutions to terrorist countries.
- Section 307 of the Foreign Assistance Act of 1961 requires withholding of the U.S. proportionate share of the programs of international organizations for several named countries including Syria.
- Section 512 of the Consolidated Appropriations Act for FY2000 bans aid to countries in default of obligations to the United States for over 12 months (this provision, which appears annually in foreign operations appropriations, is known as the "Brooke-Alexander Amendment").
- The Anti-Economic Discrimination Act of 1994 bans sale of defense articles to countries enforcing the Arab boycott of Israel and denies State Department contracts to foreign persons complying with the boycott.

In addition, Section 6(j) of the Export Administration Act of 1979 requires prior congressional notification and a validated license for export of commodities that could increase the military capability of a country on the terrorism list. Under a related provision of the same act (Section 6(a)), the Department of Commerce lists 31 categories of exports requiring a validated license for shipment to Syria. According to current guidelines, there is a presumption of denial for export of these items to military end users in Syria or for export of dual use equipment to Syria regardless of the end user.

Several steps would be necessary to restore aid or reestablish normal trade relations with Syria. First, the Secretary of State could remove Syria from the terrorism list, after notifying Congress. Second, Congress could exempt Syria from the "Brooke-Alexander Amendment" and remove Syria from other legislation that imposes sanctions on Syria by name. Also, the President could waive the application of several legislative sanctions against Syria where he has the authority to do so; for example, the Anti-Economic Discrimination Act of 1994 has been waived on behalf of several Arab countries that have good relations with the United States.

LEGISLATION

H.R. 4811, the Foreign Operations Appropriation bill for FY2001. Section 507 continues to ban direct assistance to Syria and Section 523 continues to ban indirect assistance to Syria. This bill is awaiting conference.

Chapter 23

LIBYA: AN OVERVIEW OF ECONOMIC SANCTIONS

Clyde Mark

ISSUE

On January 31, 2001, the three-judge Scottish court found one Libyan innocent and one Libyan guilty in the 1988 bombing of Pan American Airways flight 103 over Lockerbie, Scotland. United Nations sanctions against Libya were "suspended" pending the end of the trial. Should the United States oppose action within the United Nations to drop entirely the sanctions against Libya? Should the United States maintain its sanctions against Libya until Libya accepts responsibility for the Pan Am 103 bombing and agrees to pay compensation for the victims? Has Libya demonstrated that it no longer supports international terrorism and that it has abandoned its quest for weapons of mass destruction? Congress has extended the Iran-Libya Sanctions Act until August 2006.

BACKGROUND

In 1973, Libya announced that the Gulf of Sidra in the Mediterranean Sea was a closed bay and part of Libya's territorial sea. The United States disagreed with the Libyan position, maintaining that Sidra was too large to be a closed bay and that there were no precedents for the Libyan claim. The Gulf of Sidra disagreement led to a series of air and sea encounters in which Libyan ships and aircraft tried to deny U.S. ships and aircraft access to the contested areas. In the mid-1980s, reports circulated that Libya was using chemical weapons against government rebels in the Chad civil war and that Libya was seeking chemical and nuclear weapons. In the past, Libyan leader Muammar al-Qadhafi stated that he supported international terrorism, and defended terrorism in wars of national liberation. Because of that support, the United States named Libya a state sponsor of terrorism on December 29, 1979.

The United States suspected that the Libyan government was involved in the April 5, 1986, bombing of a Berlin nightclub frequented by U.S. Armed Forces personnel. Three U.S. soldiers died in the blast. On April 15, 1986, United States Air Force and Navy aircraft bombed three target areas in Libya in retaliation for the Berlin incident. The United States and the United Kingdom accused Libya of complicity in the December 21, 1988 explosion of Pan American Airways flight 103 en route from London to New York that crashed in Lockerbie, Scotland, killing 259 passengers and crew and 11 people on the ground. Also, France suspected that Libyans were involved in the bombing and crash of UTA flight 772 over Niger in Africa in 1989. The United States has noted al-Qadhafi's recent recantations on his support for terrorism with some skepticism and caution.

The United States imposed sanctions banning trade, aid, and financial transactions with Libya because of Libya's support for terrorism, apparent involvement in terror attacks against the United States, attempts to acquire weapons of mass destruction, and belligerency over its territorial claims. United Nations sanctions banned air flights to Libya, weapons sales, and the transfer of oil drilling equipment to Libya until Libya presented for trial two Libyan nationals accused of placing the Pan Am 103 bomb. In April 1999, the Libyan Government turned over the two Libyans to United Nations officials, and the United Nations suspended the sanctions. The trial began in The Hague, Netherlands, on May 3, 2000, under Scottish legal procedures, and ended on January 31, 2001, with the acquittal of one defendant and a guilty verdict for the other. A five-judge panel will hear an appeal of the guilty verdict in mid-June 2001; the court has granted the defendant three six-week extensions to prepare the appeal.

The United States imposed sanctions on Libya through four executive orders:

(1) EO 12538 &November 15, 1985, prohibited petroleum product imports from Libya (19 USC 1862 note);
(2) EO 12543 of January 7, 1986, prohibited trade and financial transactions with Libya (50 USC 1701 note);
(3) EO 12544 of January 8, 1986, froze Libyan assets in the United States (50 USC 1701 note);
(4) EO 12801 of April 15, 1992, banned air traffic between the United States and Libya (50 USC 1701 note).

To restore U.S. trade and other economic relations with Libya, the Department of State could remove Libya from the terrorism list, and the President could revoke or amend the four executive orders.

Note: The Iran Libya-Sanctions Act (*P.L. 104-172*, August 5, 1996, 110 Stat. 1541, 50 USC 1701 note) imposes U.S. sanctions on any country or foreign company that invests $20 million or more in developing Libya oil resources, but the law does not affect directly U.S. companies or U.S. trade relations with Libya. The law expires in August 2001.

LEGISLATION

In the FY2002 foreign operations appropriations bill, *H.R. 2506,* Section 507 bans direct assistance to Libya, and Section 523 bans indirect assistance to Libya. H.R. 2506 passed the House and has been reported in the Senate. It is highly unlikely that the United States would offer aid to Libya.

H.R. 1954 (*P.L. 107-24* of 3 August 2001) extended the Iran-Libya Sanctions Act (*P.L. 104-172*) for five years until August 2006, lowered the threshold for applying the sanctions from $40 million to $20 million, and called for a presidential report to Congress on the sanctions' effectiveness and humanitarian interests. *S.Con.Res. 23*, which passed the Senate by unanimous consent on April 6, 2001, calls upon Libya to accept responsibility for the Pan Am 103 bombing and pay compensation to the victims' families and states that it should be the policy of the United States to oppose ending economic sanctions against Libya. *S. 244*, introduced on February 1, 2001, opposes lifting sanctions against Libya and bans U. S. assistance to Libya until Libya pays compensation to Pan Am 103 victims' families. *S. 171*, introduced on January 24, 2001, would repeal the law applying sanctions to several countries, including Libya.

INDEX

C

D

E

J

K

L

M

N

T

U

V

W

Y

Z